# PATHOS AND PRAXIS

STUDIES IN CONTINENTAL THOUGHT
John Sallis, editor

*Consulting Editors*

Robert Bernasconi
John D. Caputo
David Carr
Edward S. Casey
David Farrell Krell
Lenore Langsdorf

James Risser
Dennis J. Schmidt
Calvin O. Schrag
Charles E. Scott
Daniela Vallega-Neu
David Wood

# PATHOS AND PRAXIS

## AN INTEGRATED PHENOMENOLOGY OF LIFE

Scott Davidson

INDIANA UNIVERSITY PRESS

This book is a publication of

Indiana University Press
Office of Scholarly Publishing
Herman B Wells Library 350
1320 East 10th Street
Bloomington, Indiana 47405 USA

iupress.org

© 2025 by Scott Davidson

All rights reserved
No part of this book may be reproduced or utilized in any form
or by any means, electronic or mechanical, including photocopying
and recording, or by any information storage and retrieval system,
without permission in writing from the publisher.

First Printing 2025

Library of Congress Cataloging-in-Publication Data

Names: Davidson, Scott, author.
Title: Pathos and praxis : an integrated phenomenology of life / Scott Davidson.
Description: Bloomington, Indiana : Indiana University Press, [2025] |
   Series: Studies in continental thought | Includes bibliographical
   references and index.
Identifiers: LCCN 2024045287 (print) | LCCN 2024045288 (ebook) | ISBN
   9780253072313 (hardback) | ISBN 9780253072344 (paperback) | ISBN
   9780253072337 (ebook)
Subjects: LCSH: Phenomenology. | Life. | Henry, Michel, 1922–2002. |
   Ricœur, Paul.
Classification: LCC B829.5 .D4 2025 (print) | LCC B829.5 (ebook) | DDC
   142/.7—dc23/eng/20241112
LC record available at https://lccn.loc.gov/2024045287
LC ebook record available at https://lccn.loc.gov/2024045288

*For Lupe,*
*in gratitude for the life that we have made together.*

CONTENTS

*Acknowledgments   ix*

Introduction: Life as Pathos and Praxis   1

1. From a Phenomenology of Consciousness to a Phenomenology of Life   18

2. Birth: The Pathos of Being-in-Life   42

3. Movement: The Force of Life and the Biranian Philosophy of Effort   62

4. Desire: The Henry-Ricoeur Debate over Freud   83

5. Praxis: The Henry-Ricoeur Debate over Marx   104

6. Language: Words of Life and the Living Word   123

7. Death: Being-towards-Life and the "Life after Life"   144

8. For an Integrated Phenomenology of Life   165

*Notes   179*
*Bibliography   217*
*Index   227*

## ACKNOWLEDGMENTS

THIS BOOK IS THE CULMINATION of a sustained reflection on the Henry-Ricoeur debate for the last decade. It has been a labor of love and care. Instead of rushing it to publication, I have pored through countless drafts and different ways of organizing the book, seeking to find just the right way to express the ideas contained here, in the hope of making a lasting impact.

Preliminary sketches of various elements of the book have been presented at conferences and speaking engagements over the years. I want to thank the members of the Society for Ricoeur Studies, the Fonds Ricoeur Summer Workshop, and the International Network for the Philosophy of Religion for their helpful feedback and intellectual community. For their ongoing friendship and support, I would especially like to thank George Taylor, Crina Gschwandtner, Emmanuel Falque, Johann Michel, Jean-Luc Amalric, David Pellauer, Frédéric Seyler, Karl Hefty, Steven DeLay, Janine Jones, Adam Graves, Sebastian Purcell, Nathan Ross, David Hoinski, David Cerbone, Diane Perpich, John Drabinski, Kris Sealey, Brian Treanor, Michael Johnson, Daniel Frey, Azadeh Thiriez-Arjangi, and my late colleague John Starkey. In addition, I acknowledge Greg Dunaway, dean of the Eberly College of Arts and Sciences at West Virginia University; Sharon Ryan, chair of the Philosophy Department at WVU; and Amy Cataldi, dean of the Petree College of Arts and Sciences at Oklahoma City University for their support of this research project. I thank Anna Francis and her team at Indiana University Press for taking on this project and carrying it through production. Last but not least, I thank my family, who have been tremendously supportive and such wonderful company during this journey.

# PATHOS AND PRAXIS

# Introduction

*Life as Pathos and Praxis*

THE PHENOMENOLOGY OF LIFE IS the best available option for the future advancement of phenomenology. For the past century (indeed, almost from its inception), classical phenomenology has been criticized internally for either misreading or neglecting important aspects of the bodily dimension of lived experience. Moreover, it has been challenged externally by other movements—Marxism, psychoanalysis, poststructuralism, and the like—that have inserted a wedge between lived experience and meaning. But the phenomenological work of Michel Henry and Paul Ricoeur is instructive in this context because it responds both to the so-called masters of suspicion (Marx, Nietzsche, Freud) by exploring what undergirds conscious thought and to the internal critics by returning to the wellspring of bodily experience. The two thinkers thus embrace an expansive view of phenomenology that returns to the topic of life and takes it seriously. This recovery of life, instead of marking a departure from phenomenology, actually renews its original impetus: life is that which classical phenomenology has always sought but never been able to capture. In their hands, the phenomenology of life is able to generate valuable new meaning and insights regarding perennial phenomenological themes such as birth, movement, affectivity, desire, language, and death.

So, what exactly is a phenomenology of life? This question is deceptively simple. In fact, the answer varies depending on how the terms *phenomenology* and *life* are construed.[1] As a phenomenology, its methodology can be distinguished from a naturalistic approach to life that typically proceeds from an understanding of the simplest organisms and gradually builds up an explanation of more complex organisms. Consider the example of biology. After identifying basic patterns and behaviors of less complex living organisms (for example, the MRS GREN list),[2] biologists then seek to account for the more complex organization and structure of human life. This naturalistic approach thereby situates the experience of a human life along a continuum with all other biological organisms in the natural world.

The phenomenology of life, by contrast, points to the fact that the biologist's cognition of the world presupposes a prior recognition of the biologist's own life. Michel Henry, for instance, raises this point when he asks, "Is it not paradoxical for anyone who wants to know what life is to go and ask protozoa or, in the best case, honeybees? As if our only relation with life was a wholly external and fragile relation with beings about whom we know nothing—or so very little! As if we ourselves were not living beings!"[3] In contrast with the naturalistic approach that moves from the simplest to the most complex organisms, Henry contends that our best access to life comes through what is most familiar and most directly known to us—that is, our own lived experience. Our own experience of life is what we know best. After all, if someone were to ask you whether you're alive, you wouldn't need to consult some other source of information to verify whether it is true: it's simply an experienced fact.[4] The lived experience of one's own life, according to Henry, should thus serve as the starting point and focus of any inquiry into life.

To be clear, neither Henry himself nor phenomenology in general would advocate a wholesale rejection of biological knowledge. The point is not to deny our ability to know other forms of life or to dismiss the importance of this field of study; instead, the aim is to highlight a basic difference between the observation of other living organisms and the experience of one's own life. In fact, a similar observation is made by legendary biologist John Haldane. In his book *What Is Life?*, Haldane notes that "we know what it feels like to be alive, just as we know what redness or pain or effort are."[5] We know these simple facts directly, he continues, and "cannot describe them in terms of anything else." His point, in other words, is that no matter how much our scientific knowledge of living organisms might advance, a certain type of knowledge—the knowledge of the subjective qualia of life—remains inaccessible to it in principle. Science can observe living beings, analyze their composition, and study their various functions and processes, all in an effort to explain how life works. Nonetheless, it runs up against its limits with respect to the lived experience of life: external observations of life will always fall short of knowing what it is like to be alive. That is a qualitatively different type of knowledge that requires a different type of access. The phenomenology of life is necessary and relevant precisely because it provides access to this realm of experience. It is the field that studies the qualia of life—or, what it is like to be alive—through a rigorous inquiry into what one can know directly through the firsthand experience of one's own life.

This way of answering the question "What is the phenomenology of life?" might surprise some readers due to its focus on the first-person, subjective experience of life. It implies that the phenomenology of life stands closer to the project of a philosophical anthropology than to either naturalism or environmental philosophy.[6] Accordingly, it may be helpful to situate the phenomenology of life in relation to Kant's anthropological question posed in *Anthropology from a Pragmatic Point of View*: What is it to be human? Kant's response is to divide the "knowledge of the human" into two separate areas: a physiological perspective that studies humans as natural objects and a pragmatic perspective that examines humans as freely acting beings.[7] The Kantian division between these two different ways of knowing the human, in my opinion, captures the difference between the two prevailing approaches to the phenomenology of life today—the one developed in the work of Michel Henry and the other proposed more recently by Renaud Barbaras.[8] Let me situate their approaches in terms of the difference between their responses to the anthropological question.

Setting aside the physiological aspect of the human body, Henry's phenomenology of life approaches the question of the human—what is it like to be a living individual?—through an exclusive focus on the pragmatic side of the Kantian division. Henry's account of the human focuses on what he calls the experience of one's own "original flesh" [*la chair; Leib*].[9] This experience, he insists, is completely separable from the natural world and the organic functions of the body. It can be accessed only through a subjective firsthand feeling of one's own living flesh, which Henry calls the auto-affection of life. This auto-affective experience, which will be analyzed later in much closer detail, is a fundamental experience of life that touches each and every living individual most deeply at their core. Phenomenology is needed precisely because this basic experience usually and for the most part escapes our notice. As Ovid famously observed, "One lives and remains unaware of one's own life" [*"Vivit et est vitae nescius ipse suae"*].[10] Since we often go through life without being aware of the simple fact of our own living, this forgetting leads us to lose a grip on life as well as ourselves. By returning to this most basic question about who we are, Henry's phenomenology of life seeks to restore our original contact with an auto-affective experience of life that resides within us at all times. It is only after we have regained this contact with life that it becomes possible to pose an authentic question of the meaning and purpose of one's own life. The recovery of one's own life thereby goes beyond the establishment of a fact and acquires a practical significance: it serves as a necessary precondition for the pragmatic task of living authentically, or living well.

Renaud Barbaras's phenomenology of life, by contrast, emerges as a critical response to Henry's suspension of the natural world. While Henry occupies the pragmatic side of the Kantian divide, Barbaras emphasizes the physiological approach to the anthropological question and deploys a phenomenological reduction *to* the world. Inspired by Merleau-Ponty, Barbaras begins with the living body's original immersion in the natural world and focuses on the physiological dimension of the body. For example, he emphasizes the metabolic functions that sustain bodily life. Building from the most basic organic functions of bodily life, his analysis gradually extends to increasingly complex life functions such as movement, perception, and desire. In contrast with traditional accounts of the human that emphasize intellect or the will, desire plays a pivotal role for Barbaras. It attests to a lack that thrusts the self outside itself and directs it toward the world in search of its fulfillment. The phenomenology of life is necessary for Barbaras because we have lost touch with the movement of life. We ordinarily think and live on the level of static oppositions between things—for instance, between subject and object, thought and its content, or an activity and its goal. Returning these abstractions to their prior origin in desire, Barbaras's phenomenology of life shows that life is fundamentally a movement and a temporal process of becoming.

Even if we grant, for the sake of argument, that each of these projects is internally consistent and unfolds logically from its own initial set of assumptions, the Kantian framing of the anthropological question offers a valuable insight into the potential limitations of both projects. It suggests that these two phenomenologies, taken solely on their own, only offer a partial answer to the anthropological question. On the one hand, Henry's phenomenology embraces the pragmatic aspect of the human but neglects the physiological perspective. How, as Emmanuel Falque asks, is it really possible to speak about flesh without a body? On the other hand, Barbaras's phenomenology of life adopts the physiological perspective but neglects the pragmatic aspect of human life. How, one could legitimately wonder, could his focus on natural desire ever allow him to account for human freedom and the role of reason in setting goals for desire? These critical questions suggest that each of these approaches to the phenomenology of life only glimpses one aspect of the broader whole of a human life. Accordingly, a more comprehensive and integrated account is needed.

The development of such an account motivates this book's turn to the hermeneutic phenomenology of Paul Ricoeur. Unlike either Henry or Barbaras, Ricoeur explicitly links his own philosophical project to Kant's philosophical anthropology.[11] In a 1960 essay titled "The Antinomy of Human Reality and the Problem of Philosophical Anthropology," Ricoeur contends that an answer to the question "what is it to be human?" must adopt both the pragmatic and physiological perspectives toward the human.[12] Yet at the same time, he recognizes that there is an inevitable tension that makes them difficult to reconcile. To be human is to be situated perilously on a fault line between subjective and objective reality, between freedom and necessity, between the rational will and organic needs. The fault line between these two perspectives defines the fragility of a life which is both capable [*homo capax*] of action but also vulnerable to suffering cuts and wounds.[13]

This brief reference to Ricoeur's anthropology and its potential contribution to the phenomenology of life generates its own series of questions, undoubtedly. For example, if it can be said that there is an implicit philosophical anthropology contained in Henry's phenomenology of life, can the reverse be said for Ricoeur? That is to say, even though Ricoeur never describes his work as a phenomenology of life, can it be said nonetheless that an implicit phenomenology of life is operative in his philosophical anthropology? If so, what exactly would his embrace of Kant's dual perspectives on the human—in which he emphasizes the experience of disproportion over and above a simple additive approach to the two—entail for a phenomenology of life?[14] Can it deliver a more comprehensive account of the human than what can be found in either Henry or Barbaras alone?[15]

## Background of the Henry-Ricoeur Relationship

Neither Michel Henry (1922–2002) nor Paul Ricoeur (1913–2005) needs much in the way of an introduction at this point. Their impact on the landscape of contemporary phenomenology is evident and widely acknowledged, and many useful overviews of their thought have already been written.[16] Due to the sheer volume and scope of their work, it is a massive undertaking even to address either one of these thinkers on their own. Henry is the author of a dozen books, plus several posthumous works, including a five-volume collection of his articles.[17] Likewise, Ricoeur is the author of more than forty books and hundreds of articles translated into English.[18] Moreover, thanks to the excellent work of the Fonds Henry in Louvain and the Fond Ricoeur in Paris, new source materials are accessible and continue to be published regularly. Henry studies and Ricoeur studies are both thriving on an international level, and secondary scholarship continues to proliferate across many different disciplines. This profusion of research material means that no single project can provide an exhaustive account of either thinker or anticipate all the possible linkages between the two thinkers.[19]

This project, accordingly, is focused more narrowly. It examines the explicit and sometimes implicit points of exchange between Henry and Ricoeur with a view toward the development of a more comprehensive phenomenology of life. As a result, it goes beyond simple comparison and contrast between two different orthodoxies or a partisan advocacy for one thinker or the other. Instead, it carries out a productive dialogue with the following aims: (1) to uncover specific aspects of their thought that, without this comparison, might otherwise remain implicit and underdeveloped; (2) to expand the points of contact between the two thinkers beyond their actual historical exchanges; (3) to ameliorate what might otherwise be regarded as shortcomings or oversights in their work. This latter point is essential, insofar as the integrated phenomenology of life proposed here aims to establish a freestanding position that moves beyond the limitations of each thinker to arrive at a more comprehensive view.

To contextualize this dialogue, let me provide some historical context for the relationship between Henry and Ricoeur. Their personal relationship could not be described as a particularly close friendship or mentorship, although they do express an "immense esteem" for one another.[20] Their acquaintance dates back at least to the 1950s, when Ricoeur served as a member of Henry's dissertation committee and continued afterward through occasional correspondence and several more formal intellectual exchanges over the course of their careers.[21] This means that Ricoeur would have been exposed to Henry's original thought already at the earliest stages of its development in the 1950s and early 1960s, because Henry's doctoral thesis included his first major publication, *The Essence of Manifestation* (1963), as well as his detailed reading of Maine de Biran in *Philosophy and Phenomenology of the Body* (1965), which applies the insights of the former work to the topic of the lived body. Yet it is unclear what type of impact, if any, these early works might have had on Ricoeur's own thinking because Ricoeur does not make any direct references to Henry's thought in that early period. Likewise, it is hard to tell whether, or exactly how, Ricoeur's early work might have influenced Henry's trajectory at this stage. If any such influence were to be found, it would likely be attributed either to *Freedom and Nature* (1950) or, more likely, to the early essays in which Ricoeur helped to introduce Husserlian phenomenology to the French-speaking world.[22] But Henry doesn't cite Ricoeur in his early publications either.

Although there is no direct evidence of a mutual influence at this early stage in their careers, they do have a shared intellectual inheritance characteristic of many French scholars of their generation.[23] Both thinkers were trained in the very distinctive philosophical program that included a shared canon of historical refence points as well as the major movements of the time: training in French reflexive philosophy,[24] enthusiasm for the "return to the concrete" promised by Husserlian phenomenology,[25] and concern about the challenge to the cogito raised by the "masters of suspicion" (Marx, Nietzsche, Freud). While the influence of all these movements will be examined in this study, it turns out that later debates over the interpretation of Marx and Freud are the terrain on which the actual exchanges between Henry and Ricoeur take place. Those debates are especially generative for thinking about how the future development of the phenomenology of life can respond to the challenges posed by Marxism and psychoanalysis.

The two thinkers engage one another directly through several lengthy review essays. In the late 1970s, Ricoeur responded to Henry's 1975 book on Marx in an extended book review, "Le Marx de Michel Henry."[26] Henry, in turn, later responded to Ricoeur's 1965 book *Freud and Philosophy* in the essay "Ricoeur and Freud: Between Phenomenology and Psychoanalysis,"[27] which was presented at the August 1988 Cerisy-la-Salle conference organized in honor of Ricoeur. These two published exchanges prove to be quite valuable because they serve as the vehicle through which each thinker identifies the fundamental differences that separate their philosophical projects. But in the context of the immense body of work that each thinker produced over a lifetime, the results of these discussions remain quite limited.[28] Interpretive work is needed to show that the differences that surface in the actual exchanges between the two thinkers are emblematic of deeper differences extending throughout their entire work.

Let me anticipate two plausible objections to a sustained study of the Henry-Ricoeur dialogue: the first is substantive while the second is methodological.

The first possible objection to a Henry-Ricoeur dialogue would be based on the substantive differences in the focus and content of their philosophies. Most importantly, Henry's philosophy is defined, from beginning to end, by its profound and concentrated reflection on the concept of life. Separating his concept of life from any of its usual biological connotations, Henry defines its original phenomenological essence as a radical inwardness. His thought thus continually returns to the intimacy of one's own experience of being alive. Whereas each one of Henry's books and articles returns to this essential teaching about life, Ricoeur's work does not appear to be guided by any single organizing theme. And even if one were to select a set of keywords or themes to describe his work, life would probably not figure among them, either. Indeed, Ricoeur confides in a late interview that he "had always fled" the topic of life due to his suspicions about "*Lebensphilosophie*, of the very idea of a philosophy of life."[29] As a result, one could object that their philosophies are simply so different that they are left with nothing profound to say to one another. Does Ricoeur actually have something substantive to offer to the phenomenology of life?

While we have noted Ricoeur's self-admitted reluctance to address the topic of life in an interview, it is important to consider what he goes on to say in that interview. Ricoeur adds that, despite his caution concerning the notion of a philosophy of life, he does intend to take up the questions of time, memory, and history "under the sign of the *Zusammenhang des Lebens*, the cohesion of a life. How does a life follow after itself? I stress the fact that this is indeed a life and not a consciousness."[30] The full quote thus offers a much more positive signal of an implicit phenomenology of life in his work. Indeed, the theme of life does emerge in his later thought. Consider, for example, the provocative and profound closing lines of *Memory, History, Forgetting*: "Under history, memory and forgetting. Under memory and forgetting, life. But to write a life is another story. Incompleteness." Additionally, we will later examine Ricoeur's interesting reflections on the relation between life and death in the posthumously published book *Living Up to Death*.

Yet, the theme of life does not simply surface out of nowhere at the end of Ricoeur's career. The confrontation with Henry helps to highlight its presence across the entire trajectory of his philosophical journey, starting from his first major work, *Freedom and Nature*, and continuing up to his final writings. Elsewhere I have documented the very interesting account of the involuntary dimension of life developed in *Freedom and Nature*,[31] and the chapters to follow will pick up this theme at other important junctures of Ricoeur's career. The topic of life is thus comparable to a mysterious underground river that, in the words of Frédéric Worms, resurfaces at various points along Ricoeur's way.[32] Though it emerges as an explicit theme only in an isolated and intermittent manner in his works, there is a continuous underlying current of reflection on life across his career. By bringing this to the surface, we can envision what Ricoeur might have written if, in his own words, he would have "had another life" and if he would have been able to write "a philosophy of life."[33] The chapters that follow will imagine this possibility and envision its potential contribution to the phenomenology of life.

A second possible objection to the prospect of a Henry-Ricoeur dialogue could be based on their methodological differences. The two thinkers exemplify two rival conceptions of phenomenology. Drawing from the work of Dominique Janicaud, this difference can be characterized in terms of the contrast between a "maximalist" and a "minimalist" phenomenology.[34] The Henryan approach, on the one hand, is resolutely maximalist, which is to say that it embraces phenomenology in virtue of its radicality. Influenced by Husserl's tendency to frame phenomenology as a first philosophy or metaphysics, it returns to the foundation, the original *arche*, of experience. Proponents of this view, including not only Henry but, perhaps most notably, Jean-Luc Marion, regard phenomenology as the only conceivable path for metaphysics today, in the wake of the twentieth-century deconstruction of classical metaphysics. Henry's maximalism is evident in his repeated attempts to conceptualize life in its radicality and to establish it as the absolute foundation or ground of all experience. In this foundationalist endeavor, Henry's project is an exemplar of a phenomenological approach that stands in the lineage of classical metaphysics, even while challenging specific assumptions of that tradition.

A minimalist phenomenology, by contrast, follows a different tendency in Husserl's work. Terminologically, it eschews all pretenses to reach the absolute, to be apodictic, and to establish a new foundation for metaphysics. Instead, phenomenological minimalism speaks more modestly in terms of testing hypotheses within a larger project, seeking out the morphology of a set of appearances, or dealing with some phenomenon solely in its uniqueness. This minimalist alternative is more consistent with Ricoeur's hermeneutic phenomenology, and in fact, Janicaud applauds Ricoeur as an exemplar of this more cautious approach. To be sure, Ricoeur's work could hardly be described in terms of its radicality or its search for a foundation. Instead of rejecting the philosophical tradition, Ricoeur's tone is usually humble and conciliatory. His impulse is to carry out the work of mediation. He seeks to reconcile the seemingly opposed and irreconcilable views that divide various philosophical movements.

But this cautious hermeneutic would not qualify as sufficiently radical in the eyes of Michel Henry, for whom the entire history of philosophy is marked by the forgetting and concealment of the true reality of life. For Henry, to mediate between traditional disputes, as Ricoeur does, is to confine oneself to a history of error that cannot be improved or redeemed. The discovery of a radical first truth—such as the auto-affection of life in its radical immanence—requires a complete break with history, interpretation, and representation. In words that seem to target Ricoeur directly, Henry observes that "thoughts of mediation are superficial. To know what we are, they always take a detour: either our true being is mediately constituted or our knowledge of it is mediate."[35] Instead, it is necessary to return to what can be known immediately and directly about life.

Henry's maximalist approach to the phenomenology of life is evident in the three basic theses that govern his thought.[36] First, Henry establishes a distinction between two fundamental modes of appearing: immanence and transcendence. This duality structures the entire field of Henryan oppositions: the invisible versus the visible; flesh versus physical body; auto-affectivity versus intentionality; the language of life versus the language of the world; life versus death. Second, Henry asserts that these oppositions are governed by a founding relation, such that the latter terms are ontologically dependent on the former terms and thus unable to stand on their own.[37] Third, Henryan phenomenology identifies the immanence of auto-affectivity with life, thus making life the fundamental precondition of all appearing whatsoever. Henry explains the generative force of life as follows: "Life is phenomenological in an original and founding sense. It is not phenomenological in the sense that it too would be shown as a phenomenon among other phenomena. It is phenomenological in the sense that it is creative of phenomenality."[38]

While these three points provide evidence of the radicality of Henry's phenomenological maximalism, the Henry-Ricoeur dialogue will bring forth a series of questions about this methodological approach: What if Henry were to abandon his commitment to the maximalist enterprise and its foundationalist claims about the pathos of life?[39] What if the pathos of life, instead, were treated simply as one mode of appearing (immanence) alongside another mode of appearing (transcendence)? What if these two different modes of appearing, instead of being governed by the dependency of a founding relation, were cogenerating and cofounding? What if their interdependency were studied hermeneutically through a patient and careful investigation of the entanglement between life and the world?

Exploring these questions, the Henry-Ricoeur dialogue helps us to envision what Henry's phenomenology of life could look like if it were developed along the alternate path of a minimalist phenomenology. This allows a latent possibility to emerge from Henry's work. Instead of seeking to recover a ground of all experience that stands apart from the world, a minimalist approach would chart a new future course for a phenomenology of life that is hermeneutical and nonfoundational. Instead of privileging one term of an opposition over the other, this minimalist approach would instead discern the significance of life precisely in and through their interrelation. It would thus highlight the mutual interaction between one's own life and the lifeworld, between immanence and transcendence, between affect and representation, and, most importantly, between pathos and praxis.

Putting to rest any concerns about the fruitfulness of a Henry-Ricoeur dialogue, this project at once steers Henry in the direction of a minimalist phenomenology and unearths an implicit phenomenology of life in Ricoeur's hermeneutics. In so doing, it identifies a new possible direction of thought: an integrated phenomenology of life.

## Outline of Chapters

The integrated phenomenology of life is able to ground the concrete meaning of the two perspectives described by Kant's anthropology. On the one hand, the physiological perspective toward the human can be anchored in the phenomenological structure of being in life. This structure includes the various elements that comprise what it means to have a life [*Leben*], such as the various physiological givens of a life situation—for example, one's own birth, genetic inheritance, sociohistorical circumstances, and so forth. To be in life is to be a natural body affected by other natural bodies and by a broader set of life circumstances in which a living individual is situated. On the other hand, the practical perspective toward the human can be linked to the phenomenological structure of being toward life. This structure is linked to the various elements that enable a living individual to give shape to the practical task of leading a life [*Erleben*], such as the abilities to perceive, move, desire, speak, etc. Each of these capabilities, though, is exposed to the limits of the life one has, which includes both the passive reception of these capabilities and their vulnerability to the circumstances of the life in which one acts. An integrated phenomenology of life thus discloses two fundamental aspects of the experience of the living individual as a being who is capable of acting and leading a life yet vulnerable to life circumstances and the threat of suffering.

Each chapter of this book, in its own way, contributes further insight into this twofold structure of the living individual who at once has a life [Leben] and leads a life [Erleben]. The givenness of being in life or having a life will be treated directly in chapters 2 and 7, dealing with the phenomenology of birth and death, though this structure is woven into the fabric of the other chapters as well. The phenomenology of the capabilities of the living individual and their corresponding vulnerabilities is the primary focus in chapters 3 to 6 of this book. Let me offer a brief preview of how the argument unfolds in each chapter.

The first chapter establishes an initial contrast between the phenomenology of life and the traditional phenomenology of consciousness. Husserlian phenomenology is undoubtedly a major influence on both Henry and Ricoeur.[40] Even though both thinkers are critical of Husserl's Idealist tendencies, the critique of Husserl plays an important role in launching each philosopher's own contribution to phenomenology. For Henry, it prepares the passage from a phenomenology of consciousness to a material phenomenology of life. Henry's material phenomenology discloses an original cogito that precedes all forms of intentional consciousness; this original cogito is revealed in the givenness of a pure auto-affection of life. Likewise, for Ricoeur, the critique of Husserl leads to the development of a phenomenology of the involuntary that exposes the self to the experience of necessity and later leads to the development of his hermeneutical phenomenology. Setting aside the methodological differences that may divide Henry and Ricoeur, both provide a phenomenological defense of the passive and nonvoluntary dimension of life. This is accomplished by taking the full experience of the living body—capable of both acting and suffering—as their starting point.

To sharpen the contrast between the phenomenology of consciousness and the phenomenology of life, the second chapter takes up the phenomenology of birth developed by Henry and Ricoeur, respectively. Birth is a limit situation for phenomenology because it is a condition of consciousness but not an experience for consciousness. To make this limit experience intelligible, this chapter draws from the Cartesian circle, which includes both an *ordo essendi* and an *ordo cognoscendi*. On the one hand, birth marks a radically passive exposure to Life. Like the Cartesian ordo essendi, Life brings the self into existence prior to any initiative. The self finds itself in life before it can even be aware of itself as a self. On the other hand, birth does not merely signify a passive suffering of life; it also marks the emergence of a self. Like the Cartesian ordo cognoscendi, birth is a beginning that puts the living individual in possession of its own body and its various capabilities; it becomes capable of acting in life. The phenomenology of birth thus includes the pathos of having a life (being born from Life) as well as the praxis of leading a life (the birth of a self). But there is something quite odd about Henry's assertion that Life gives birth to a self. Isn't it a mother who gives birth? Doesn't a child descend from parents and not from Life as such? Ricoeur's phenomenology of birth provides a minimalist alternative that eschews discussion of a transcendental birth and instead passes through biology to elucidate the subjective meaning of birth. The difference between these approaches is substantive: it leads Ricoeur to emphasize the role of genetics, which indicates the reception of a genetic inheritance that ties me to ancestors and endows me with a set of tendencies that shape my own future. But this genetic inheritance and its influence on the course of one's life is wholly absent from the Henryan account.

Chapter 3 turns to the active side of bodily life by taking up the force of bodily movement. This theme alludes to the work of the French thinker Maine de Biran, whom Henry crowns the "prince of philosophy" and credits as his only true influence. Biran's great contribution is the notion of the living body [*corps propre*], which is not only the object of experience but also a subject of experience, or a bodily cogito. This chapter compares the two thinkers' respective interpretations of what Biran calls "the primitive fact." For Biran, the bodily cogito is anchored in the feeling of effort when my body's movement encounters an external resistance. The experience of effort discloses the body as an active force, an efficient cause, that marks one's personal presence in the world. Ricoeur accepts the importance of Biran's insight, but he calls into question the purported primacy of the primitive fact and the special status it affords to the force of life in Henry's work. The feeling of effort, according to Ricoeur's approach, is an abstraction from a prior effortless involvement in the world. As an alternative, Ricoeur develops the notion of a docile body that undergoes a prior immersion in the surrounding world.

The next two chapters examine actual exchanges between Henry and Ricoeur. While chapter 4 treats their debate over the interpretation of Freud, chapter 5 turns to their debate over Marx. On the surface, these confrontations might seem to raise purely exegetical questions about other thinkers, but these chapters suggest that their debates serve as proxies that illuminate core points of contrast between their respective approaches to the phenomenology of life.

Freud's discovery of the unconscious poses a deep challenge to phenomenology because it detaches meaning from lived experience and undoes the subject's pretentions as a master of meaning. Ricoeur's book on Freud sought to reconcile phenomenology and psychoanalysis by linking both discourses to a shared search for meaning. Against Ricoeur's hermeneutic reading of Freud and a similar drift in Freud's own work, Henry calls for a rethinking of the phenomenology-psychoanalysis relation. Freud's discovery of the unconscious, he contends, can be illuminated by a material phenomenology of life that shows that the unconscious is not simply the unrepresented but the province of life. The unconscious is thus comprised of affects, drives, and instincts of life that cannot be translated into the realm of consciousness. The key point of contention in this debate concerns the question of whether desire—understood as the force of life—can be brought to the level of shared meaning and representation. Whereas Ricoeur argues that Freud offers a mixed discourse combining the language of force and the language of meaning, Henry denies the possibility of an undistorted translation from one register to the other. The chapter concludes with an assessment of some of the challenges raised by Henry's maximalist attempt to detach desire from the natural world.

Disagreement between Henry and Ricoeur also comes to the surface in a brief discussion that followed Henry's presentation of "Rationality According to Marx," which launched Henry's two-volume *Marx*. In his reply, Ricoeur attests to the significance of Henry's undertaking but suggests that it commits an interpretive violence that steers Marx's thought toward Henry's own philosophy. Ricoeur locates this violence in the strict dividing line that Henry establishes between a praxis that is anchored entirely in the subjective experience of a lived body and an economic reality that would be completely objective and separate from subjective experience. According to Ricoeur, Henry goes too far in insisting that only one side of this division—namely, the subjective dimension of lived experience—constitutes the ultimate basis of Marx's thought. As a result of this interpretive decision, Henry minimizes the unchosen economic circumstances [*Umstände*] that situate praxis. This leads Ricoeur to propose, as an alternative, that praxis involves an individual acting in circumstances they did not create. To develop the significance of this proposal, the chapter then turns to Ricoeur's most extensive treatment of Marx: his *Lectures on Ideology and Utopia*. Chief among the conditions that the individual does not create is ideology. In his treatment of ideology, Ricoeur confronts the questions of whether it is possible for an ideology to be nondistorting and whether it is ever possible, as Henry contends, to escape ideology. If we are always situated inside one ideology or another, then the living individual can be accessed only through some interpretive lens or another. Without direct access to the praxis of the living individual, the phenomenology of life is inevitably hermeneutic.

Taking up the suggestion that there is a language of life in Marx and a language of the force of life in Freud, chapter 6 explores the topic of language in more detail. Ricoeur wrote extensively on the problem of language from the 1960s to the 1980s, whereas Henry addressed this topic only in a few essays. Language, however, poses a significant challenge for a phenomenology of life that describes life as a radical immanence that admits no light, no representation, and no exteriority. It therefore cannot be conveyed by what Henry calls "the language of the world" or, in other words, the referential aspect of language. If this were the sole function of language, language would only betray life. But according to Henry, there is another aspect of language—the language of life—that is suited to the appearing of life. After examining the Henryan account, the chapter draws from Ricoeur's philosophy of language to provide a more sophisticated set of tools for thinking about language in minimalist terms—that is, without separating from ordinary language. In particular, the chapter taps into the pragmatics of language that includes living utterances and speech acts. This locates the language of life concretely in the living word of the living individual who speaks.

Chapter 7 examines the opposite end of a lifespan from the study of birth in chapter 2. If life precedes birth, is it equally the case that life survives one's own death and continues to live after? In place of the traditional concept of the afterlife, this chapter contends that a phenomenology of immortality is possible if life is defined in minimalist terms as living after. The meaning of this concept is elucidated through a multistage analysis. Henry describes the immortality of Life as an eternal present that survives and continues to live after the death of the finite individual. But the metaphysical assumptions surrounding this notion make it more appropriate to a doctrine of faith. In contrast, Ricoeur develops a horizontal sense of survival that can be justified phenomenologically; it refers to the way in which an individual is oriented toward others who live after oneself. To probe its phenomenological significance, the chapter turns to Samuel Scheffler's recent work on death and the afterlife. Scheffler helps to clarify that immortality is not simply about one's own desire for self-preservation. It extends the realm of care to the horizontal survival of others and, more generally, of Life as such. This horizontal conception of survival conveys the phenomenological meaning of living after. Beyond the finite scope of being-towards-death, living after introduces a broader attunement of being-towards-life. The structure of being-towards-life transcends the bounds of the concern for one's own life and opens the realm of practical concern to the furtherance of Life as such.

One result of this Henry-Ricoeur dialogue is to combat the simplistic temptation to depict Henry as the philosopher of pathos and Ricoeur as the philosopher of praxis. To be sure, Henry is widely known for his account of the pathos of life and is often identified alongside fellow defenders of passivity like Emmanuel Levinas and Jean-Luc Marion. But it is sometimes forgotten that Ricoeur too challenged the phenomenological primacy of the active dimension of the human and already developed extended analyses of the themes of pathos, vulnerability, and suffering in his early works in the 1940s and '50s. The pathos of life, accordingly, is characteristic of his thought just as much as it is of Henry. Conversely, an equal and opposite oversight is evident in the prevailing scholarship on Henry's thought. While Ricoeur is well-known for his introduction of the Anglo-American theory of action into the French context and for his careful analyses of human action, the practical dimension of Henry's phenomenology is all too often overlooked. Our analyses show that the praxis of life, or the field of human action, is just as essential to Henry as it is to Ricoeur. It follows that both thinkers make significant contributions to thinking about the full scope of praxis *and* pathos. Ultimately, the integrated phenomenology of life aims to unite their contributions around the pathos of having a life and the praxis of leading a life.

Yet, at this juncture, what still remains an open question for an integrated phenomenology of life is the question of how to think what Ricoeur calls the "sharp-edged dialectic between pathos and praxis."[41] In other words, it does not suffice to pursue the meaning of either pathos or praxis in isolation; we need to examine the dialectical interplay between them. Hence, if there is both a pathos and a praxis of life in Henry's work, we need to ask: How does Henry's account of the experience of the pathos of life link with his account of the praxis of the life that one leads? And conversely, how might the praxis of life relate to the pathos of the life that one has? Similar questions need to be raised with respect to the role of pathos and praxis in Ricoeur's work. If Ricoeur configures the meaning of pathos and praxis differently from Henry, how might this affect his own understanding of their relation and their mutual influence on one another? Might his account of their interrelation somehow lend increased nuance and complexity to an integrated account of having a life and leading a life?

The studies that follow pursue these essential questions in order to discern the phenomenological structure of life as pathos and praxis. By providing clarity about this structure, it will then be possible for the phenomenology of life to forge ahead and explore new horizons. It will provide an opening to the vital question of how an integrated account of life can help us to think anew about the practical question of how to live.

# 1

## From a Phenomenology of Consciousness to a Phenomenology of Life

THE PHENOMENOLOGY OF LIFE DRAWS inspiration from the conceptual reservoir of life deployed in Husserlian phenomenology—including such notions as lived experience, the lived body, the living present, and the lifeworld, among many others. Insofar as Husserl exerts a profound and enduring intellectual influence on both Henry and Ricoeur, a discussion of their relation to Husserl's phenomenology serves as more than a historical backdrop. It is essential to understanding the trajectory of their work because it serves as the springboard from which they launch their own unique contributions to phenomenology. The aim of this chapter, accordingly, is to situate their rival approaches to the phenomenology of life in a Husserlian context by detailing their respective criticisms of Husserl and explaining how they motivate the development of their own distinct versions of a phenomenology of life.

Ricoeur played an instrumental role in Husserl's initial reception in France. He published a French translation of Husserl's *Ideas I*, which he prepared during his years as a prisoner of war.[1] This translation, together with an extended commentary on the book, formed one part of Ricoeur's doctoral thesis in 1948.[2] In addition, he wrote a number of early introductory essays on Husserl, many of which are collected in English under the title *Husserl: An Analysis of His Phenomenology* (1967); several more are included in the French collection *À l'école de la phénoménologie*.[3] Together these projects positioned Ricoeur at the vanguard of the phenomenological movement in France. Given Ricoeur's important role in introducing Husserl's work to French readers, there is little doubt that Henry would have been familiar with his writings on Husserlian phenomenology, which remains a continual reference point throughout his own career as well, starting with his magnum opus, *The Essence of Manifestation* (1963), continuing with his close reading of Husserl in *Material Phenomenology* (1990), and culminating with the phenomenology of the body developed in *Incarnation* (2000). Due to the sheer breadth and depth of their respective engagements with Husserlian phenomenology, a detailed discussion of this topic itself could easily warrant a book-length study.[4]

This chapter will concentrate more narrowly on showing that Henry and Ricoeur belong to "the history of Husserlian heresies" and that the content of their heretical positions can be found in the phenomenology of life.[5] The so-called Husserl heretics include an array of thinkers who, though inspired by Husserl's thought, do not adhere to the letter of his doctrine and go beyond it in various ways. Like other Husserl heretics, Henry and Ricoeur challenge certain aspects of Husserl's thought. In particular, they both criticize the Idealist tendencies of Husserl's phenomenology of consciousness, which privilege the active dimension of the ego over its passive dimension and posit the ego as the source of all meaning.[6] Consequently, although it is true to say that Henry and Ricoeur stand in the lineage of Husserlian phenomenology, for them this legacy includes not only what their respective phenomenologies of life borrow but more tellingly what they leave behind.

To trace this development, the chapter begins with an overview of Ricoeur's early (prehermeneutic) work on phenomenology, revealing a strong continuity linking his earliest essays on Husserl to the development of his own phenomenology of the will in *Freedom and Nature*.[7] For Ricoeur, the essence of Husserl's phenomenology is located in his rejection of naturalistic explanations of conscious experience and his corresponding discovery of intentionality. Although Ricoeur praises the phenomenological method in *Freedom and Nature*, his phenomenology of the involuntary deploys a "diagnostic method" that carefully describes the interaction between the voluntary and involuntary in the lived experiences of an embodied cogito. In contrast to Ricoeur's cautious minimalist approach, Henry's writings on Husserl embrace the phenomenological method in its radicality. This maximalist approach questions back to the radical origin of appearing but rejects Husserl's identification of this origin with intentionality. Prior to intentional consciousness, Henry's phenomenology of life recovers a more "original cogito" that undergoes the pure impressionality of the stamp of life and experiences life as a pure pathos of life.[8]

This account of Henry's and Ricoeur's relationships to Husserlian phenomenology will shed light on the significance of the passage from a phenomenology of consciousness to a phenomenology of life more precisely. The phenomenology of life, as this chapter shows, shifts the focus of phenomenology away from the realm of pure thought and turns it to the lived experience of a bodily cogito. In so doing, it reveals the self as a mixture of activity and passivity, freedom and necessity, capability and vulnerability. For both Henry and Ricoeur, the life of the living body becomes the concrete point of intersection between the praxis of action and the pathos of suffering.

## The Critique of Husserl's Idealism

To condense my treatment of Ricoeur's long and multifaceted engagement with Husserl, I will forego consideration of Ricoeur's later development of a "hermeneutic phenomenology" in the late 1960s and focus exclusively on his earlier engagement with Husserl.[9] This period includes Ricoeur's first original work, *Freedom and Nature*, as well as his early commentaries on Husserl collected in *Husserl: An Analysis of His Phenomenology*. These two projects were produced around the same time (late 1940s) and display a strong continuity.[10] In fact, it is possible to link specific observations made in Ricoeur's essays on Husserl to points that are developed more fully in *Freedom and Nature* and vice versa.

*Freedom and Nature* draws inspiration, above all, from Husserl's practice of the phenomenological reduction. The reduction begins with the performance of an *epoche* that suspends or brackets the so-called natural attitude, in which one engages with the world straightforwardly by taking its reality to be out there and ready-made. With this bracketing of the natural attitude, the reduction initiates an act of reflection in which one turns back toward one's own conscious activity and becomes newly aware of its involvement in constituting the meaning of the world. Ricoeur employs the phenomenological reduction in *Freedom and Nature* to bracket two different sets of considerations from his eidetics of the will. The use of the epoche, first of all, allows him to exclude more speculative notions about the will, such as those of the fault and transcendence. The concept of the fault is tied to the problem of the bad will and thus raises the value-laden question of evil, while the concept of transcendence introduces broader questions concerning human innocence, guilt, forgiveness, and reconciliation. By employing the epoche, Ricoeur is able to set aside these normative and more speculative considerations for later treatment and focus solely on the task of providing a value-neutral description of the essential structure of acts of the will.

The second important function of the epoche involves the bracketing of naturalistic explanations of willing.[11] Naturalistic accounts explain human behavior by tracing it back to a more basic level of causal explanation. In this respect, naturalism constructs human behavior as if it were a house whose foundation is anchored in the nonvoluntary dimension of organic life. Physical, biological, and chemical processes serve as the basis for its explanations of increasingly complex layers of willing.[12] By bracketing all causal explanations of behavior, the phenomenological epoche allows the top layer of the conscious experience of willing to be described directly and exclusively on its own terms.

Before proceeding any further, it is worthwhile to pause and note how the phenomenological reduction shapes the broad contours of a phenomenological approach to life. Through the use of the epoche, a phenomenology of life brackets all naturalistic explanations of life, which means that it sets aside theories that explain the experience of life in terms of the laws that govern biological or chemical processes. In addition, it sets aside speculative accounts that would situate life within some sort of metaphysical construct that stands apart from experience. This bracketing allows a phenomenology of life precisely *as* a phenomenology to return to the surface layer of the first-person, subjective experience of life and to describe it exclusively on its own terms.[13]

While Ricoeur embraces Husserl's methodology, the core of his disagreement with Husserl emerges as early as his commentary on *Ideas I*, which expresses the suspicion that Husserlian phenomenology is "an Idealism, even a transcendental idealism."[14] To be sure, Ricoeur is careful to distinguish Husserl's phenomenology from traditional Idealism of the Berkeleyan, Kantian, or Hegelian variety by noting that, at least in *Ideas I*, Husserl's adoption of Idealism is supposed to be "methodological rather than doctrinal."[15] That is to say that even if Husserl utilizes the technical vocabulary of Idealism in the elaboration of his phenomenology, he refrains from making metaphysical commitments to the ultimate reality of consciousness and its objects. The practice of the phenomenological reduction, in this context, simply belongs to the broader description of how to conduct phenomenology as a neutral observer who describes conscious experience in terms of its own sense.[16]

But Ricoeur detects a fundamental shift that occurs in the *Cartesian Meditations* when Husserl makes "a metaphysical decision about the ultimate sense of reality and exceeds the methodological prudence by which consciousness is only interrogated."[17] This metaphysical decision in favor of Idealism can be demonstrated by Husserl's account of the constitution of sense. The ongoing challenge for Husserl involves the question of how to strike a balance between the self-givenness of the reception of what appears (the self as passive) and the sense-giving activity of consciousness (the self as active). Ricoeur describes this as a tension pulling in two opposite and competing directions: "1) As a description restricted to the things just as they are given, phenomenology is a generous effort to respect the diversity of appearing and to restore to each of its modes (perceived, desired, willed, loved, hated, judged, etc.) its quota of strangeness, and, if I may say so, of otherness; 2) in its capacity as an idealistic interpretation of its own descriptive activity, Husserlian phenomenology is a radical effort to reduce all otherness to the monadic life of the ego, to ipseity."[18] In Husserl's early studies of constitution, Ricoeur observes, Husserl emphasizes the receptivity of what is self-given in its diversity and otherness. From that starting point, the work of intentional analysis involves patiently sorting out the multiple intentions that intersect and flow into the sense of what is initially given. But this trajectory is reversed in the *Cartesian Meditations* such that what appears "for me" now also comes "from me."[19] When all forms of appearing are reduced in this way to the ego as their source, the shift from a methodological to a substantive Idealism has been completed. This leads Ricoeur to conclude that "the *Cartesian Meditations* are the most radical expression of this new Idealism for which the world is not only 'for me' but also derives 'from me' all of its ontological validity."[20] Sections 40 and 41 of the *Cartesian Meditations* provide evidence in support of Ricoeur's contention. Consider, for instance, Husserl's assertion that "the final accounting of the self for the self coincides with phenomenology as a whole."[21] This makes phenomenology tantamount to an egology.

However, when sense does become the exclusive product of consciousness, Ricoeur observes, this marks both the culmination and crisis of the ego. It is a culmination of the ego inasmuch as the ego has become the absolute source of meaning. But at the same time, this produces a crisis in the ego, to the extent that it turns the ego into a *solus ipse* and removes all forms of alterity from the ego. The cost of Husserl's promotion of the absolute ego is solipsism—the elimination of everything that is other. In this respect, Husserl's account of an absolute ego falls prey to what Ricoeur elsewhere identifies as the three "transcendental illusions" of the ego's desire to be absolute. This "threefold wish of absolute consciousness" includes the following features: *"the wish to be total,* that is, without the finite perspective associated with a particular character; *the wish to be transparent* in the perfect correspondence of self-consciousness with intentional consciousness; *the wish to be self-sufficient*, without the necessity for being dependent on the nutritive and healing wisdom of the body which always precedes the will."[22] These three illusory desires—to be total, self-transparent, and self-sufficient—might be described as a permanent temptation for a phenomenology of consciousness. According to Ricoeur's assessment, Husserl succumbs to this temptation most clearly in the *Cartesian Meditations* when he gives pride of place to the active, sense-giving performances of the ego.[23] Accordingly, Ricoeur's aim in *Freedom and Nature* is to counter this temptation and to develop a more restrained, non-Idealist variation of phenomenology. This offers a first indication of Ricoeur's minimalist approach to phenomenology.

## Beyond Husserl's Idealism: Ricoeur's Phenomenology of Life

The most innovative feature of Ricoeur's phenomenology of the will, to be sure, is his thesis concerning "the reciprocity of the involuntary and the voluntary."[24] This implies, first of all, that a phenomenology of the will cannot proceed solely through a description of voluntary experience. Such an approach would easily fall prey to the temptation of Idealism, to which Husserl allegedly succumbs. Instead of being defined solely through voluntary acts of self-positing, Ricoeur emphasizes, the will "lives on what it receives and in a dialogue with the conditions in which it is itself rooted." Accordingly, a full account of the will must include reference to the involuntary dimension that precedes and "constantly overflows" the voluntary will.[25] The involuntary does not simply exist in separation from the voluntary, either. Its meaning arises precisely through its various interactions with the will "as that which gives it its motives and capacities, its foundations, and even its limits."[26] As a result, Ricoeur's "phenomenology of the involuntary" seeks to introduce the involuntary dimension of experience into the "very core of the Cogito's integral experience."[27]

To accomplish this, Ricoeur proposes, phenomenology ought to insert itself into "the course of the blood stream" and begin with bodily existence.[28] The living body is the concrete location where the dialectical relation between the voluntary and the involuntary is played out. In this dialectic, each of the three moments of voluntary action—deciding, moving, consenting—is accompanied by an involuntary dimension of receptivity.[29] To decide, for example, is to act for freely chosen reasons, but these reasons are initially motivated by the involuntary needs of the body. I might decide to get a drink, but I do not choose to be thirsty. An act of voluntary decision thus emerges against a background set of biological motivations that I do not choose. Moving, likewise, can be described as a voluntary act that I freely initiate, but it too is made possible by a prior set of capabilities that I do not choose, such as the ability to use my limbs, to coordinate my muscular system, and so forth. This leads Ricoeur to observe that "all power is immersed in life and seems superimposed on a 'tacit' structure which assures the essential tasks of life before all reflection and effort."[30] Last, in consent I can choose or accept who I am, but there is a profound sense in which the reality of the self is unchosen and unwilled. This refers to an absolute involuntary dimension of experience—which Ricoeur describes in terms of character, the unconscious, and biological life—that defines the facticity of my life situation. Through this brief outline of three levels of mutual reciprocity between the voluntary and the involuntary, it is clear that a full account of the lived body must be situated within a dialectic of "decision and motive, action and possibility, consent and situation."[31]

This transition from a phenomenology of pure consciousness to a phenomenology of the embodied cogito involves more than an application of transcendental phenomenology to the empirical world. Instead, it issues a direct challenge to the desire for the absolute that Ricoeur detects in Husserlian thought. The experience of the involuntary exposes the embodied cogito to its limits and limitations. In light of its encounter with the involuntary, "the Ego must more radically renounce the overt claim of all consciousness, must abandon its wish to posit itself, so that it can receive the nourishing and inspiring spontaneity which breaks the sterile circle of the self's constant return to itself."[32] The body's receptivity to the "nourishing and inspiring spontaneity" of the world conveys its exposure to the wide range of nonvoluntary influences—such as bodily reflexes, circulation, respiration, digestion, and countless others—that shape what the body can do. While there are many different examples of the involuntary, the most fundamental and all-encompassing of these, for Ricoeur, is the involuntary dimension of life.

Ricoeur is not widely recognized to have a phenomenology of life, even among Ricoeur scholars. But we are now in a position to show that Ricoeur does articulate a phenomenology of life as early as *Freedom and Nature* (1950), even though it is not presented or systematically developed as such. His phenomenology of life is motivated precisely by his critique of Husserl's phenomenology and thus is a key feature of Ricoeur's original contribution to phenomenology.[33]

In *Freedom and Nature*, Ricoeur describes life as an "experienced necessity" that is "both willed and undergone."[34] This "experience of necessity" is designed to avoid the pitfalls of two alternatives: either a wholly subjective account of experience in which meaning would be established entirely by the voluntary activity of the ego (Husserl's Idealism) or a wholly objective account of necessity in which meaning would be established by external determinants (naturalism). Instead, the experience of necessity is a "mixed concept" that assigns a meaning-giving role for consciousness in response to an unchosen reality.

Life, as an experienced necessity, combines the voluntary and the involuntary. On the one hand, life involves an experience of necessity in the sense that life precedes and conditions all lived experience. This pregivenness of life is explicable in terms of what Husserl calls the *hyletic data*, or in other words, the impressional material that is initially given to conscious experience. In relation to this initial exposure to life, the ego can only be in the position of a response to something that is already there and already given. With respect to life *as given*, one finds oneself always already in life [*en vie*]. Yet, on the other hand, one also has an experience of life as a necessity. In this sense, life is something experiential that one lives though [*Erleben*]. With respect to life *as experienced*, the ego retains the resources to respond to what is given and to shape its meaning. As a result of this duality, it can be said that the experience of life is both undergone and willed, both a source of our actions and something that we act upon, both a source of value and something that is valued.

Ricoeur's first and most extensive treatment of the topic of life occurs in part III of *Freedom and Nature*, which is titled "Consenting: Consent and Necessity." There, Ricoeur examines life in the context of the experience of the absolute involuntary. There are three levels of the absolute involuntary: character, the unconscious, and life. His treatment of these levels is arranged regressively, such that each level points back to a deeper degree of involuntary experience that culminates with the unchosen circumstances of life. In this way, life—which Ricoeur calls "the pure fact of existing 'in life'"[35]—forms the ultimate horizon of the absolute involuntary that situates all the voluntary choices that we make and goals that we pursue.

There are three different ways in which the involuntary dimension of life manifests itself: (1) as a structure that regulates my body, (2) as a temporal development through the process of growth, and (3) as the ultimate facticity of my birth. In dealing with these aspects of life, Ricoeur observes that there is a temptation to confine life to the realm of objective necessity in which "the will can appear as an effect of structure, as a product of evolution of the living, or even as a result of its heredity."[36] But in keeping with the notion that life is an experienced necessity, Ricoeur shows that a subjective experience is woven into each of these involuntary aspects of life.

First of all, life as a structure marks the static component of Ricoeur's analysis. Living creatures are distinct from objects in the sense that they carry out biological functions. The structure of life creates a balance among the various functions of life, such as respiration, digestion, temperature regulation, and so forth. These functions are necessary to sustain life, but they happen automatically without my input; they are, as Ricoeur says, "a problem resolved as though by a greater wisdom than myself."[37] They function in me but without me. These organic functions establish and maintain an equilibrium between myself and the surrounding environment. Although I do not need to do anything to operate the somatic processes of the body, I do have an important role to play in caring for my body. For example, I do not have to be concerned with the beating of my heart, but I can play a role in caring for the health of my heart. I do not have to be concerned with my digestion, but I can be mindful of what I eat. It is in this sense that the involuntary and the voluntary are intertwined in life as a structure.

Whereas the focus on life as a structure offers a static analysis of the involuntary functions of life, the dynamic movement of life is highlighted by Ricoeur's discussion of the process of growth. Ricoeur briefly engages what he calls "a psychology of ages" or what today is called developmental psychology.[38] Each developmental age, he contends, has its own perfection and is a peak in its own way. This makes it possible to respect the multiple aspects of humanity and avoid reducing the teleology of growth to a single developmental point in a lifespan, such as the mature human adult. It includes all the developmental stages on the way to becoming an adult as well as those of aging.

Growth and aging are comparable to life as structure in the sense that they can be described as both a resolved problem and a task. Aging has an element of fate in the sense that it takes place regardless of what I might happen to do or want. I may grow up and eventually grow old, but age is not simply a matter of constraint and limitation. Quite the contrary, Ricoeur observes, "the field of an unlimited freedom opens only within these finite bounds."[39] Each developmental stage of life opens its own type of freedom in relation to the possibilities afforded by the organic processes of growth and aging. Through lifestyle choices and behaviors, I can influence how the aging process unfolds and what it means to me. In growth and aging, we thus find ourselves situated within a dialectic between the voluntary and the involuntary.

The third essential involuntary feature of being *in life* is the fact of birth. While the next chapter will examine this topic in detail, for now it suffices to note that Ricoeur takes the phenomenon of birth to show that the ego is not an absolute beginning. I am always already in life before I am even aware of it. In this way, the fact of my birth points back to beings who existed before me. My birth, my beginning, is the result of a prior series of events. This implies that "the explanation of my being will be alienation. I leave myself in order to place myself in a being outside my control, my ancestors, and follow out a chain of effects down to myself."[40] My birth is the necessary result of a prior set of circumstances, but at the same time, it points to the contingency of my own existence. To be myself, I had to be born with this specific set of genes, in this particular place, and at this particular time, but the fact that this occurred is not necessary. Other genetic combinations, for example, were possible and would have led to the birth of someone else: "This is the alienation which I inflict on myself in genetics," as Ricoeur says.[41] Birth is an interesting concatenation of necessity and contingency: to be myself, I necessarily had to be born in this particular time and place to these particular parents, but the fact that I was born remains purely contingent. Everything could have happened otherwise.

Taken together, these three features of life—structure, growth, and birth—articulate a fundamental life situation that shapes and nourishes all lived experiences. To be alive is to be an organized body, to grow according to a vital impetus, and to descend from ancestors. These facts of my life situation are given to me without my choosing. Although my life situation imposes a set of limitations and constraints on my possibilities, it does not undermine my freedom. For, as we have already noted, life is at once "a task and a resolved problem."[42] It is resolved in the sense that this life situation is established and maintained independently from my will, yet it remains a task in the sense that the will has a role in shaping the meaning and direction of the involuntary. In other words, it is only within a given life circumstance that I can become the particular individual I am, that I can value what I value, or that I can accomplish what I accomplish. This conception of a freedom situated within the involuntary circumstances of life is perhaps summed up best by the closing lines of *Freedom and Nature*, which state that "to will is not to create."[43]

In the context of this chapter's overall argument, the main takeaway point from this section is that Ricoeur does indeed develop a phenomenology of life, even if he does not explicitly use this phrase and is not widely known for this aspect of his thought. Ricoeur's conception of life as an *experienced necessity* is designed to challenge Husserl's Idealism, which construes the transcendental ego as an absolute source of meaning. The experience of the involuntary (which encompasses all the unchosen aspects of life) exposes the bodily cogito to a reality that it does not will. Life precedes and conditions it. It follows that the bodily cogito finds itself always already *in life* and acting in response to a given life situation that it did not create.[44] For Ricoeur, the passage from a pure phenomenology of consciousness to a phenomenology of life reveals a bodily cogito that is situated at the intersection of the voluntary and the involuntary, activity and passivity, creativity and givenness, aspiration and limitation.

## Henry's Critique of Husserl

Just as Husserlian phenomenology is central to Ricoeur's own thinking, so too for Henry it signifies "the principal movement of our time" and defines what it means to do philosophy today.[45] Husserlian phenomenology acquires this prominent role for Henry in virtue of its radicality; it alone is able to renew the question of appearing as such.[46] This radical conception of phenomenology is associated, first and foremost, with the practice of the phenomenological epoche. As noted earlier in this chapter, the epoche involves the suspension of metaphysical constructions and scientific explanations of experience. Bracketing or neutralizing all such presuppositions, phenomenology seeks to return to concrete lived experience. This return does not simply lead, as with Ricoeur, to a patient description of the active and passive dimensions of various mundane bodily experiences. Instead, in the Henryan approach, phenomenology is assigned a more ultimate and radical task: it inquires into the origin of appearing and asks how anything comes to appear in the first place. In sharp contrast with Ricoeur's minimalism, Henry's material phenomenology embraces (and perhaps even radicalizes) the maximalist trajectory in Husserl's thought.

By identifying the task of phenomenology with a return to the origin, or the *radix* [the root], of all possible appearing, Henry is aligned with "the

Cartesian way" into Husserlian phenomenology.[47] In contrast with other ways into phenomenology—such as the ways through descriptive psychology and the lifeworld—the Cartesian way is characterized by its attempt to provide an ultimate foundation for all appearing. Inspired by the Cartesian search to establish a first starting point of knowledge, Henry goes so far as to call the Cartesian cogito "the birth of phenomenology itself."[48]

Although both Husserl and Henry identify the Cartesian cogito as the birthplace of phenomenology, it is interesting that neither one of them actually endorses the famous Cartesian formulation "I think, therefore I am." In the *Cartesian Meditations*, Husserl criticizes Descartes for missing the significance of his own discovery. In his haste to secure knowledge of the external world, Descartes passes over and neglects the cogito itself as a distinctive region of being. This prepares the way for Husserl's own discovery concerning the essential structure of conscious life: intentionality. Husserl extends the very same certainty of the *ego cogito* to the intentional structure of consciousness in the following passage: "However I might perceive, imagine, judge, infer . . . it remains absolutely clear that with respect to perception I am perceiving this or that, that with respect to judgment, I am judging this or that, etc."[49] According to Husserl, we can know with certainty that consciousness has an intentional structure, such that every act of consciousness is an *ego cogito cogitatum*.

Henry, however, is critical not only of the Cartesian *cogito, ergo sum* but also of Husserl's *ego cogito cogitatum*, contending that both formulations conceal the true reality of the cogito. To make sense of Henry's criticism, it is helpful to take a step back and situate it in the context of a basic principle of phenomenology that was introduced by the Marburg school: "so much appearing, so much being."[50] Henry accepts this formula as a legitimate phenomenological principle, provided that it does not impose any undue constraints on the scope of appearing and remains fully open to the question of the *how* of appearing. In the actual development of phenomenology, Henry contends that Husserl violates this principle by narrowing the scope of appearing in two specific respects: (1) methodologically, through the adoption of the eidetic reduction; (2) substantively, by privileging intentional consciousness over other modes of experience.

Husserl employs the eidetic reduction, according to Henry, as a reduction to transcendence. That is to say it converts each *cogitatione* into a *cogitatum*. It casts the *cogitationes* themselves out into the external realm of the visible and puts them on display in the light of the outside and places them in front of [*Vor-stellung*] consciousness. By performing this transfer, the eidetic reduction provides a pure seeing, or insight, into the form [*eidos*] of what appears. This is exemplified by Husserl's adoption of the Cartesian standard for cognition: the criterion of clear and distinct perceptions. In determining what counts as phenomenological evidence, Husserl follows Descartes in asserting that "with Descartes we can now take the additional step (*mutatis mutandis*): whatever is given through clear and distinct perception, as it is in any particular cogitation, we are entitled to accept."[51] But, Henry notes that the evidence of "clear and distinct perception" is suitable only to the visual perception of external objects. As a result, it narrows the scope of appearing to the horizon of the visible, or, in other words, to the external mode of appearing.

To develop Henry's claim, we can identify three defining features of intentional consciousness: (1) exteriority, (2) objectification, (3) correlation. First, intentional consciousness imposes a distance between the consciousness that lets something be seen and the object that is seen by consciousness. Just as the vision of a thing establishes a distance between the observer and the observed object, so too is intentional consciousness fundamentally ek-static. It is not directed toward itself but instead points outside itself, toward its objects. Second, intentional consciousness defines being in terms of objects or beings. According to its Latin etymology, an object is something that is thrown against or stands in the way of something else; in this case, the intentional object is something that is thrown in front of consciousness. As such, the being of the intentional object is defined by its relation to consciousness; it is placed in front of consciousness and stands there as something available for consciousness. Third, intentional consciousness establishes a correlation between subject and object. On the one hand, intentional consciousness is a consciousness that is for object while on the other hand, the intentional object is an object that exists for consciousness. This correlation between the intentional subject and object establishes an equivalence between the philosophy of consciousness and the philosophy of being, leading Henry to observe that "the subjectivity of the subject is only the objectivity of the object."[52] To appear comes to mean being an intentional object—that is, an object of and for consciousness. As a result, Husserl's phenomenology is ultimately a phenomenology of the visible.[53]

The problem with Husserl's phenomenology, then, is that it is not sufficiently radical.[54] Although Husserl's practice of the eidetic reduction is suited to the ek-static mode of appearing that characterizes the visible, it misses the true origin of appearing when it turns away from what is actually given in consciousness—or what Henry calls the cogitationes. This shift from the actual lived experience to the seeing of its formal structure is not simply an exchange of one type of givenness for another; instead, it marks a fundamental distortion of the original mode of appearing.[55] As a result, Henry contends that Husserl's account of intentional consciousness captures only a secondary cogito.

To recover the truly radical origin of appearing, Henry's material phenomenology moves in the opposite direction from Husserl and performs what might be called a reduction to immanence. In so doing, it returns to the immanence of the original cogitationes that precede intentionality and are its material conditions. These cogitationes, in their material reality, are not externalized or represented by consciousness; instead, they are experienced purely and simply in the pathos of living through them: in the experience of thinking, desiring, acting, and so forth. Here Henry discovers the original cogito as a cogito without a cogitatum. The study of this hitherto unexplored region, with its own unique structure and set of laws, defines the task of Henry's own phenomenology of life.

To unpack this discovery of the original cogito, Henry provides an example through a reading of Article 26 in Descartes's *Passions of the Soul*.[56] There, Descartes returns to the hyperbolic doubt that is cast over everything that appears in the world and confronts the prospect that it could all just be a dream. Under such conditions, certainty can be found only in that which does not owe its reality to the experience of the world. If I have a scary dream, for example, it could be the case that everything that appears in my dream is false. "But," Descartes writes, "we can't be misled in that way with regard to the passions, because they are so close, so internal to our soul, that it can't possibly feel them unless they are truly as it feels them to be." The affective experience of fright, even though it might be experienced in a nightmare, cannot be doubted. It still exists precisely as I experience it.[57] This example highlights a specific type of cogitatione—an affective experience—that is freed from the intentional structure that would put it in relation to the external world and, precisely in that sense, can be called invisible. The self-revelation of this affect reveals itself immediately and directly to oneself.

Prior to Descartes's purported discovery of the cogito, Henry detects this other mode of appearing through a careful rereading of Descartes's Second

Meditation. In particular, he calls attention to a passage in which Descartes observes that *"at certe videre videor"* ("it seems that I see").[58] Henry interprets this as the release of the cogito from any relation whatsoever to a cogitatum. Everything that is seen or represented as a cogitatum is considered potentially dubious and uncertain. This phenomenological residue of this suspension of all relations to the external modes of appearing is the disclosure of an original self-relation conveyed in the statement "it seems that I see" [*videre videor*], which signifies an entirely different type of appearing—an auto-affective relation to one's own seeing.

This distinction supports Henry's thesis concerning the fundamental duality of appearing: the transcendence of intentionality versus the immanence of auto-affectivity. Recall that intentionality can be described as a transcendent mode of appearing with the following characteristics: (1) exteriority; (2) objectifying activity; (3) correlation. By contrast, Henry describes auto-affectivity as an immanent mode of appearing with the precise opposite set of characteristics: (1) interiority; (2) nonobjective pathos; (3) self-relation. First, in contrast with the externalizing direction of intentionality, the immanent mode of appearing does not involve any ek-static relation to the outside. It is a cogito without a cogitatum, which involves only the self's relation to itself. Second, unlike intentionality's active bestowal of meaning on objects, this immanent mode of appearing is accomplished as a pathos that is undergone and felt without being converted into an object, like the cogitationes described earlier. As a result, the intentional correlation between the subject and object is broken; the immanent mode of appearing does not open onto anything outside itself. It does not admit any distance between lived experience and its contents. In this self-relation, the self relates directly to itself in the immediacy of its own embrace. According to Henry's view, this auto-affective experience reveals the true phenomenological meaning of life: life is rooted in the lived experience of one's own living and nothing other than itself.

At this point, the legitimate meaning of Henry's phenomenology of the invisible is clear.[59] Henry is not invoking some sort of mystical or otherworldly experience with this phrase. Instead, its meaning must be situated in the Husserlian context in which it is deployed. We have seen that Henry redirects the phenomenological reduction from the transcendent mode of appearing to the immanent mode of appearing. Insofar as Husserl's reduction promotes a transcendent mode of appearing, his phenomenology unfolds entirely within the horizon of visibility. By contrast, Henry's reduction to immanence can be described aptly as a recovery of the invisible. To be precise, it reveals a different mode of appearing that escapes from the horizon of visibility. For this reason, Henry's phenomenology remains within the bounds of phenomenology and offers a new phenomenological breakthrough. It introduces a new mode of appearing—a radical immanence—that was glimpsed but overlooked in both Descartes's and Husserl's thought.[60]

Still, an important set of questions about Henry's phenomenology of life remain unanswered thus far. That is, how does Henry go beyond this thesis concerning two irreducible modes of appearing—transcendence and immanence? How does Henry justify his further claim that one of these modes—immanence—is a radical origin while the other mode of appearing—transcendence—is dependent on it? What, in other words, justifies his claim that the immanent mode of appearing alone serves as the radical origin of all appearing? These questions can be pursued through a close reading of Henry's book *Material Phenomenology* (1990), which offers the most detailed articulation of his relation to Husserlian phenomenology.

## A Material Phenomenology: Beyond Husserl's Phenomenology of the Visible

The book's title originates from a question posed by Didier Franck in 1987 in conjunction with a special issue of the journal *Philosophie* devoted to Henry's thought. In the process of preparing that issue, Franck sent a list of questions that specifically asked Henry to clarify the relation between his own material phenomenology and Husserl's hyletic phenomenology. In response to Franck's question, Henry's chapter "Hyletic Phenomenology and Material Phenomenology" in *Material Phenomenology* is especially instructive. It shows how and why Henry's material phenomenology grants primacy to the nonintentional experience of life over and above intentional consciousness of the world.[61]

To distinguish himself from Husserl, Henry draws a contrast between their respective approaches to the concrete starting point of phenomenological analysis: the givenness of sense impressions.[62] Husserl discusses this topic extensively in *Ideas I* (1913) and in his *Lectures on the Internal Consciousness of Time* (1905). For instance, his early analysis of intentionality includes a distinction between the form [*morphe*] and the matter [*hule*] of an intention. The form refers to the conscious activity that confers a meaning onto the sense impression; it thus serves as the intentional component of this pair.

By contrast, the matter is that which is passively received by consciousness and contributes sense data for the intentional act. But Husserl is quite clear that these impressions, though providing the support for intentionality, are not themselves intentional. As a simple example, consider the perception of a tree. It includes various sense impressions (color, shape, etc.) that are given as the material content of the perception. Through them, the act of perception confers a meaningful form onto these data and is directed toward the tree as a real object that transcends consciousness. But already with this very simple example, a question about Husserl's account arises: which of these two components of the intentional experience—the form or the matter, the active bestowal of meaning or the passive reception of material—is fundamental? The key point of divergence between Husserl's account of the hyletic data and Henry's own material phenomenology can be located in their respective answers to this question.

Although Husserl does acknowledge that the hyletic data should be included in a full account of conscious experience, Henry contends that he makes a series of interpretive decisions that grant a primacy to the formal element over and above the material component of intentionality. Examples of these interpretive decisions can be provided with respect to the previous example concerning the form and the matter of intentionality as well as his treatment of impressions in his *Lectures on the Internal Consciousness of Time* (1905).[63] In a nutshell, Husserl devalues the nonintentional matter [hule] in each of these cases because he considers it to exist only for the sake of receiving intentional form. This point is illustrated in a particularly illuminating passage, which I quote at length:

> Everything that is given is given to us, so to speak, two times. The first givenness, the *Empfindung*, is mysterious. It is the type of givenness and given in which the mode of givenness is itself the given. Affectivity is both the impression's mode of givenness and its impressional content. It is the transcendental in a radical and autonomous sense. And then, this first given, which is always already given and presupposed, is given a second time in and through intentionality, as a transcendent and irreal thing, as its "vis a vis." "Transcendental" phenomenology, as intentionality, is limited to the description of this second givenness, to the analysis of its essential modes and the various types of noeses and noemas corresponding to it. But it has set aside what it constantly presupposes, the first givenness.[64]

The key here is to recognize two types of givenness: the first givenness of the material impression and the second givenness of the irreal intentional object. Even though Husserl acknowledges that the impressional element is necessary to intentional consciousness, his interpretive decisions yield the result that "the phenomenology of *hyle* is diverted into a phenomenology of intentionality."[65] By privileging the second type of givenness over the first, Husserl turns away from the materiality of what is first given.

Henry's material phenomenology, in contrast, could be described as an attempt to restore and revalue the first givenness of the hyletic data, or what we earlier called the cogitationes. The hyletic data are impressed on consciousness, and without their initial givenness, intentional consciousness would be unable to lay any claim to an external reality. In this respect, Henry emphasizes that intentional consciousness is ontologically dependent on the first givenness of the hyletic data.

This provides the phenomenological ground for the second central thesis of Henry's phenomenology of life: the two irreducible modes of appearing—immanence and transcendence—have a founding [*Fungierende*] relation in which immanence founds transcendence. Henry asserted this thesis as early as *The Essence of Manifestation*: "The original act of transcendence reveals itself independently from the movement by which it projects itself outside of itself, reveals itself in itself, in such a way that this 'in itself' signifies: without bypassing itself, without leaving itself. What is not bypassed, what is not thrown outside of itself but remains in itself without leaving itself or going outside of itself is, in its essence, immanence. Immanence is the original mode in which the revelation of transcendence is accomplished and as such, the original essence of revelation."[66] While Henry's assertion lacked phenomenological grounding at that time, his material phenomenology grounds the primacy of the immanent mode of appearing in the first givenness of material impressions. It shows that the immanent mode of appearing conditions all intentional experience. Intentional consciousness, accordingly, is only a secondary mode of appearing, which is dependent and founded on the prior reception of material impressions. The task of material phenomenology is to investigate the structure and significance of the material impressions, the hyletic data, on which all intentional consciousness depends.

Yet, one might legitimately wonder whether Henry accidentally falls back into the Idealism he just criticized in Husserl. By advocating for the primacy of the immanent mode of appearing, isn't Henry ultimately repeating the same mistake of elevating the ego to the rank of an absolute origin—a foundation—of all meaning? Henry is careful to dispel this suspicion in a passage I quote at length:

> Experiencing each of its powers while it exercises it—and in the first place, the power it has of exercising them—the ego now assumes it is their source, their origin.... As somehow the absolute source and origin of the powers that compose its being (the effective and active being with which identifies and by which it defines itself), the ego considers itself also the source and origin of its own being. *Thus is born the transcendental illusion of the ego*.... Exercising its power and taking itself as its source, as the ground of its Being, the ego believes that it perceives its true condition and so suffers under the similar illusions of forgetting and of falsifying that condition. It forgets Life, which in its Ipseity gives it to itself and at the same time gives it all its powers and capacities.... In the transcendental illusion, the ego lives the hyper-power of Life—self-generation as self-givenness—as its very own.[67]

Like Ricoeur, in this passage Henry criticizes Husserl—and others who conceive the ego as an absolute origin—for falling prey to a transcendental illusion produced by the ego's desire to be the absolute source of its own powers and its own intelligibility. While the ego does possess such powers to act and make sense, Henry continues with a word of caution that this is only one aspect of its reality:

> The ego's transcendental illusion is not totally illusory, in fact. It carries a portion of "reality" and "truth," which we have to deal with simply because it is essential.... Once given to itself, the ego is really in possession of itself and of each of these powers, able to exercise them: it is really free.... The "I Can"—the activation of each of my powers—is the contrary of an illusion, as is the "I am" born of this "I can." Thus the effectuation of this "I Can" / "I Am" covers over [*vient-elle recouvrir*] the fact that this living "I can," this living "I am," has come about only thanks to the endless work of Life in it.[68]

In other words, Henry concedes that the powers and sense-making activities of the ego are real, but he emphasizes that they do not originate entirely from the ego itself. Instead, Life is the original source that brings these powers of the self into existence. Here, it becomes clear that Henry surpasses Husserl by carrying out an additional step of phenomenological reflection that results in a more radical questioning. On the one hand, Husserl's phenomenological reflection questions back from the object in order to disclose the constituting activity of the ego. It reveals the ego as the absolute source of the object's meaning. On the other hand, Henry adds a second layer of heightened reflection—a reflection on reflection—that poses the question about the source of the ego's own power to constitute meaning. How does the ego acquire its power to act and constitute meaning? Henry challenges the primacy of the ego by observing that the ego does not give this power to itself but instead receives it from a source outside itself. Life, in a word, is the source of the ego's capacities. The following passage is one instance, among many, in which Henry notes the involuntary and passive reception of life: "The movement through which the life tirelessly comes into the self . . . is not willed. It does not result from any effort; instead, it precedes effort and makes it possible. . . . All effort and all abandon is always already given to oneself on the Ground of being-given-to-an effort and to act."[69] This passage highlights life's role as a ground of the living individual, which gives rise to and continually supports the living individual. In this respect, life exists in a founding relationship to all conscious activities. Prior to any act of will or consciousness, life has always already placed its stamp on the self. Life is the original and all-encompassing source of meaning for the objects of consciousness as well as the powers of the ego. It is the true first givenness and the true condition on which all intentional experience depends. This brings the key difference between Husserl and Henry to the surface: whereas the transcendental ego is the phenomenological absolute for Husserl, life becomes the phenomenological absolute in Henry's phenomenology.

While the next chapter will inquire more thoroughly into the phenomenological structure of Henry's account of the relation between life and consciousness as well as the duality of pathos and praxis implicit in it, let me sum up a few important takeaway points from this brief overview of Henry's relation to Husserlian phenomenology. We have shown that Henry's phenomenology of life is motivated by the concern that Husserlian phenomenology narrows the scope of appearing to the horizon of the visible and the transcendent mode of appearing. In response, Henry's reduction to immanence first establishes a nonintentional mode of consciousness that is distinct from and irreducible to intentional consciousness. Second, it shows that intentional consciousness is ontologically dependent on the prior reality of the nonintentional, material impressions of life. This prior reality reveals the passivity of the ego with regard to its original and inescapable exposure to life, with its material impressions, affects, and drives. In this respect, our study of Henry's phenomenology yields an unexpected point of convergence with Ricoeur. Both thinkers, as it turns out, go beyond Husserlian phenomenology by tapping into the involuntary dimension of life. They both contend that a full account of the living individual must include not only what is actively willed or chosen by the ego but also account for the unwilled dimension of the ego's exposure to life.

## Conclusion

This chapter has shown that Husserlian phenomenology is indispensable for understanding the motivations and significance of the passage from a phenomenology of consciousness to a phenomenology of life. To make sense of this trajectory in Henry and Ricoeur, respectively, it is of equal importance to discern how they depart from Husserlian orthodoxy and to identify what remains phenomenological about their work.

The fact that their respective phenomenologies of life remain phenomenology can be attributed to their shared commitment to Husserl's method—specifically, to the use of the phenomenological epoche.[70] The epoche signifies a suspension or bracketing of metaphysical and naturalistic explanations of consciousness. Instead of reducing consciousness to either some type of metaphysical construct or a set of biochemical processes, the phenomenological approach returns to the surface layer of lived first-person experience and seeks to disclose its structure and meaning on its own terms. This methodological decision has significant consequences: it entails the bracketing of all metaphysical and naturalistic explanations of life. This orients the phenomenology of life toward a reflection on the meaning of lived first-person experience. It discloses what might be called the subjective qualia of life, in which one experiences what it is like to be alive. This type of experience remains inaccessible to the objectively oriented approach to life in the natural sciences. On this point, Henry is fond of quoting François Jacob's quip that "biologists no longer study life today," which he takes to mean that biologists study only algorithms but not life in its true phenomenological sense.[71] The principal aim of a phenomenology of life, accordingly, is to recover the subjective experience of life, to uncover its fundamental structures and laws, and to demonstrate their significance in a human life.

Moreover, both Henry and Ricoeur challenge the orthodoxy of Husserlian phenomenology by invoking two main points of criticism.[72] First, they accuse

Husserl of being (mis)guided by the model of visual perception. Ricoeur, for instance, asserts that "the phenomenology of Husserl remains an analysis of seeing; phenomenology itself aims at seeing; its descriptions are an exercise of visions applied to vision."[73] This phenomenology of the visible, as Henry's analysis further shows, results in an undue restriction and narrowing of the scope of appearing. Second, both thinkers criticize Husserl's Idealism, or, in other words, his emphasis on the active role of the ego in constituting the meaning of lived experience. This leads to a sort of voluntarism in which the ego is mistakenly believed to exert its will and mastery over the scope and meaning of what appears. As a result of these two criticisms, Henry and Ricoeur both turn to the phenomenology of life in an effort to reveal a prior dimension of passive, involuntary experience that conditions the activities of the ego.[74]

To accomplish this task, both thinkers return to the wellspring of the lived experience of the embodied cogito whose significance can be summed up with three final points. First of all, the turn to the embodied cogito signifies more than the disclosure of a different region from that of pure consciousness: the embodied cogito belongs primarily to the realm of praxis rather than thought. Ricoeur refers to the practical self as a *homo capax* while Henry speaks about it as a fundamental *I can*. Considered as a power to act, the practical self is endowed with a set of bodily capabilities through which it can act and do things in the world. This field of practical capacities and bodily know-how is a source of cognition, perhaps even its original source as some recent proponents of embodied cognition have argued.[75]

Second, the embodied cogito is understood in terms of its capacity for both acting *and* suffering. Whereas Husserl's phenomenology of consciousness emphasizes the active dimension of the self, the phenomenology of life returns to the original fund of lived experience and discloses the body's passive exposure and vulnerability to life. Indeed, while developing this theme in his own work, Ricoeur praises Henry as one of the great defenders of the passivity or the pathos of the lived body. This passivity, as Henry elucidates, includes one's encumberment with burdens, needs, and desires as well as the various types of pathos that accompany it, ranging from the sorrows of pain, loss, and evil to the elation of pleasure, love, and joy. It also includes, as Ricoeur shows, an exposure to the external limits and limitations imposed by the surrounding world, others, and sociohistoric factors.

Yet, while acknowledging this passive exposure to life, it is important to keep in mind that the lived body is a point of intersection between praxis and pathos. This duality is found not only in Ricoeur's thesis concerning the reciprocity of the voluntary and the involuntary but also, perhaps unexpectedly, in Henry's account of life as a source of possibility and impossibility. Hence, a phenomenology of life ought to articulate the "sharp-edged dialectic" that takes place in bodily life between the pathos of life (the passivity of what it undergoes) and the praxis of life (the activity of what a body can do).[76] To call this a dialectic does not imply a simple merger of the two, as if passivity were simply the other side of activity. Here, we are not simply dealing with the relative type of passivity that allows sense impressions to make the activity of seeing possible or the reverse process in which a conscious activity fades from attention and slides into the background. To be clear, the phenomenology of life aims to describe a more radical sense of passivity that, for the sake of contrast, might be called an absolute passivity. Echoing what Levinas famously described as a passivity more passive than any passivity, this type of passivity cannot simply be converted into an activity or an idea. It signifies the suffering of a pathos that is purely undergone, such as the suffering of insomnia, pain, depression, trauma, or evil. Instead of thinking about these as experiences [*vécus*] that one has, they are described more fittingly as trials or ordeals [*épreuves*] that one goes through. Life, as a radical passivity or an absolute involuntary, is not like the experience of an object; instead it is a condition and an ordeal that one goes through.[77]

The third point to note is that, even though Henry and Ricoeur arrive at this shared insight into life as both pathos and praxis, they arrive there by two very different methodological paths. We have seen that Henry adopts a maximalist approach that embraces phenomenology in its radicality. He seeks an Archimedean point that is even more radical than Husserl's Cartesian starting point: an original cogito that stands on its own without any support from the material world. Through a reduction to a radical immanence, the original cogito is revealed in a pure auto-affection of life that serves as the starting point for his further investigations into the meaning of lived experience. By contrast, Ricoeur deploys a minimalist approach that, instead of retreating from the natural world, inserts phenomenology "into the blood stream" of the lived body. This is evident in the diagnostic method adopted by *Freedom and Nature*, which holds that "any moment of the Cogito can serve as an indication of a moment of the object body . . . and each moment of the object body is an indication of a moment of the body belonging to a subject."[78] This method, which anticipates Ricoeur's later development of hermeneutics, carefully demonstrates the intertwining of activity and passivity in life as an "experienced necessity." Commenting on their two different ways of doing phenomenology, Henry was therefore not wrong to say that "I took the inverse option. Ricoeur and I are at two poles of phenomenology."[79]

This key contrast sets the stage for a pair of broad questions that will be pursued in the chapters to follow: What is at stake in this methodological difference between a maximalist and a minimalist approach to the phenomenology of life? How do these methodological differences between the two thinkers translate into substantive differences in their respective accounts of life as pathos and praxis?

# 2

## Birth

*The Pathos of Being-in-Life*

WHILE BOTH RICOEUR AND HENRY propose a phenomenology of life in response to the perceived limitations of Husserlian phenomenology, the previous chapter also reinforced Henry's observation that "Ricoeur and I are at two poles of phenomenology."[1] This is evident in their two rival methodological approaches. While Henry adopts a maximalist phenomenology that establishes life as an origin and source of meaning, Ricoeur's phenomenology of life follows a minimalist path that discloses life through a patient description of mundane lived experiences. Building on this point, this chapter takes another important step in advancing the overall argument of the book. Through a study of the phenomenology of birth, it shows that these two different methodological approaches result in substantive differences. Both thinkers elucidate the meaning of birth through the pathos and praxis of life, but they turn out to have two very different conceptions of what these terms mean.

First of all, however, it should be noted that this overarching claim concerning life as pathos and praxis becomes problematic conceptually in the context of Henry's phenomenology. Recall that one of Henry's central theses involves the duality of two different modes of appearing: the transcendent appearing of the world and the immanent appearing of life. Whereas the transcendent mode of appearing is characterized by the distance that separates subject and object, immanence is described as an immediate affective embrace of life—that is, a pure auto-affection of life. This distinction encounters a difficulty when it is placed alongside the claim that his phenomenology includes the duality of pathos and praxis. Are these two claims truly compatible? Can the active/passive distinction be introduced into the structure of life without contradicting Henry's claim about the alleged immediacy of the auto-affective experience of life?

This presents a difficult dilemma. On the one hand, if, as Henry claims, the immanent appearing of life is truly immediate and without any separation, division, or difference, this would seem to entail the inability to distinguish between activity and passivity. Difference is implicit in the distinction between activity and passivity. Indeed, a lack of difference might even threaten Henry's own notion of auto-affectivity. After all, to be affected entails being acted upon by something that is somehow other. The experience of life, described as a pure immediacy, clashes with the notion of affectivity, and more problematically, runs the risk of becoming ineffable. Like the Parmenidean One, it would allegedly exist, but nothing meaningful could be said about it without introducing some type of separation, division, or difference.[2] It would be neither active, nor passive, and it would have none of the attributes that imply some element of activity or passivity, either. All Henry could say about it is simply that it is. But, on the other hand, if the affective pathos of life is retained, this would seem to require Henry to renounce his claim about the alleged immediacy of the experience of life. If the cogito experiences life as a pathos, this implies the prior reality of a life that precedes itself and acts on oneself. Life, rather than the cogito, would be the active source of this pathos, and as such, would entail some degree of separation, division, or difference from oneself. This distance and separation between life and the cogito, however, would undermine many of the common descriptors invoked in Henry's phenomenology of life—such as the description of the experience of life as immediate, without distance, without difference, without division, and so forth. As a result, Henry's phenomenology of life is confronted with a difficult dilemma: either it must remove the language of activity and passivity from its description of the immediacy of the experience of life, or it must abandon its claims concerning the immediacy life's appearing and embrace the language of difference. How should this dilemma (which, to the best of my knowledge, Henry does not answer or even seem to recognize) be resolved?

The solution requires another important step in the overall argument of this book: that there is an implicit concept of difference operative in Henry's phenomenology of life. Even though Henry speaks the language of a philosophy of the immediate, this study of the phenomenology of birth shows that he actually relies on a specific type of difference. The root problem here is that Henry fails to recognize the possibility of distinguishing between two kinds of difference: external and internal. An external difference refers to a difference between two separate things whereas an internal difference emerges within a single entity. The limitation in Henry's own discourse about life, therefore, can be attributed to the fact that he conceptualizes difference only as external difference. This leads him to ascribe difference only to the transcendent mode of appearing that is characterized by the division between inner and outer, subject and object, and so forth. To justify his sharp contrast between the transcendent and immanent modes of appearing, Henry therefore resorts to speaking about the immanence of life in terms of its pure immediacy and lack of any (external) difference. But Henry fails to recognize that an internal difference, or self-differentiation, could govern the phenomenological structure of the appearing of life and still preserve its distinction from transcendence.

This self-differentiation of life, though it goes unnamed, is actually evident in Henry's phenomenology of life. Indeed, his phenomenological description of birth becomes coherent only when it is explained through the notion of an internal difference. This language of self-differentiation enables the phenomenology of life to go beyond the static language of immediacy and articulate a more complex and dynamic account of life. It opens the possibility of describing the temporal development of life through the stages of birth, growth and decline; additionally, it allows for a more complex and rich account of the structure of the relationship between consciousness and life as such. By introducing this concept of internal difference, it becomes possible to adjust the terminology of Henry's phenomenology in such a way that it provides a more coherent and compelling account of the immanence of life without compromising the insights of his actual phenomenological studies.

To accomplish this retooling of Henry's phenomenology, this chapter proceeds in a series of steps. First, it returns to Descartes's Third Meditation. This starting point draws inspiration from Ricoeur's observation that "only the first two Meditations count for Husserl." His point is that Husserl's Idealism becomes possible only if and when Descartes's *Meditations* are narrowed to the Second Meditation which establishes the certitude of the cogito. Accordingly, his Idealism can be overcome by an appreciation of the full scope of Descartes's argument. The point here is not simply to extend phenomenological analysis to the Third Meditation. Ultimately, what matters is the rediscovery of the Cartesian circle that highlights the relation between the Second and Third Meditations.[3] Whereas Husserl's reliance solely on the Second Meditation leads to an absolute cogito without any limits, the Cartesian circle reveals the cogito in a dual sense: the cogito is aware of itself as well as its own limitations.

By adopting this model, the phenomenology of life is able to surpass Husserl's Idealism and articulate the internal self-differentiation of life between life and the living individual and between pathos and praxis. This becomes evident through Henry's description of the birth of the self. The birth of the self both puts the natal self in possession of itself and makes it aware of its own limitations. Although these two aspects of the natal self are present in Henry's account, their connection is never clearly articulated or justified there. This disconnect, I contend, can be repaired by the proposed retooling of the Henryan approach. Instead of emphasizing only the immediacy of the original cogito, I propose that birth (and the phenomenological structure of life more generally) should be articulated through the model of the Cartesian circle. The two sources of evidence in the Cartesian circle allow us to articulate the relation between Life and the living individual as an internal difference, or, in other words, as a process of self-differentiation that governs life's immanent mode of appearing.

After showing how this phenomenological structure elucidates Henry's phenomenology of birth, the chapter will conclude by drawing a contrast with the Ricoeurian approach to the phenomenology of birth. Adopting a minimalist approach, Ricoeur's account is informed by the intersection between the discourses of phenomenology and biology. As such, it reveals a dimension of birth that is plainly obvious yet surprisingly absent from the Henryan account: the natal bond with a mother and a genetic ancestry. This biological dimension of life lends initial support for the broader conclusion that Henry's account of the internal self-differentiation of life alone is insufficient and that a more thoroughly integrated phenomenology of life is necessary.

## The Cartesian Circle

The path to overcoming Husserl's Idealism is paved by a rereading of Descartes's *Meditations*.[4] What Husserl fails to appreciate, according to Ricoeur, is that the cogito is not the only ground of cognition. To be sure, Descartes's Second Meditation establishes the cogito as the epistemological source of the evidence of ideas. But the reality of these ideas is secured only later in the Third Meditation, where Descartes establishes the ontological ground for ideas, including even the idea of the cogito itself. Ricoeur explains that the phenomenological significance of Descartes's Third Meditation does not reside so much in its proof of the existence of God or in its proposed solution to the problem of knowing the external world. Instead, what matters most is that it offers "a displacement of the center of gravity toward the infinite being."[5] Through its decentering of the cogito, Descartes's Third Meditation reveals the limitations of the cogito and its dependence on something other than itself.

This broader reading of Descartes's *Meditations* surmounts Husserl's exclusive focus on the first two Meditations and yields two irreducible types of evidence: the cogito and the idea of the Infinite. Whereas the Second Meditation describes the *ratio cognoscendi* of knowledge (the way of knowing) through its establishment of the evidence of the cogito, the Third Meditation offers the *ratio essendi* of knowledge (the way of being) through its use of the ontological argument. Commenting on these two distinct forms of evidence, Ricoeur observes that "the central intuition of Cartesianism is the bond between the 'Cogito' and the ontological argument."[6] In other words, neither type of evidence—neither the ratio cognoscendi nor the ratio essendi—stands alone in the Cartesian circle: what matters is precisely the relation that links them together. These two modes of evidence overlap to create a mutually reinforcing bond.[7]

For Ricoeur, this relation between the two forms of evidence in the Cartesian circle becomes a model for thinking about the full reality of the cogito as a being who is capable of acting *and* suffering. While an exclusive focus on the Second Meditation would highlight only the active dimension of a self-certain cogito who is in possession of itself, the Third Meditation dispossesses the self and provides the context in which "passivity takes on its functional sense" in the life of the cogito.[8] The idea of the Infinite exposes the cogito to an involuntary reality that precedes it ontologically and reveals its own limits and limitations. By following the model of the Cartesian circle, it then becomes possible for Ricoeur to situate the self within a dialectic of activity and passivity that engages both the voluntary and involuntary dimensions of experience.[9]

Whereas Ricoeur fully embraces the Cartesian circle, no positive references to the Cartesian circle are to be found in Henry's phenomenology of life at all. This is because Henry (mis)reads the Third Meditation as the culmination of a gradual descent into a transcendent mode of appearing. Everything that follows after the discovery of the original cogito, which occurs early in the Second Meditation, is aligned with Descartes's shift to the cogitatum and the external mode of appearing. In Descartes's Third Meditation, the cogitatum—that is, the idea of the Infinite—becomes the focal point of the entire analysis. Henry contends that with Descartes's ontological proof of the reality of this idea, the slide toward the cogitatum comes to its full completion. It establishes a cogitatum that escapes doubt. Once a cogitatum itself becomes indubitable, Descartes is then able to ground all appearing on the model of the *cogito cogitatum*—that is, the transcendent mode of appearing. As a result, Henry concludes that the Third Meditation signals the culmination and completion of the Cartesian turn to the object and its forgetting of the original immanent mode of appearing located in the expression *videre videor* [it seems that I see].

However, in my opinion, Henry's rejection of Descartes's Third Meditation results in a missed opportunity. Reading against the grain of his negative assessment of the Third Meditation, I propose there is another more positive interpretive possibility available for his phenomenology of life. The key here is that, instead of treating the idea of the Infinite in the Third Meditation solely on its own, Henry could have invoked the Cartesian circle in a fashion similar to Ricoeur. As such, it would open the possibility for two types of evidence of life. The full phenomenological structure of life, accordingly, would consist of an original relation—a bond—between the living cogito and Life.

This reappropriation of the Cartesian circle actually helps to shed light on a persistent but unresolved ambiguity in Henry's phenomenology of life. Henry frequently invokes two very different senses of life: (1) life with a lowercase *l* (as a subjective lived experience); (2) Life with an uppercase *L* (as an absolute origin of life).[10] The ambiguity of these two different usages of the term *life* is noted in Dominique Janicaud's critique of Henry in *French Phenomenology and the Theological Turn*.[11] Janicaud willingly accepts the validity of Henry's phenomenological descriptions of life in the lowercase sense—for instance, in his description of the feeling of one's own power to act or to move. But what strains credulity for Janicaud is Henry's subsequent shift to a different register of discourse about life in the uppercase sense of Life, which is said to exist on its own and generate all lived experience. For Janicaud, this shift in Henry's discourse from the lowercase to the uppercase signals an unjustified passage beyond the limits of phenomenology. Although Henry does not back down in the wake of Janicaud's criticism and continues to utilize these two senses of life, it is also fair to say that he never provides a clear or compelling answer about his understanding of their distinctive meanings or the exact structure of their relation, either. Our reassessment of the Cartesian circle, however, helps to fill this explanatory gap in Henry's work.

How would the relation between life in the lowercase sense (the lived experience of the individual ego) and Life in the uppercase sense (absolute Life as such) be conceptualized within the Cartesian circle? The gist of Descartes's argument is that as an imperfect or finite being I can produce only the ideas of other imperfect or finite beings; I myself cannot manufacture the idea of a perfect or infinite being. Since the idea of the infinite cannot have come from me, Descartes infers that it must come from a perfect or infinite being itself. In contrast with all other ideas, the idea of the Infinite thus has two distinctive features: (1) in putting the more into the less, it is an idea that exceeds me; (2) insofar as I myself cannot produce this idea, it must have been placed in me as a radical passivity or what Levinas calls a passivity that is "more passive than any passivity."[12] In light of these two unique features, the idea of the infinite breaks up intentional consciousness and exposes the cogito to a reality whose meaning exceeds the scope of its powers.

Perhaps Henry would have been correct to describe this as a descent into the cogitatum or noema if the focus of Descartes's argument was solely on the idea of the infinite as such. But the essential point of the Cartesian circle (which Henry misses) is that the evidence of the infinite does not stand alone. As we have noted, it establishes one of two different sources of evidence: the certitude of the cogito and the certitude of the Infinite. It is precisely the relation between these two different modes of evidence—the ratio cognoscendi and the ratio essendi—that is useful for articulating the relation between the two different senses of life invoked in Henry's phenomenology. Accordingly, the original living cogito can be said to articulate the ratio cognoscendi of life, the way in which it is revealed in our own experience, whereas Life conveys the ratio essendi, through which the cogito enters into existence and is maintained there. My hypothesis, in short, is that this establishes the formal structure of the relation between the living individual and Life and that this relation, in turn, helps us to articulate the relation between the pathos and praxis of life.

This hypothesis can be tested by applying it to Henry's phenomenology of birth (and, by implication, to his phenomenology of life as a whole). The guiding questions for this test can be formulated as follows: How, if at all, does the formal structure of the Cartesian circle apply concretely to Henry's phenomenological description of birth? In other words, to what extent is the birth of the self comparable to the starting point of the cogito in the Second Meditation, and to what extent does my birth in Life resemble the ontological dependency invoked by the idea of the Infinite in the Third Meditation? To what extent does a full account of the phenomenon of birth entail the adoption of both perspectives and the overlapping of these two different forms of evidence?

## Henry's Phenomenology of Birth

What is the phenomenological significance of one's own birth? The topic of birth has been widely overlooked and ignored in the philosophical tradition, which has focused much more extensively on the topic of death at the other end of the spectrum of life.[13] Birth is ordinarily described in mundane terms as a biological process that marks a living individual's arrival in the world as an independent being. But Henry's 1994 essay "The Phenomenology of Birth" sets out to understand this phenomenon in a more radical phenomenological sense by addressing the question of what the fact of one's own birth signifies in one's own life. The first step in his analysis is to distinguish between the coming into being of a thing and the coming into life of a living individual. Henry explains, "Coming into being is a fact for every being: for rocks, for air, for water. Yet, none of these things results from a birth; they are neither born nor do they die, except metaphorically. Being born is a fact for the living and for the living alone."[14] To come into being simply means to come into the world and to be located there. But if this were equally true for the living, then the existence of a living individual would be the same as that of the rock; there would be no phenomenological difference between the inanimate and the animate. Their difference would reside only on an ontic level, so to speak, as a distinction between two different types of beings: the living and the nonliving.

With this point, Henry is taking aim at Heidegger's account of facticity and thrownness in *Being and Time*, which, according to Henry's reading, reduces the meaning of birth to coming into the world.[15] While Heidegger himself misses birth's distinct significance altogether, Henry finds his own point of departure with a statement made elsewhere by Heidegger: "life has its own kind of being, but it is essentially accessible only in Dasein."[16] Insofar as Heidegger understands appearing only in one manner—namely, as a form of ek-stasis or of being outside of oneself—he is unable to discern the full significance of his own statement. If indeed Dasein is always outside of itself, the question for Henry is how it can ever gain access to itself—that is, to its own being in life. Denying that life can ever be attained outside of itself, Henry insists that "the material phenomenological heterogeneity between the pathos of appearing in which life fulfills itself and the ek-static appearing which unfolds in the difference of the world and things, is radical, irreducible, and insurmountable."[17] This means that Dasein, defined solely in terms of being outside itself, could never gain access to the pathos of its own life. "If the character of being alive," Henry asks, "is not derived from the appearing proper to Dasein, *then where does its phenomenological origin reside?*"[18] To answer this question concerning Dasein's own appearing, Henry contends that it is necessary to understand how one enters into life and, in so doing, to discern the genuine meaning of birth.

To be born, as we have said, is not to come into the world but to come into life. In its original phenomenological meaning, Henry sets out to disclose what he calls a "transcendental birth." This refers to "an original birth, an *Ur*-birth which no longer has anything to do with what we understand naively by birth. The *Ur*-birth about which we will now speak escapes from the sciences that relate to the world as well as traditional philosophy that has only thematized this type of relation."[19] To clarify this notion of an original or transcendental birth, Henry sets aside the biological account of birth and introduces an additional distinction between two different senses of the expression *to come into life*.

First of all, it means for an individual "to come to life, to enter into it and to arrive at this extraordinary and mysterious condition of being alive."[20] To be sure, the elucidation of this mysterious character of life—the wonder of being alive—is one of the essential tasks for a phenomenology of birth. But Henry also wants to call attention to a second and more profound sense of the expression *to come into life*. In this second sense, to come into life means that "it is in life and only on the basis of life that this arrival [*venue*] can occur. To come into life means to come from life, such that life is not the destination but the point of departure for birth, if one can speak in this way."[21] If to come into life means to come from life, this suggests that each birth is situated in relation to the prior reality of life, and this is why the individual living being is not a self-positing or self-generating *arche*. The living ego, as Henry explains, "cannot be understood on the basis of itself but only on the basis of this essence of life that eternally precedes it in the very process by which it continues to engender it as something that results necessarily from it, by which it continues to give birth to it."[22] As such, Life is the generative source from which the self is able to come into life, and in this sense the living individual can be described aptly as lifebound.

Insofar as the self is bound to life and generated from life, Henry observes that birth reveals "the fact that the singular Self is expressed and must be expressed first in the accusative as a 'me' [*moi*] conveys the fact that it is engendered. It does not bring itself into its own condition of experiencing itself as a Self, but it derives this condition from the eternal auto-affection of life."[23] In contrast with a transcendental I standing in the nominative case, the natal self is assigned to the accusative case, which indicates that it is not the cause of its own being: "I go through the experience of myself without being the source of this experience; I am given to myself without this givenness being derived from myself in any way."[24] So if Henry's phenomenology of birth reaches into oneself to disclose the meaning of one's own birth, his reflection on birth ends up turning the self inside out and shows that the self is the passive recipient of its own life.

In reflecting on its own birth, the self discovers a principle outside itself; it recognizes itself as the recipient of the gift of life. Birth reveals the self's passive exposure to a life that precedes itself, and with this realization, the self discovers that it owes its own being to life. The gift of life gives rise to the pathos of birth, which Henry describes in the following terms: "This pathos . . . is the pathos of that which, in experiencing itself, experiences the experience that absolute life has of itself [*éprouve l'épreuve de soi de la vie absolue*], such that its radical passivity with regard to itself is its radical passivity with regard to life. . . . This mode of passivity is the most constant trait of every life resulting from a birth, of a life like ours. The condition of the ego is the pathos of its presupposition. The life of the transcendental ego is the phenomenology of its birth."[25] Due to the self's passive exposure to the prior reality of life, it follows that to live is essentially to suffer, though not necessarily in the ordinary sense in which life might be described as toil or hardship. The suffering of life does not simply signify pain; in its original or ontological sense, the suffering of life refers to the radical passivity of having been born into life without one's own initiative or choosing. It is an experience of the involuntary. Life, as Henry shows, places its stamp on me long before I ever become aware of it or able to do anything about it. To be born into life is to undergo the suffering of a lifebound subject who bears the weight of a life that is already given.

But pathos—the suffering of life—does not encapsulate the whole meaning of birth. Alongside the passive dimension of birth, Henry also invokes a transcendental birth, or, in other words, the birth of a cogito. To be born, in this transcendental sense, is to be born as a self and as the living individual I am. In this respect, Henry explains that birth puts me in possession of myself and of the various powers that belong to me: "It (the living individual) enters into possession of itself at the same time as it is able to exercise each of the powers that traverse it. A new capacity is conferred to it. . . . This is the self's [*moi*] ability to be in possession of itself, to be one with it and with everything that is contained within itself and that belongs to it as the many real components of its own being. Among these components, there are the powers of the body, for example, those of grasping, moving, touching, etc."[26] The birth of the self, in its transcendental sense, grants the self a hold over itself, putting it in possession of itself and granting it power over all its powers and capacities. This self-possession—or power to act—is what makes freedom of the will possible. This experience of the voluntary entails that the meaning of birth cannot be reduced to the pathos that binds me to life; it also binds me to myself and makes it possible for me to be a self who is capable of acting.

This brief overview of Henry's phenomenology of birth might seem to equivocate insofar as birth has been described in two very different ways: (1) as the active side of a self who enters into the powers of its "I can"; (2) the passive side of a self who is generated from Life itself. How should we make sense of these two different discourses? Do these two different senses of birth refer to two separate realities, or can they be reconciled somehow? Henry's account does not answer this question. Yet, my claim is that, instead of being either an equivocation or an assertion of two irreconcilable perspectives, the Cartesian circle can be utilized to place these two discourses about birth in an overlapping relation [*surimpression*]. That is to say that Henry's analysis of birth can be interpreted in terms of the two types of evidence—both the ratio cognoscendi and the ratio essendi—established by the Cartesian circle. First of all, *the birth* of the self invokes the passive dimension of coming into life from life. This aspect of birth runs parallel to the structure of Descartes's idea of the infinite, which exposes the cogito to a reality that precedes it and guarantees its being. As a ratio essendi, the stamp of life precedes me and is placed within me, without any initiative or consent from me. In this sense, birth becomes a sign of the limitations of a self who does not create or generate itself. It signals the ontological dependency of the self on the prior reality of Life. Yet, the phenomenological significance of birth cannot be reduced to the pathos of suffering under the weight of Life. In addition, the birth *of the self* parallels the Cartesian discovery of the cogito. As a ratio cognoscendi, this marks the emergence of the subject as a living cogito. In this transcendental sense, birth marks a first starting point, a beginning, of selfhood. The self is able to bear the weight of life, precisely because life puts it into possession of itself and the various powers and abilities that it can exercise. It follows that life is tied to praxis and the self's ability to act. Each new birth marks not only a new beginning for a self but also the possibility to make something new happen; it is a source of renewal and hope in the world.[27]

This analysis of birth confirms two important hypotheses. First, it shows how the formal structure of the Cartesian circle can provide a coherent account of the relation between two different aspects of Henry's analysis of birth. Henry's phenomenology of birth follows the logic of a double genitive.[28] That is to say that the birth of the self runs parallel to the ontological dependency of the cogito described in the Third Meditation. In that sense, it places the self in the accusative, meaning that it shows how the self comes from life. But the birth of the self also signifies the self's birth. Returned to the nominative position, it marks the beginning of a living cogito who is capable of action. In this sense, it parallels the evidence of the cogito in the Second Meditation.

By modeling Henry's phenomenology of birth in terms of the Cartesian circle, a second important hypothesis is affirmed. Even though Henry describes his own phenomenology of life as a philosophy of the immediate, it suggests that his actual practice of phenomenology relies implicitly on the concept of internal difference. Of course, Henry adamantly rejects any thinking of life in terms of the difference between immanence and transcendence, subject and object, inner and outer, or life and the world. But his arguments are directed against the notion of external difference and never contemplate the possible role that internal difference, or self-differentiation, could play within life. This type of difference is evident in the immanent relation between the two senses of life: Life and the living individual. Instead of being separate or unrelated, these two different senses of life indicate that an internal difference, a self-differentiation, is operative within life itself. This is evident in Henry's assertion that Life brings the living individual into life and at the same time brings the living individual into itself. This internal differentiation of life between life and the living individual will be tested in subsequent chapters to determine whether it is able to yield increased clarity and insight for other phenomena as well.

## Ricoeur's Phenomenology of Birth

Long before Henry's 1994 article "The Phenomenology of Birth," Ricoeur takes up the topic of birth in a section of *Freedom and Nature* entitled "Life: Birth." As is the case for Henry, Ricoeur's phenomenology of birth is designed to counter the Idealistic tendencies of Husserlian phenomenology. Although birth is an undeniable given for each living individual, the facticity of birth poses a deep problem for a phenomenology of consciousness. It marks a significant event in my life that escapes the realm of my own lived experience. My very own beginning as a living individual—my birth—is essential to me but yet it is not an experience or event that is available to me. Thus, the phenomenological question is: what significance does this event, which exceeds the bounds of my own lived experience, nonetheless have for me?

As noted in the previous chapter, the central thesis of Ricoeur's *Freedom and Nature* involves the reciprocity of the voluntary and the involuntary. In response to Husserl's tendency to overlook the involuntary, Ricoeur sets out to recover the full significance of the involuntary dimension of life and to show how it interacts with the voluntary. The unchosen circumstances of life, following his analysis, include three components: (1) character; (2) the unconscious; (3) life. The deepest level of the involuntary is represented by life.

Birth is emblematic of the involuntary dimension of life. Indeed, it seems to sum up everything that is unchosen about my life. Although birth is an undeniable given for each and every living individual, the facticity of birth poses a problem for a phenomenology of consciousness. My own beginning as a living individual is not a lived experience for me. My own birth exposes me to a prior reality that cannot be returned to an original perceptual experience or be reproduced in memory. By the time I emerge as a conscious self, I find myself already born, already in life, and already in a given life situation. All of this happens without my own doing and even without my own awareness. For this reason, birth can be described as a limit experience for a phenomenology of consciousness.

Due to the inaccessibility of my own birth, the direct route through lived experience is barred for a phenomenology of birth. Ricoeur thus proposes that a phenomenology of birth must proceed indirectly and pass through an external consideration of birth provided by scientific explanation. Yet, it would be a mistake to stop with the objectification of birth, insofar as biology "without an apperception of the cogito, alienates me" from myself.[29] Accordingly, the contributions of biology will require a subsequent recovery of the self in which I become able "to understand in myself what I had explained in terms of the other."[30] With this indirect approach to the phenomenon of birth, we find a proto version of the hermeneutic circle that is developed later in Ricoeur's career. The phenomenology of birth, like a hermeneutic circle, passes from an initial understanding of birth to its objective explanation by science and then culminates with a better self-understanding of its significance for me.[31]

As the first stage of this circle, Ricoeur alludes to three features of our initial understanding of birth: (1) as the beginning of my life; (2) as an indication of my dependency on others; (3) as the reception of a genetic inheritance. Ricoeur offers a brief account of each of these features and notes some initial perplexities pertaining to each of them. The first of these features is the notion that birth marks the *beginning* of my life. What makes this fact puzzling is that the beginning of my life remains obscure and hidden from my experience. There is a gap between the beginning of my life and the beginning of my lived experience: I am always situated *after* the event of my birth. Due to the inaccessibility of this past to my lived experience, a methodological question arises: can there be a phenomenology of birth, properly speaking? The antecedence of life in relation to lived experience suggests a second key feature of birth: my *dependency* on others. My birth is an event for others who are there before me. I depend on them to shed light on this event for me afterward—for example, through their recollections, stories, or recorded documents. More deeply, I depend on others who bring me into existence in the first place. This prior ontological dependency raises a question: if my birth points to my dependency on others, how does the filial relation affect my own identity as an independent self?[32] The third and final feature of birth deepens this dependency further: my birth involves the reception of an *inheritance* from others in the remote past. My ancestors are like donors whose genes have been passed down to me. This biological inheritance influences me even after my birth, to the extent that it provides a structuring principle that guides the subsequent development of my life—that is, my inherited traits, genetic predispositions, and so forth. And this genetic inheritance raises deep questions concerning my own identity: to what extent does this genetic inheritance—the genetic self—define and even predetermine who I am?

Ricoeur's treatment of these three features of birth next examines each of them along their objective (biological) aspect and then returns them to their subjective (phenomenological) significance. Working in reverse, let me begin with his account of birth as a genetic inheritance. When ancestry is defined as a genetic inheritance, the focus expands beyond my own specific DNA and extends more broadly to the entire genetic ancestry of humanity that precedes me, leading most broadly to the entire species. Genetically speaking, I am simply the product of my heredity, a recipient of the chromosomes contributed by a mother and father who were themselves recipients of them and so on. My genetic identity gives rise to questions of whether, and to what extent, my genetic inheritance defines who I am. Indeed, some thinkers have gone as far as to posit that the subjective experiences of consciousness, reason, and free will are illusory; deep down, these phenomena are ultimately conditioned and determined by a prior set of genetic motives. That said, Ricoeur's question is, "What does heredity mean to me?"[33]

This question marks a shift from a purely objective account of heredity to a consideration of its lived phenomenological significance. It is true that heredity refers to my reception of a set of genetic traits from my ancestors, but Ricoeur contends that these traits must ultimately be anchored in the unity of my own life. I inherit physical traits or perhaps some predispositions, but the point is that these are *my* physical traits or *my* personality traits, plus the idea of an ancestor. Of course, I do have genetic ancestors, but *their* traits no longer exist because they are no longer living; their influence is internalized such that they become my specific traits. What genetics means to me is thus not tied so much to the ancestral past as to how it influences my future. This is evident in the sense that one's genetics establishes a sort of pre-personal habitus, a set of predispositions and tendencies that delineate the course of one's future. Through this genetic habitus, my future choices as well as their consequences continue to be influenced by the fact of my birth. Importantly, this shows that the significance of my birth does not only pertain to the past but also continues to weigh on my future.

The next feature of birth that Ricoeur considers is the dependency of the filial relation. This refers to the fact that my own birth is primarily a choice and experience that belongs to others. Considered objectively, the biological account of filiation focuses on a history of choices that were made by my biological parents. A whole series of contingent encounters and circumstances had to occur and combine in order for me to be born. If any one of them had not happened, then I would not have been born. But Ricoeur notes that this emphasis on the prior history leading up to one's birth produces a sort of self-alienation, such that "I leave myself in order to place myself in a being outside my control, my ancestors, and follow out a chain of effects down to myself."[34] From the perspective of one's genetic lineage, one's own being comes to be explained as one particular combination of genetics that occurred among an immense statistical set of possible combinations. One's own birth appears in its stark contingency. This gives rise to two questions: What makes this specific combination of contingent events me? Am I anything but this specific combination of contingent events that happened to occur?

Whereas the objective explanation of filiality treats birth as the result of a chain of contingent events that can be traced ever more deeply back in time, the subjective consideration of filiality returns to the experience in which "to be born is to be engendered."[35] By emphasizing that I am begotten from particular parents, this subjective orientation focuses on the singularity of the filial bond. Here, Ricoeur makes a brief but insightful observation that the umbilical cord is an indicator of both the lesion as well as the suture of the self's dependence on others.[36] The umbilical cord points to the self's prior physical dependency on a mother. And with the severing of the umbilical cord at birth, there is an initial sign of the independence of the self (even if the dependency on care exists long—and for parents of young adults sometimes too long!—afterward). But this lesion does not disappear, either; it leaves behind the physical trace of a scar—an umbilicus—that remains in the future. The navel is, in this way, the physical reminder of a prior and continuing vital bond between mother and child. This scar indicates that the filial relation is neither fully erased nor eliminated; the self's dependency on the filial relation continues to live on after the event of birth.

The third and final feature of Ricoeur's phenomenology of birth involves the notion that birth marks a beginning of life. My own beginning, as we have noted, presents a limit situation for consciousness and remains an elusive mystery to me. To the extent that birth escapes my own consciousness, I might turn to biology in search of some type of objective explanation of this beginning. But the problem here is that biology does not offer any beginning of the self whatsoever; it situates my birth in relation to a genetic lineage and traces a line of descent that extends ever more deeply back in time. It traces the transmission of a genetic inheritance back to an ancestral past and perhaps even to a genetic kinship with an entire species, if not with all living creatures.

From the perspective of this genetic lineage, one's own individual life has a continuity with all the other lives that precede oneself. In biology, there is no beginning but only continuity.

Due to the biological absence of an objective beginning to one's life, it is necessary to turn to a subjective consideration of birth as a beginning of life. Here, Ricoeur introduces an insightful distinction between two different senses of the word *beginning*.[37] We can speak of a beginning in an immanent sense, where birth signals the beginning of one's own freedom—that is, the beginning of my freedom to act. But we can also speak of a beginning in a transcendent sense, in which it signifies a beginning of one's own life: here, a beginning takes on the sense of a state or condition for me. Considered together, these two different senses of a beginning yield a sort of paradox in thinking about the birth of the self, such that "the 'I' is at the same time older and younger than itself."[38] These two different beginnings, in other words, introduce a sort of delay structure into the self, such that I arrive late to myself. My beginning in birth is older than the beginning of my lived experience, yet both of these beginnings define me.

This paradox of two beginnings can be resolved, however, by returning to our earlier discussion of the Cartesian circle. Just as the Cartesian circle was utilized to elucidate Henry's account of the birth of the self, it can also be applied here to Ricoeur's account of the dual sense of the beginning of the self. This means that birth, on the one hand, includes the antecedence of a life into which one is born; in this sense, it signifies the radical passivity of my placement into life before I emerge as an independent self. In this passive sense, Ricoeur observes that birth "is not an experience but the necessary presupposition of all experience."[39] I am born from life, and in this sense, life is given to me without my choosing or input. But, on the other hand, the limitations imposed by my life situation do not annul the possibility of my freedom. Quite the contrary, they make it possible for me to begin as a self. It is only within a given life situation that I can become the particular individual I am, that I can value what I value, or that I can accomplish what I accomplish. In this sense, birth marks the self's beginning as a living cogito who enters into possession of itself and is able to act in life. Accordingly, Ricoeur's account of the beginning of the self can be structured in terms of the same dual evidence—a ratio cognoscendi and a ratio essendi—that has been shown to guide the Henryan account of the birth of the self: a double beginning, at once the ratio essendi of a life that brings me into existence and the ratio cognoscendi of the self's beginning as a self.

Despite the parallel structure that links Henry and Ricoeur on a formal level, it is important to acknowledge the significant differences between their respective accounts of birth. In particular, this difference can be located concretely around the notion of a homo umbilicus. To describe the human in this way—as an umbilicus—is to draw attention to the materiality of a physical body and, in particular, to the navel that bears the trace of the severed umbilical cord that linked mother and child. This physical aspect of birth, while not denying the profundity of Henry's reflection, illustrates what gets lost as a result of Henry's shift from biological birth to the notion of a transcendental birth.

The Henryan account develops a phenomenology of birth that does not need an umbilicus. Due to the bracketing of the biological dimension of birth, there is no physical umbilicus and no singular relation to a mother and to one's genetic ancestry. All of this comes to be replaced by an impersonal relation to Life. Accordingly, for Henry, to be lifebound means first and foremost that the natal self is inscribed in a relation with Life in general; the bonds with other living individuals are subsumed under this more general relation. By contrast, Ricoeur's reference to the navel—the umbilicus—provides a rich carnal symbol of the condition of homo umbilicus, or a natal self.[40] The navel offers a physical reminder that we are not self-sufficient or self-creating beings; it recalls the original limitations and physical dependency of the self. This dependency, moreover, does not simply consist of a general or impersonal relation to life; it refers more precisely to a specific bond between mother and child: a singular bond between this mother and this child during gestation. Genetically, this bond can be traced back further to include the self's unique genetic kinship with the ancestral past. Due to this emphasis on the specificity of these umbilical and genetic ties, to be lifebound means something different for Ricoeur from what it means for Henry: in place of a general bond to life, to be lifebound means to have singular material bonds with concrete others who define one's own life situation.

The methodological differences between Henry and Ricoeur thus yield different results for a phenomenology of birth. Their difference can be conveyed by the following contrast: whereas Henry discloses the internal relation between life and the living individual in the birth of the self, Ricoeur's phenomenology of birth discloses a physical connection between living individuals who are external to one other. Examples of this physical connection between self and other include the umbilicus that connects materially to a mother, the genetics that connect me to an ancestral past, and the social significance of my birth for others. These physical bonds to others are missing from the Henryan account.

## Conclusion

The theme of birth is central to the broader project of this book on multiple levels. First of all, birth illustrates the contrast between a phenomenology of consciousness, which takes self-certitude as its starting point, and a phenomenology of life, which begins with the birth of the living individual. The phenomenology of consciousness, as Henry and Ricoeur allege, grants a privilege to the active and voluntary dimension of the self, but the phenomenology of life challenges the pretenses of the self's claim to be independent and self-sufficient. The phenomenon of birth is important insofar as it highlights the passivity and prior dependency of the self. The natal self does not create itself or support itself; instead, it is begotten. It receives the gift of life and is thereby bound to life and others prior to any of its own lived experiences.[41]

Second, after examining the phenomenology of birth in Henry and Ricoeur, the chapter reframes their analyses by introducing the formal structure of the Cartesian circle. Although Henry himself rejects Descartes's Third Meditation as symptomatic of external difference, this chapter suggests that Henry's phenomenology operates with a concept of internal difference. This internal difference, or self-differentiation, of life can be made intelligible by the structure of the Cartesian circle, which establishes two different but co-equal types of evidence: a ratio cognoscendi and a ratio essendi. The phenomenology of birth, as we have shown, describes the birth of the self from these two different perspectives. Considered from the perspective of Life as a ratio essendi, the fact of my birth reveals a radical passivity at the beginning of my life. I find myself *in life* prior to any activity or willing on my own behalf. But considered from the perspective of the living individual as a ratio cognoscendi, the self's birth can be described as the beginning of a self who is able to act and make a new beginning in the world. It follows that birth cannot be defined solely by the pathos of suffering; birth also introduces a new beginning into the world, a source of joy and hope. This latter aspect of the birth of the self—which Henry calls "force" and Ricoeur calls "the power to make something happen"—will be the primary focus of the next chapter.

The Cartesian circle is part and parcel of Ricoeur's own critique of Husserl, but it is worth mentioning that this duality is not entirely antithetical to

Henry's own thinking, either. For example, Henry himself speaks about the "controvertibility"—or the reciprocity—between affect and force.[42] This suggests that a full phenomenological account of life must include the language of affect as well the language of force; accordingly, it should describe the affective pathos of having a life as well as the active force through which one is able to lead a life. Our hypothesis moving forward is that the Cartesian circle lends increased clarity and insight into the interrelation between the affect and force of life in Henry's own work.

Third, while the Henryan and Ricoeurian accounts of birth clearly yield two different sets of results concerning the significance of birth, these two accounts do not necessarily contradict one another. In reality, it might not be necessary to choose between them because they are dealing with different aspects of life. What we find in the Henryan approach is an emphasis on the internal self-differentiation of life. This form of difference between Life and the living individual is generated within the lived experience of life as such. In contrast, the Ricoeurian approach proceeds through a reflection on the external difference between the living individual and the objective determinations of life in the natural and social world. Instead of placing these two approaches in competition with one another, perhaps an integrated phenomenology of life could show how they are compatible and even mutually reinforcing. This integrated approach, which will be tested in subsequent chapters, opens the possibility of a more comprehensive account that includes the living individual's relation to world of Life (as internal difference) as well as its immersion in the lifeworld (as external difference).

# 3

## Movement

*The Force of Life and the Biranian Philosophy of Effort*

THE PRECEDING CHAPTER ADOPTED THE model of the Cartesian circle to show how the phenomenology of life can articulate the internal self-differentiation of life. This phenomenological structure was detected in Henry's phenomenology of birth, which identifies the dual significance of a cogito that is exposed to the pathos of being born into life and also put in possession of itself as an origin of its own power to act. This chapter will investigate the phenomenology of bodily movement and show that it too is governed by the duality of pathos and praxis.

Bodily movement, or locomotion, is commonly recognized as a defining feature of living bodies. Aristotle, for example, identifies a fundamental difference between the motions of inanimate and animate bodies. Living bodies are moving bodies whose source of movement [*arche*] is located within themselves, whereas the principle of movement for inanimate bodies is always external to them. Accordingly, life can be defined at least in part as a principle of self-movement, and the living body is thus capable of being an efficient cause—that is, an active source of its own movement. With the rise of modern science, the Aristotelian account of movement is displaced in favor of the view that every physical movement is situated within a causal nexus and can be attributed to a prior moving cause. Consequently, for the moderns the idea of freedom is no longer a cosmological idea located in the material world. Where, then, is the power to act voluntarily grounded? Instead of saving the idea of freedom as Kant does, for example, by securing it in the realm of suprasensible ideas, the phenomenology of life follows the "way through the body" and anchors freedom in the subjective lived experience of a bodily *I can*.[1]

On the surface, it might seem that this reference to the lived body would lead back to Husserl's famous distinction between the objective body [*Körper*] and the subjective lived body [*Leib*]. While Husserl's analysis of the living body undoubtedly serves as a touchstone for both Henry and Ricoeur, their own studies of the body go beyond the Husserlian distinction between the objective body and the lived body.[2] Who, then, is the source of inspiration for this study of bodily movement?

For Henry, the answer is unmistakably clear: his one (and only) stated influence is the French thinker Maine de Biran (1766–1824). In response to a question about whether he ever encountered a thinker who helped him in the development of his phenomenology of life, Henry answered:

> Yes, Maine de Biran. The only true aid that I received is his to the extent that my effort was to show that subjectivity is a concrete subjectivity, individual and carnal, affective. The reading of Maine de Biran let me anticipate what I later called ontological dualism, that is, the fact that appearing is double. It is either appearing in the world outside of oneself or appearing in the impressional and pathos-filled immediacy of life. They are two heterogenous ways of appearing. By studying the phenomenon of the body in Maine de Biran, I discovered—what was truly the philosophical revelation of my journey—that by deepening Descartes's cogito he affirmed that this cogito is an "I can" and that this "I can" is my subjective body—the body-subject that is at the origin of all experience.[3]

The work of Biran is key to Henry's phenomenology of life, and in fact, Henry completed a book-length study of Biran in 1949. Although this study was initially designed to serve as a single chapter of *The Essence of Manifestation*, it blossomed into a stand-alone project that was published in 1965 under the title *Philosophy and Phenomenology of the Body: An Essay on Biranian Ontology*.[4] There, Henry crowns Biran as the "prince of philosophers" and identifies him as the first philosopher to have understood "the need to determine originally our body as *a subjective body*."[5] One can gain further appreciation of the full depth of Biran's influence by reading Henry's 1987 foreword to the second edition of the book. Looking back, Henry says that he would "change nothing about this text" and that "its essential findings are developed in my later investigations," citing its influence in particular on his study of Marx.[6] Life, he adds, presupposes nothing and doesn't need anything else in order to be given: "it is self-givenness [*auto-donation*], the primitive fact."[7] Drawing from the Biranian notion of the primitive fact, this assertion links Henry's central intuition about life to Biran and suggests that Henry's phenomenology of life is Biranian from beginning to end.

Could it possibly be said, likewise, that Ricoeur's work is Biranian through and through? No, at least not to the same degree as Henry. Ricoeur, in *Freedom and Nature* and elsewhere, endorses Biran's motto "*homo simplex in vitalitate, duplex in humanitate*" as an appropriate description of the embodied self's dual belonging to the voluntary and the involuntary. Moreover, in *Oneself as Another* Ricoeur praises Biran as "the first philosopher to introduce the personal body [*corps propre*] into the region of non-representational certitude."[8] Aside from these endorsements of Biran's work, however, Ricoeur does not undertake a study of Biran that is comparable to the depth of Henry's book. His most extensive engagement occurs in a section of *Freedom and Nature* entitled "Limits of a Philosophy of Effort: Effort and Knowledge," which will be studied later in this chapter. Thus, instead of emphasizing the direct influence of Biran's work, it would be more fitting to say that Biran exerts an indirect influence on Ricoeur through the tradition of French reflexive philosophy. Ricoeur credits reflexive philosophy as one of his major influences, but what exactly does the label *reflexive philosophy* mean?

French reflexive philosophy, which is not widely known in the English-speaking world, can be traced back to the writings of Maine de Biran (1766–1824) and extends through the work of Félix Ravaisson (1813–1900), Jules Lachelier (1832–1918), Jules Lagneau (1851–1894), and Jean Nabert (1881–1960).[9] French reflexive philosophy's influence on Ricoeur is apparent in at least three specific ways. First of all, Ricoeur penned a master's thesis in 1934 on two reflexive philosophers entitled *Méthode réflexive appliqué au problème de Dieu chez Lachelier et Lagneau*. The protagonists of the book—Jules Lachelier and Jules Lagneau—were two influential French reflexive philosophers in the latter half of the nineteenth century.[10] Second, the continued influence of reflexive philosophy is discernible more than a decade later in Ricoeur's "philosophy of the will," which includes detailed readings of Maine de Biran and Ravaisson in *Freedom and Nature* (1950)[11] as well as *Fallible Man* (1960), which is dedicated to Jean Nabert.[12] Third, and most importantly, its influence is directly acknowledged in the 1980s when Ricoeur defines his own philosophical approach in the following terms: "it stands in the lineage of a reflexive philosophy; it remains in the movement of Husserlian phenomenology; it seeks to be a hermeneutic variant of this phenomenology."[13] This indicates that reflexive philosophy is more than just an early influence that would later be outgrown; quite the contrary, it continues to serve as an orientation throughout Ricoeur's oeuvre.[14]

In an insightful overview of French reflexive philosophy, Jean Nabert observes that the reflexive tradition, instead of forming a shared orthodoxy, develops along two distinct trajectories.[15] For some (the Kantian path), it leads to a reflection on the conditions of the possibility of true knowledge and of the universality of reason; for others (the Biranian path), it is the intimacy of conscious life that prevails. Within the present context, the Kantian path can be set aside in order to focus on the question of how the Biranian path shapes the reflexive tradition and thereby exerts an indirect influence on Ricoeur. What characterizes the Biranian path, first and foremost, is its challenge to the impersonal nature of the Kantian reflection on the ego. As an alternative, it seeks to "promote a self-consciousness that does not lack the dimension of intimacy that is missing from the transcendental consciousness of criticism."[16] Accordingly, reflection is assigned the task of recovering the intimacy of a personal dimension of the self. Nabert describes the Biranian mode of reflection in the following manner: "It is therefore true that in all of the domains where the spirit reveals itself as creative, reflection is called on to retrieve the acts which works conceal, because, living their own life, these works are almost detached from the operations that have produced them. It is a question of bringing to light the intimate relationship between an act and the significations in which it is objectified."[17] The activity of reflection, then, is prompted by a self-forgetting that occurs with respect to the acts and events that are objectified in the world. Insofar as actions and events can always be detached from their agents and their initial purposes, we can easily lose sight of our personal involvement in the objective world. Reflexive philosophy thus attempts to restore what Nabert calls the "intimate relationship" between the power to act and the products in which it is objectified. In so doing, it reveals the self's personal presence and freedom to act in the world.[18]

This chapter envisions what it would look like to situate both Henry and Ricoeur along the same Biranian path. It shows that Biran's thought is central to their own attempts to reclaim the personal dimension of the lived body and to ground its force or power to act as an efficient cause in the world.[19] This becomes especially clear with respect to the Biranian analysis of "the primitive fact," which serves as the first truth and starting point for his reflection on the bodily cogito. While both Henry and Ricoeur challenge Biran's account of the primitive fact, this chapter shows that they develop two very different lines of criticism. For Henry, Biran's analysis is criticized for privileging the voluntary and active exertion of bodily effort against a physical resistance and thereby for failing to identify life as a fundamental source of resistance and passivity. Ricoeur, by contrast, develops a more radical critique of Biran's primitive fact. He calls the primacy of the so-called primitive fact into question. Prior to the experience of effort and resistance, Ricoeur posits a docile body that is already connected with the external world and serves as a precondition for any experience of resistance whatsoever.

What ultimately results from these interpretive differences about Biran's primitive fact? Does the phenomenology of movement yield comparable results to the phenomenology of birth? That is, does the phenomenology of movement reveal the duality of life as pathos and praxis? And if so, does it also show that Henry and Ricoeur conceptualize this duality in two decidedly different ways?

## The Primitive Fact in Henry's Philosophy and Phenomenology of the Body

To begin our exploration of the phenomenology of movement, this section will provide a brief introduction to Maine de Biran's thought. Biran's work can be described as a deepening of the Cartesian cogito that surpasses the *I think* and affirms the bodily cogito as an *I can*.[20] It is noteworthy that Biran's discovery of the bodily cogito is already anticipated by Descartes himself.[21] In the "Fifth Set of Objections" to Descartes's *Meditations*, Gassendi famously wonders why, instead of saying "I think, therefore I am," one couldn't infer his own existence from any of his activities. Descartes's response is unexpected but telling. He answers that indeed the proposition "I walk, therefore I am" would be correct, provided that one understands walking in a particular way, that is, in terms of the subjective awareness that I have of walking. This remark becomes an important reference point for Biran, insofar as it alludes to a subjective experience of walking and more broadly of the body in general. This subjective experience is not displayed externally through physical movement in the world; instead, it belongs to an inward experience of one's own body. In this original subjective relation to one's own movement, Biran discovers a bodily cogito—a bodily *I can* that takes the place of the *I think* as the origin and first starting point of all knowledge.

At the outset of his careful study of Biran, Henry highlights the novelty of Biran's discovery by distinguishing between three different layers of the body.[22] First of all, the body can be understood as an objective reality. As such, it is an object that exists among other objects and whose reality can be observed, measured, and quantified. Second, there is the living body in the sense of an organic body that carries out various life functions (some voluntary, some involuntary) such as respiration, digestion, movement, etc. Third, there is the properly human body, which Henry calls the "transcendental body" here and which he refers to as the "original flesh" [*chair*] in his later writings.[23] The body so understood is a condition of the possibility of subjective experience, or, in other words, "a body which is an 'I.'"[24] The significance of Biran's philosophy, according to Henry, is that he was "the first and actually the only philosopher who . . . saw the necessity for originally determining our body as a subjective body."[25] Biran's breakthrough, in other words, is the discovery of a personal body [*corps propre*].

To explore this new region of the personal body, Biran introduces a methodological distinction between two different types of reflection: what he calls concentrated reflection as opposed to specular reflection. The activity of specular reflection is akin to intentionality, insofar as it refers to the activity of observing or representing an object. This conforms to our ordinary ways of thinking about reflection as more or less synonymous with the activity of introspection, understood as a way of looking into oneself. But Biran rejects the view that reflection would simply redirect inwardly the vision that is previously oriented toward the external world. In bodily reflection, *there is nothing to see*.[26] Concentrated reflection, in contrast, bypasses seeing and directly grasps the subjective experience of my very own exercise of bodily activities.[27] Importantly, these two types of reflection in Biran's work are the precursor to Henry's thesis concerning the two different modes of appearing. While specular reflection refers to the transcendent mode of appearing, concentrated reflection opens the immanent mode of appearing in which the body reveals itself as an auto-affection—that is, through a feeling of one's own body from within.

To illustrate the contrast between these two types of reflection, consider the experience of moving my own hand. Under specular reflection, the movement of my hand is observed as an external object like other objects in motion. The hand can be rotated and viewed from different angles. It can move from one location to another, its movement across space can be measured, and so on. But unlike other objects, this hand belongs to my own body: it is *my* hand. This means that in addition to being able to observe its movement through specular reflection, I also can experience the act of movement itself from the inside, so to speak. Through concentrated reflection, I am intimately acquainted with the movements of my hand. I am aware of them directly and able to perform them without the need to pass through any visual or mental representation of them.

In more contemporary terms, this inner relation to one's own body resembles what is called proprioception, referring to the awareness of one's own body position, and this form of bodily awareness is what allows us to do things with our own bodies, precisely without representing or observing those activities. Based on proprioceptive awareness, I am able to press my foot on a car's accelerator without having to watch my legs do it, my hand is able to reach out for the turn signal without looking at it, and so forth. This proprioceptive awareness signifies a direct and immediate control of my own body's performance of various acts. And more broadly, it should be added that I become aware of my body as a field of capabilities that can be exercised by me. That is to say that in proprioception, I am aware not only of the actual exercise of my foot in driving or the actual exercise of my fingers in playing the piano; my bodily awareness also includes an awareness that I possess the capacity to use these powers [*dunameis*] and to do so in a wide range of possible manners.

This discovery of an inner or personal relation to one's own body constitutes what Biran calls a primitive fact. "The human being does not perceive or know anything," Biran says, "without the internal awareness of itself. This is the primitive fact of the inner sense, the basis or the beginning of all science."[28] Based on this claim that internal (bodily) self-awareness is fundamental, the Biranian cogito departs from the Cartesian cogito. The self is not simply a thinking thing [*res cogitans*] or a self-same substance; instead, the truth of the Biranian cogito resides in the bodily feeling of one's own power to act. That is to say that the bodily cogito knows itself first and foremost through the feeling of itself as an efficient cause of its own actions; it experiences itself as a power to act and to will.[29]

Yet, Henry rightly cautions that the primitive fact should not be taken to imply a mere reversal that would place the domain of practical action—the *I can*—above the theoretical realm of the Cartesian *I think*. For Biran, both the *I think* and the *I can*—both the theoretical and the practical realms—are grounded in the bodily cogito.[30] What is most basic is "to be in this state called '*conscium*' or '*compos sui*' where one is directed toward oneself or in oneself, in contrast with this other state that ordinary language distinguishes very well by the formulation: being outside of oneself."[31] Without this prior bodily self-relation in a compos sui, Biran's claim is that there would be no possibility of any knowledge and no possibility of any action whatsoever. The reflexive relation to one's own body is thus the first starting point—the Archimedean point—for all forms of human activity and cognition whatsoever.

Biran's demonstration of the primitive fact is based on the experience of bodily effort or volition, which, according to him, "is the true primitive fact of the inner sense [*le sens intime*]."[32] To illustrate this claim, consider the placement of a rock on my outstretched hand. The weight of the rock gives rise in my body to a feeling of resistance; I feel something external that is not me and that is pushing down against me. And along with this sensation of the rock's resistance, I have a corresponding feeling of effort exerted against this rock. As I exert my body to hold up the rock, I become aware of my own body's role as a productive cause. This example leads Biran to observe that the feeling of effort—this bodily self-awareness—would not emerge unless it encountered some form of obstacle; it would not occur without a resistance. But if effort has meaning only in its exertion against some resistance, and, conversely, if resistance has meaning only in opposition to a bodily force, then this would seem to suggest that the so-called primitive fact is actually comprised of two factors: the subjective force of my body and the objective resistance of the rock. This gives rise to an important interpretive question: does Biran's primitive fact have a single or a double origin? If it were single, then which of these two factors is truly primary? And if instead it were a double origin that included both factors, could it legitimately be called a primary fact any longer?[33]

## Henry's Interpretation of the Primitive Fact

Henry's interpretation of the primitive fact emphasizes the subjective experience of effort and dismisses the external source of resistance entirely. What the primitive fact reveals, according to Henry, is the absolutely subjective origin and meaning of the notion of force. To elaborate this point, Henry praises the following sentence from Maine de Brian as "one of the most laden with meaning that the philosophical tradition has ever produced." It reads, "There is no force that is absolutely foreign."[34] Commenting on this sentence, Henry observes that the force of effort cannot reside in any milieu external to the self. That is to say that it cannot be disclosed by any representation or observation of movement. Observed from the outside, the force behind an action does not appear; what is observed is only the action itself. The action remains the same, regardless of whether there is any subjective force behind it. The concept of force emerges only when movement is approached from a first-person perspective involving "concentrated reflection."[35] To experience myself as the source of the effort behind an action is precisely to feel the force of my own power to act, to be in possession of it, and to take hold of it. Since every force can be traced back to this original self-possession of the power to act, Henry interprets Biran's claim that "no force can be absolutely foreign" to mean that the subjective feeling of effort is the primitive fact; it alone is the Cartesian first principle.[36]

Drawing from the primitive fact, Henry's phenomenology of bodily movement can be summed up by three fundamental claims: (1) bodily movement reveals itself directly; (2) it is in our power; (3) it is not an instrument or intermediary between the ego and the world.[37] Because it is known directly, my bodily movement can be grasped without distance and without relying on anything outside itself. In this sense, bodily movement can be called a self-revelation that reveals itself on its own. But we have also seen that this inner experience of movement reveals me to myself. I discover myself as the active source of the movement of my own body [*corps propre*]. For Henry, this dual revelation—the self-revelation of movement and the revelation of myself—is the central meaning of the primitive fact.

Despite crowning Maine de Biran as the "prince of philosophers," chapter 6 of Henry's book, which is titled "The Problem of Passivity," criticizes Biran's analysis of the subjective body for overemphasizing the active dimension of effort and the force of the will. In this respect, his criticism of the Biranian cogito resembles his criticism of the Husserlian cogito discussed in the first chapter of this book.[38] Henry writes: "Maine de Biran, after having identified the ego and effort, is totally lacking when he must account for affective life, the imagination, and sensibility. He is then limited to borrowing conceptions from other philosophies that seem to be an integral part of Biranism, but that in reality only mask its essential lacuna: the absence of any theory of the affective, imaginary, and sensible life, that is to say, *the absence of any ontological theory of passivity.*"[39] In asserting that Biran lacks an ontological theory of the passivity of the subjective body, Henry is not denying the fact that Biran does talk about the passive dimension of experience. His contention, instead, is that when Biran does discuss passivity, he treats it without originality and uncritically relies on the views of his predecessors.[40] As a result, Biran's analysis slides back into a traditional view of the distinction between the involuntary and the voluntary, which privileges the voluntary dimension of human life over the involuntary realm that is associated with animal nature.

The traditional distinction holds that when one yields passively to the influence of appetites and desires, the result is a loss or diminishment of one's own humanity. The humanity of the self, by contrast, is revealed precisely by those instances in which the body frees itself from the constraints of impulse and asserts itself actively. Due to the influence of this traditional conceptual framework, Biran relegates the passive dimension of subjective experience—as expressed in drives, sensibility, affectivity, and imagination—entirely to the organic or animal body.[41] This leads Biran to call for a mixed psychology that would include both a physiological and a reflexive approach to the body: the physiological account would deal with the involuntary and passive dimension of the organic body while the reflexive approach would study the hyperorganic, voluntary will that is specific to the human body.[42]

What Biran fails to appreciate, according to Henry, is that *"activity and passivity are two different modalities of one and the same fundamental power which is nothing other than the original being of the subjective body."*[43] The experience of passivity is more than the result of an external influence. For Henry, it is intrinsic to the experience of the total subjective body, just as much as the experience of activity. Activity and passivity comprise two modes of the same bodily reality. Consequently, Henry maintains that an account of the total reality of the subjective body must include both the activity of force and the passivity of affect, or in other words, both praxis and pathos.

To illustrate the implications of Henry's claim, we can return to our previous example of the rock that is placed on one's outstretched hand. The weight of the rock resists my hand, but it would be a mistake to interpret the passive dimension of this experience—undergoing the weight of the object—simply as the discovery of an external reality or of the rock's physical density. To do so would be to define passivity externally—that is, as the product of an interaction between two different things: my hand and the rock. Instead, by integrating passivity into the reality of the total subjective body, it follows that the primitive fact not only establishes the feeling of my effort to hold up the weight but also my suffering of its weight. This explains why the total subjective body cannot be defined simply as either active or passive. Its full reality includes an experience of an active power that exerts its own force as well as an experience of its own weight as an encumbrance that is passively undergone.

Although Henry traces the experiences of force and pathos back to the single reality of a total subjective body, one might legitimately doubt whether the feeling of effort can be grounded in a purely immanent self-relation. One might reason, following Derrida, that this feeling itself can emerge only as the result of a prior passive exposure to the world. To support this claim, Derrida cites a passage from Biran's introduction to *The Influence of Habit*: "We can already begin to perceive that activity, as that which is distinctive of the ego and its ways of being, is directly attached to the faculty of moving, which ought to be distinguished from that of feeling, as a main branch is distinguished from the trunk of the tree, or rather as twin trees are distinguished which cling together and grow into one, with the same stem."[44] Drawing from this metaphor of two trees that have grown together into a single trunk [*dans la même souche*], Derrida emphasizes that what appears to be a primitive fact is not in fact single (the single trunk) but actually is double (the twin trees). The primitive fact, following Derrida's reading, thus comprises two necessarily distinct elements: the inner feeling of effort and the outer resistance.

If indeed the primitive fact can be traced back to a double origin as Derrida proposes,[45] this casts doubt on whether it is possible to speak any longer about a "bodily ownness" [*corps propre*] that is exclusively one's own [*propre*]. For Derrida, the auto-affective experience of one's own body—that is, the feeling of one's own effort—entails a prior exposure to an external reality—that is, to the external object that resists me. Without the resistance of the external world that acts against it, there would be no feeling of one's own effort. The feeling of one's own bodily effort depends on a prior exposure to what is other.[46]

This alternate interpretation of Biran gives rise to a series of questions. Is it plausible any longer to speak, as Henry does, of a purely intimate or personal [*propre*] bodily awareness that would not entail a prior, pre-personal [*impropre*] exposure to alterity? Or is it necessary to acknowledge a double origin of the primitive fact in which the internal and external, the self and other, are mutually implicated? And if so, does this necessitate a return to Biran's mixed discourse, which Henry rejected? Amid these alternatives, where would Ricoeur's own reading of Biran be located?[47] Might his own analysis of the primitive fact escape this impasse somehow?

## The Mark of Subjectivity in Ricoeur's Freedom and Nature

Although Ricoeur mentions Biran at various points in his work, he does not provide a comprehensive discussion that would be comparable in scope to

Henry's book. This section will focus on his most extended engagement with Biran, which takes place in the chapter "Limits of a Philosophy of Effort: Effort and Knowledge" in *Freedom and Nature*.[48] Ricoeur's thesis of "the reciprocity of the voluntary and the involuntary" informs his assessment of Biran's primitive fact and leads him, like Derrida, to emphasize the necessary co-relation and interaction between the activity of subjective effort and the passivity of objective resistance. The feeling of effort is a mixture of activity and passivity that stands, in Ricoeur's words, "at the confluence of the activity which descends from the self into its corporeal density and of 'simple affection.'"[49]

Applied to perception, Biran's philosophy of effort highlights the interaction between the active and passive dimensions of sense experience. The senses, of course, are receptive to what is given and register input from the external world. But there is also an active dimension of perception (which he distinguishes from the passivity of mere sensation), which refers to perceiving not just as seeing or hearing something but rather as an active and directed looking at or listening to something. In an active perception, Biran maintains that we can feel our own involvement in perception, just as we can feel the movement of our own hand when it reaches out to grasp an object in the world. Accordingly, I see *by* looking, I hear *by* listening, I smell *by* inhaling, I feel *by* touching, and so forth.[50] Sometimes these perceptual activities are accomplished quite effortlessly, but other times they may require considerable effort and difficulty. Yet, all of the various modalities of perceptual activity—ranging from the easy to the difficult—involve some underlying level of effort that marks one's own personal role in perception. This feeling of effort, according to Biran, underlies every act of perception and applies more broadly to every subjective experience whatsoever.

While Ricoeur concedes Biran's claim that "a complete characterization of the will is possible only in the context of effort," he also notes the limitations Biran's philosophy of effort.[51] First of all, Ricoeur rejects the view that effort can serve as the basis of an entire theory of perception as well as an entire theory of knowledge.[52] While the Biranian theory of perception works well for the sense of touch, it does not apply equally well to the distance senses. Biran simply asks too much from the single example of the effort to touch or move an object, according to Ricoeur, and goes wrong by extending this example to all types of perceptual experience. Second, Ricoeur contends that there comes a point where effort must yield to knowledge. "The pair action-passion, effort-resistance," Ricoeur asserts, "does not govern my relation to the world either exclusively or even essentially."[53] The active exertion of the will alone, on the one hand, is not sufficient to produce theoretical knowledge; at best, it can be said to promote only a particular way of knowing. On the other hand, the external world does not simply acquire meaning through its resistance to me; quite apart from any opposition to me, it signifies the actual presence of something that is other than me. Due to these two limitations, Ricoeur concludes that Biran's philosophy of effort is unable "to constitute a theory of knowledge."[54]

Ricoeur's most important and penetrating objection, however, challenges the alleged primacy of the so-called primitive fact. The feeling of effort, he contends, is derived from a more fundamental bodily relation.[55] Ricoeur points out that effort is itself a secondary effect; it is "primarily resistance of the thing or body or some aspect of myself which brings about this awareness of effort."[56] If effort is the result of a prior encounter with an object that resists it, it might at first seem as if Ricoeur were endorsing the view that the resistance of the object—its alterity—is the primary fact instead. But the true problem, Ricoeur suggests, can be attributed to the example itself.[57] The focus on the effort-resistance pair misses a more fundamental form of nonresistance and effortlessness that makes this experience possible in the first place: what Ricoeur calls the "docility of a yielding body."[58]

The docile experience of the body is effortless. It points to the availability of my own body in an immediate, transparent, and pre-reflective manner. Without any resistance at all, my will traverses the docile body and accomplishes tasks in the world. That is to say that the body is not the object or aim of my actions; it is instead a power—a know-how—that I use in order to carry out projects in the world. The docile body is primary, but it easily gets overlooked precisely due to its effortlessness and transparency: "docility is transparent, resistance opaque."[59] While bodily effort attracts our attention, it is actually secondary and "can only be understood as a complication of the very docility of the body, which, from another viewpoint, corresponds to willing."[60]

The experience of resistance already presupposes the idea of the docile body, according to Ricoeur. For it is only in the process of carrying out some type of action that something can be said to disrupt and resist it. In this way, "resistance is a crisis of the unity of the self with itself."[61] When I encounter obstacles, I become aware of the role of my body in mediating between my aims and the world. But this reflection on effort and resistance can also falsify our understanding of the body. "It tempts us to reduce the description of moving to one of its forms, namely, to the relation between effort and organic resistance.... We no longer see anything but the opposition between willing and the body."[62] To draw from Biran's motto "*homo duplex in humanitate, simplex in vitalitate*," what turns out to be dual for Ricoeur is the opposition between effort and resistance, but what is simple is the life of the docile body that unifies the self and the world.

But, if the docile body (rather than effort) actually turns out to be the primary fact, this gives rise to a new difficulty. How can we access this transparent relation of the body to itself? How, if reflection requires resistance, would this transparency ever reveal itself in reflection? Ricoeur does not answer this question directly in *Freedom and Nature* or elsewhere. But to make sense of the transparent relation to one's own body and its contrast with the phenomenon of effort, we can glean some insight from a parallel concept introduced earlier in *Freedom and Nature*: the notion of a pre-reflexive self-imputation. My claim is that this pre-reflexive relation provides access to the docile body.

## Pre-Reflexive Self-Imputation

In the first part of *Freedom and Nature*, Ricoeur provides an analysis of decision that breaks it down into the following three essential features: (1) the relation to the project ("I want to do this"); (2) the relation to oneself ("I make up my mind to do this"); and (3) the relation to the motives for action ("I decide to do this because"). Given the context of this chapter's argument, my focus will be on the second component of decision—namely, one's self-relation in the process of deciding. Ricoeur announces the shift of his analysis from the first element of decision, which focuses on the relation to the project itself (the thing to be done), to this second element in the following terms: "leaving the intentional direction—according to which, to decide is to decide something—we must describe the reflexive direction of decision: '*je me decide*'"—I make up my mind. This ability to will oneself to do something signals a shift in Ricoeur's analysis from a Husserlian-style intentional analysis of the relation to the project to a reflexive recovery of the act of making up one's own mind.[63]

In the section titled "The Imputation of the Self: *Se Décider*,"[64] Ricoeur begins by noting that consciousness is usually directed outward toward the projects that are to be done. I am absorbed in those projects to such an extent that either I might not notice or perhaps even forget their reference to me. But the reflexive features of language serve as important reminders that decisions involve more than simply what is decided and done.[65] Through reflection, I can turn back onto myself and reflect on my own role in the process of choosing and acting. In examining this relation to oneself, Ricoeur distinguishes between two different types of reflexivity: (1) reflexive judgments in which the regard is placed on the self as a theme; and (2) pre-reflexive judgments in which one is actively involved in the process of determining oneself. These two types of reflection, I suggest, correlate with Biran's aforementioned distinction between specular and concentrated reflection.

Reflexive judgments are exemplified by Descartes's famous observation in the Second Meditation that "it is I who doubts, who understands and who desires." With the formulation *it is I*, Descartes acknowledges a self-presence that accompanies all of the conscious performances that are directed toward some object, whether it is doubt, understanding, desire, and so forth. The reflexive judgment ties me to these conscious acts by recognizing that it is I who doubts, who understands, who desires, and so forth. Likewise, practical actions are not simply events that can be described from a third-person point of view; there is a self who accompanies them. For example, when another person (or even myself in looking back at an action) asks "who did this?" I can take away the anonymity of the action and respond by staking a claim to it: "it is I who did this." In so doing, it is as if I place my signature or mark on the action. I personalize it by claiming it as *my* deed or as *my* decision. Here, the reflexive judgment—*it is I*—asserts a connection between the action and myself, such that this action really *is* mine.

Yet, if reflexive judgments were the sole basis of a self-relation, they would fall prey to two obvious limitations that are characteristic of the Kantian path of reflection. First of all, reflexive judgments miss the first-person perspective of the subject because they operate in a way that is analogous with other judgments made from a third-person perspective. For a reflexive judgment always positions me as the direct object of a judgment (*it is I who*) rather than as the subject of this judgment. They are the logical equivalent of saying "it is you (or she) who." If I entered into relation with myself only by way of reflexive judgments, then I would relate to myself only as an object (leading to the Kantian problem that there can be no experience of the self except as an object). Second, a reflexive judgment of an action is always backward looking, which is to say that it takes place only after an action has taken place and lays claim to it only after the fact. Accordingly, if I entered into relation with myself only by way of reflexive judgments, then I would relate to myself only in terms of my past. I would entirely miss the productive or forward-looking relation to myself *en marche*. In order to disclose the first-person perspective and the living presence of the self in decision-making, it is therefore necessary to go beyond the scope of reflexive judgments about ourselves.[66]

Following the Biranian path of "concentrated reflection," Ricoeur identifies a type of self-relation that occurs on a pre-reflexive level. The pre-reflexive imputation of myself does not rely on a representation or any other form of observational knowledge about oneself. Ricoeur says that "pre-reflexive self-imputation is active not observational."[67] In short, there is nothing to see or to represent in this pre-reflexive relation. Here, the self actively determines itself and is actively involved in the process of its own doing. To illustrate this type of self-relation, Ricoeur points to the unique function of reflexive verbs: "When I say '*je me décide*,' it is at the same time me who decides and who is decided."[68] So, whereas the reflexive judgment positions me in the accusative as a direct object of the judgment, the pre-reflexive judgment places me in the nominative position as the one who is making the decision or who is involved in performing the action. To be more precise, we should add that the pre-reflexive imputation of the self includes a dual reference that is directed at once to the self and to its purpose. This is conveyed, according to Ricoeur, by expressions of the form *je me décide à* [I myself decide to]. Such expressions display pre-reflexive judgments as an active relation to oneself and to a chosen project. The self is personally invested in the process of making up one's own mind and in its chosen goal. In the pre-reflexive judgment, there is an original junction between the self as a subject who is projecting a future and the self as an object whose future is projected, such that I am both choosing and chosen, so to speak.

The question becomes: what is the relation between the reflexive and pre-reflexive judgments about oneself? Ricoeur's answer is instructive. He maintains that prior to every reflexive judgment—of the style *it is I who*—there is already an implicit pre-reflexive imputation of the self. Ricoeur affirms that "self-consciousness of myself is thus originally the identity, which is itself is pre-judicial and pre-judicative, of a presence as a projecting subject and of a projected self. It is on the basis of this pre-reflexive imputation of the self in my projects that the judgment of reflection can be understood."[69] All reflexive judgments are secondary and thus entail a prior pre-reflexive "action on oneself."[70] After all, how could I recognize myself in a reflexive judgment about myself if I were not already in contact with myself? Likewise, how could I hold myself accountable for an action through a reflexive judgement if I were not already aware of my own involvement in the decision leading up to it? Hence, in a conclusion that resonates deeply with Biran's philosophy, the pre-reflexive relation to oneself is implicit in all of the self's various operations.

Returning now to the question of how to acquire access to the docile body in its transparency, Ricoeur's distinction between reflective and pre-reflexive judgments provides a useful guide. The effort-resistance opposition that characterizes the primitive fact occurs on the level of reflective judgments. Such judgments are characterized by an opposition between self and object, inside and outside. Just as the reflective judgment recovers the self through its objectification in an action (*it is I who*), the phenomenon of effort describes the confrontation between the subjective body and the resistance of the external world (*it is I who exert this effort to move*). But this identification of the self's effort is secondary. It presupposes a prior pre-reflexive, docile relation between one's own body and the world. The docile body's experience is characterized by its effortlessness. One's own actions traverse the body and calibrate with the world without any resistance or reflection. This prior union between the self and the external world provides the initial context in which one is able to accomplish the practical tasks of life. It is only against this background that the opposition of effort and resistance can subsequently emerge and acquire meaning as a disruption of this prior union.

But couldn't this original docility provide the basis for a rapprochement between Henry and Ricoeur, to the extent that it resembles Henry's own acknowledgement of the radical passivity of the original bodily cogito?[71] Indeed, Henry seems to suggest a similar point when he calls readers to "consider the feeling of effort. What is given to it is the inner tension of the existence that encounters the opposed-being and in this confrontation gives itself; it is effort. But in the way in which effort is given to itself, in the feeling of effort, there is no effort."[72] The effortlessness Henry invokes here refers to the passivity that puts the self in possession of the *I can* and grants it the ability to exercise its various powers and capabilities. But even though both Henry and Ricoeur are describing a certain effortlessness in the relation to one's own body, it remains clear that their phenomenologies of movement are operating with two fundamentally different conceptions of passivity. For Henry, the passivity of effortlessness is internal to the self-differentiation of the total subjective body (or what we have called the internal difference) while for Ricoeur the passivity of the docile body refers to its antecedent union with the external world (or external difference).

## Conclusion: The Significance of Biran and Reflexive Philosophy

This chapter on the influence of Biran and French reflexive philosophy has provided insight into the phenomenological significance of movement. From a phenomenological perspective, movement cannot be reduced to locomotion or to the observation of a body's passage from one location to another in the external world. Instead of being disclosed by its transcendent mode of appearing, the phenomenological reality of movement is revealed through reflection on the subjective experience of one's own bodily effort to move. In support of this point, Henry is fond of citing Maine de Biran's expression that "there is no absolutely foreign force."[73] Force appears solely through the feeling of one's own body [*corps propre*] and its powers [*dunameis*].[74] This affective experience of one's own power to act is the phenomenological ground of human freedom. But if the phenomenology of movement reveals the body as a force and a power to act, wouldn't it disclose only the active dimension of bodily life? If so, wouldn't the phenomenon of movement thereby pose a threat to the thesis that the duality of pathos (passivity) and praxis (activity) governs the phenomenological structure of life? Quite the contrary, this chapter has shown that the phenomenology of movement reinforces the phenomenological structure of life as a duality of pathos and praxis.

This duality emerged in our close reading of Biran's primitive fact. To be sure, Biran anchors the primitive fact in the subjective experience of one's own bodily effort, but this fact is comprised of two factors: the subjective force of one's own body and the objective resistance of an external object. Without resistance, there would be no experience of effort at all. The primitive fact is thus a dual reality that includes the pair of bodily effort and its resistance. This is the meaning of Biran's adopted motto *homo duplex in humanitate; simplex in vitalitate*. Properly understood, the duality of *homo duplex* refers to the contrast between activity and passivity while the simple (*simplex in vitalitate*) refers to their original unity in the life of the same subjective body.

To make sense of this dual presence of pathos and praxis in the primitive fact, we can retrieve the argument from the previous chapter and elucidate the phenomenological structure of movement through the Cartesian circle. Applying this structure, two types of evidence enter into Henry's reading of Biran's account of effort. The ratio cognoscendi of movement reveals the exertion of effort from the perspective of the bodily cogito. I experience the force of movement precisely in and through the feeling of my own effort to move.

This experience reveals my power to move directly without relying on any external evidence through observation or representation. This causal power is self-evident whenever I exert a bodily effort against a physical object that resists it or simply make an effort to move my own body. Beyond this identification with the specific actions and activities in which I am actually engaged, I am immediately acquainted with the field of capacities that define the scope of what my body can do. I exercise control over this entire field which is available to me, and this personal control over my bodily powers provides concrete evidence of my own freedom.[75]

Yet, Henry criticizes Biran for restricting the subjective body to the realm of voluntary activity and thereby failing to account for the pathos of suffering. To reveal the passive dimension of bodily movement, Henry introduces evidence from the ratio essendi of life. On a surface or ontic level, passivity would refer to the undergoing of resistance from an actual object during the activity of moving my body. The resistance of an object can produce bodily fatigue or exhaustion and, in so doing, give rise to the experience of one's own body as a weight and encumbrance. But going beyond this object-oriented experience of passivity, Henry introduces a more profound ontological dimension of passivity. This is revealed by posing an additional question concerning the powers of the bodily cogito: where do these powers come from? Clearly, I do not create these powers or give them to myself; instead, they are engendered in me without my own doing or willing.[76] This recalls the lesson of Descartes's Third Meditation in which the idea of the Infinite is placed within me without any initiative from me. Like Descartes's idea of the Infinite, my bodily powers are received effortlessly through a radical passivity. Just as there is a pathos of having a life that accompanies one's own birth, there is a pathos of having a set of capabilities that precedes one's power to exercise them.[77] From the perspective of the ratio essendi of life, these powers are received as a gift from life.

Following the model of the Cartesian circle, the phenomenological significance of movement is anchored in two different types of evidence. While the ratio cognoscendi of life reveals a bodily cogito that is the independent source of its own efforts, the ratio essendi of life reveals that these capacities themselves are not the cogito's own making but instead are a gift from life. A complete phenomenological account of movement thus requires an acknowledgement of "both force and affect," or, in other words, of the active and passive dimensions of bodily movement.[78] What matters here is precisely their self-differentiation in life. The phenomenology of movement, for Henry, is thus structured as an internal difference of life that includes the pathos of the capabilities that are received from life as well as the praxis enabled by the ability to use them.

Like Henry, Ricoeur turns to reflexive philosophy (including Biran) in search of the living presence of the self in the world. While Ricoeur does acknowledge that it is possible to observe physical movement from a third-person standpoint and to situate it within a causal nexus, he believes that the personal presence of one's own subjectivity "can only be reached through a reflexive method in which man recognizes himself as the author of his acts."[79] Biran's discovery of the bodily cogito recovers the self's personal presence as an efficient cause in the world. But there is also a strong emphasis on the pathos of movement in Ricoeur's thought. This is underscored by the final line of *Freedom and Nature*: "to will is not to create." Although Ricoeur does not employ Henryan terminology like *auto-affection*, it would not be inappropriate to describe his account of the docile body as an auto-affective experience. The direct acquaintance and effortless accessibility of one's own body and its capabilities are just as essential for Ricoeur as they are for Henry. But does Ricoeur really conceptualize the pathos of the primitive fact—this auto-affective experience of the docile body—in the same way as Henry?

Ricoeur's conception of the pathos associated with movement is different from Henry and actually closer to Biran's own analyses. When Ricoeur describes the pathos of the body, the primary context in which it is situated is that of the vital body. The pathos of the vital body is linked with organic needs. Although vital needs can be enabling, they also reveal the body's weight as an encumbrance. One has to take care of one's own body as part of the burdens of life. These needs resist my will and impose constraints on my ability to move in certain directions, for certain durations, or at certain speeds, and so forth. Beyond Biran, what Ricoeur adds is an additional layer of pathos in relation to the social world. Whether physically, legally, or historically, the social world can resist my will by imposing its own set of limitations and regulations of my power to move. Ultimately, what distinguishes these Ricoeurian aspects of the pathos of movement from the Henryan account is that Ricoeur retains the notion of external resistance. While the pathos of movement results from an internal resistance and limitation for Henry, Ricoeur conceptualizes its pathos as an external resistance that comes from either the natural or social world.

This contrast between Henry and Ricoeur can be traced to Ricoeur's expressed reluctance to embrace a single-minded philosophy of immanence.

Quite precociously, his 1934 master's thesis concludes with a (very Kantian) word of caution concerning the limits of the reflexive method. On the one hand, Ricoeur grants that a method of immanence is necessary, insofar as it is able to reconnect thought to a thinker or an action to an agent and thereby restore the self's living presence in the world. In that sense, it is fair to say that Ricoeur's thought continues to stand "in the lineage of a *reflexive* philosophy." But on the other hand, he proposes that the method of immanence remains incomplete and must be supplemented by a method of transcendence.[80] Elaborating on this point, Ricoeur observes that "it is not true that one can discover oneself without discovering the other. One can only descend into oneself by leaving oneself. One can only find oneself by losing oneself. One can only reach the Same through the Other. Every immanence includes some transcendence."[81] This observation, surfacing already in Ricoeur's master's thesis, is a credo that anticipates the future direction of his entire career. It entails that the practice of reflexive self-recovery must take a detour through the external world and identify the signs within it that attest to the self's living presence. We have seen this detour carried out in his phenomenology of bodily movement.

Ultimately, the two rival interpretations of Biran's primitive fact might be summed up by the following contrast: for Henry, it is necessary to be more Biranian than Biran (by enhancing reflexive philosophy with the immanence of a radical pathos of life) while for Ricoeur it is necessary to be both Biranian and Kantian (by recognizing the limits of the reflexive method and the necessary detour through the external world)!

# 4

## Desire

*The Henry-Ricoeur Debate over Freud*

IN *FREUD AND PHILOSOPHY*, RICOEUR speaks about the phenomenological structure of life in a way that resonates surprisingly with our thesis concerning the duality of life as pathos and praxis. In a remarkable passage, he writes, "The light of life, to use the language of St. John, reveals itself in life and through life, but self-consciousness remains nonetheless the birthplace of truth and first of all the truth of life."[1] Like the "light of life," the preceding studies of birth and movement have shown that life reveals itself through the pathos in which one receives the gift of life. At the same, in keeping with this reference to the role of self-consciousness, they have affirmed that life puts the cogito in possession of itself and its power to act. The phenomenological structure of life thus identifies force and affect as two irreducible aspects of the experience of life. This chapter extends the same structure to the topic of desire and uncovers it specifically in Freud's theory of the drive [*pulsion*]. A close reading of Freud shows that desire is a combination of the pathos of affect and the praxis of force: as an affect, desire refers to the pathos of being compelled by something other; as a force, it refers to the activity of desiring that manifests itself in the effort to exist and to satisfy its aims.

The development of this chapter and the next differ from the two preceding chapters, however, insofar as they have the advantage of drawing from actual philosophical exchanges directly between Henry and Ricoeur.[2] It is fitting that Henry and Ricoeur would enter into debate over the significance of Freud's work, given his sweeping influence on twentieth-century French thought. This chapter will identify the key points of difference between their rival interpretations of Freud and then conclude that a full account of desire requires a "both-and" approach that integrates the insights of both accounts.

Ricoeur's most substantial contribution to psychoanalysis is his book *Freud and Philosophy* [1965], whose primary aim is to examine the relationship between phenomenology and psychoanalysis.[3] Freud, along with the other so-called masters of suspicion, poses a challenge to the phenomenology of consciousness by showing that the ego is always susceptible to the illusions of false consciousness. Where phenomenology claims to establish its most fundamental certitude, psychoanalysis unmasks "only a prejudice, a prejudice of consciousness."[4] Despite this divergence between the discourse of phenomenology and that of psychoanalysis, Ricoeur seeks to reconnect them through a shared conception of consciousness not as a given but as a task. The task of consciousness is to search for meaning, which Ricoeur believes can be achieved through the "appropriation of our effort to exist and of our desire to be through the works which bear witness to that effort and desire."[5]

In response to Ricoeur's book on Freud, Henry penned a critical essay entitled "Ricoeur and Freud: Between Psychoanalysis and Phenomenology."[6] Henry's close reading of Freud contends that the Ricoeurian hermeneutic ultimately returns the meaning of the unconscious to consciousness and thus falls back within the confines of a traditional philosophy of consciousness. This essay is also of considerable importance to Henry's own work because it anticipates the central thesis that will be developed later in his book *The Genealogy of Psychoanalysis* (1985).[7] The unconscious, instead of being another scene of representation, is governed by an entirely different mode of appearing. It is the realm of affects and drives, which belong to the province of life. The unconscious affects and drives of life do not enter into consciousness insofar as their mode of appearing does not reveal itself within the realm of what is visible to consciousness.

It should already be clear that the Henry-Ricoeur debate over Freud hinges on the question of the relationship between the unconscious and consciousness.[8] Whereas Ricoeur believes that plumbing the depths the unconscious and bringing them to consciousness can overcome false consciousness and promote a deeper level of self-understanding, Henry bars this hermeneutic return to consciousness. The unconscious, in its own positive reality, consists of drives, passions, and energies that cannot be translated into the field of conscious representation.[9] To the extent that conscious representations inevitably alter and distort the reality of the unconscious, it could be said that for Henry, all consciousness turns out to be false consciousness. After detailing the key points in the Henry-Ricoeur debate over the unconscious, the second move in this chapter will be to consider its broader implications for a phenomenological account of desire.

My contention is that their rival interpretations of the Freudian unconscious have a direct bearing on the phenomenological meaning of desire. Informed by psychoanalysis, both thinkers reject naturalistic accounts of desire that would reduce it to a set of supposedly natural instincts or a natural teleology. The self, to be sure, is always under the sway of drives and instincts. But instead of being compelled by nature, Freudian theory highlights the self's resistances against such impulses.[10] These resistances show that human desire is supranatural in the sense that it is able to detach itself from the reign of natural influences.[11] As such, desire has a plasticity that allows it to be channeled in multiple possible directions and toward multiple possible values. But if one subscribes to this supranatural view of desire, the questions become: what is the true source of desire, where does it reside, and what does it seek?

## A Hermeneutics of the Unconscious: Ricoeur's Freud and the Henryan Challenge

In praising *Freud and Philosophy* as "one of the best expositions of psychoanalysis that is available,"[12] Henry rightly observes that Ricoeur's book offers much more than a general exposition of Freud's thought. It provides something like a Kantian critique of psychoanalytic discourse that determines its conditions of possibility as well as its limits. By steering psychoanalysis away from its naturalistic tendencies and toward questions of meaning, Ricoeur is able to produce a rapprochement between the fields of phenomenology and psychoanalysis. They come to signify two different ways of questioning back from what seems to be apparent on the surface of conscious experience to deeper meanings that remain hidden from view. Put simply, phenomenology and psychoanalysis become hermeneutic discourses. Yet, in the process of establishing this common ground, Ricoeur also takes great care to show how these two approaches differ in their respective conceptions of the meaning and role of the unconscious.

Ricoeur provocatively asserts that "phenomenology is as radical as psychoanalysis in its challenge of the illusion of the immediate knowledge of oneself."[13] In support of this claim, Ricoeur presents Husserlian phenomenology as a challenge to direct and immediate knowledge. What appears in consciousness, for Husserl, is given only incompletely or partially, and there are at least three different ways in which intentional consciousness turns out to be incomplete: (1) spatially, (2) temporally, and (3) thematically. A spatial object, for instance, is given in only one of its profiles while its other sides remain only potential and unactualized profiles. Likewise, the temporal dimension of an object is given only partially—that is, in terms of its present, even though its temporal horizon points beyond what is given in the present and toward a past that precedes it as well as a future that is yet to come. The same incompleteness characterizes consciousness itself, insofar as conscious life includes both operative and thematic intentions. Alongside the thematic intentions that are actively presented in conscious life, there is a background of operative intentions that are present but not the focus of consciousness. These operative intentions, according to Ricoeur, decouple meaning from conscious representation and, in so doing, establish the phenomenological meaning of the unconscious.

The phenomenological account of the unconscious, however, remains fundamentally different from the psychoanalytic unconscious. The phenomenological unconscious is always a potential consciousness that can be recovered and thematized in consciousness. To the extent that these unconscious meanings can be brought into view, they contribute to the broader teleology of consciousness. This leads Ricoeur to observe that the phenomenological unconscious is more closely tied to the Freudian notion of the preconscious than the unconscious.[14] By contrast, psychoanalysis separates consciousness and the unconscious by a bar that is very difficult—albeit not impossible, Ricoeur insists—to cross.[15] The work of the analyst involves more than combating ignorance and bringing hidden content into consciousness. In addition, the analyst often encounters resistance in trying to gain access to the unconscious causes of a patient's symptoms. Psychoanalysis thus develops a special set of techniques for overcoming these resistances, such as dream interpretation and word association, to name just a few examples. But this recovery of the unconscious can proceed in two different directions, which signify the point of divergence between the Ricoeurian and Henryan interpretations of the unconscious.

Ricoeur identifies a "mixed discourse" in Freudian psychoanalysis, which includes an "energetics" that describes the unconscious in terms of biochemical processes as well as a "symbolics" in which the unconscious is said to be "like a language." Freud's energetics refers to his earliest scientific attempt to provide a quantitative understanding of psychic life. Initially presented in Freud's "Project" of 1895, the notion of the "psychical apparatus" that dominates this essay "is based on a principle borrowed from physics—the constancy principle—and tends to be a quantitative treatment of energy." By explaining consciousness as the product of unconscious biochemical forces and natural processes, Freud's energetics provides a sort of "anti-phenomenology" in which, as Ricoeur puts it, there is a "reduction not to consciousness but of consciousness."[16] These natural features of the unconscious cannot be assigned a meaning or place in consciousness. As a result, Ricoeur observes, this aspect of Freud's theory poses the greatest challenge to his attempt to establish "the correlation between energetics and hermeneutics, between connections of forces and relations of meanings."[17]

Although direct access to the contents of the unconscious is blocked, we can become aware of it indirectly through its representatives: the drives. These representatives allow the forces of life to intersect with conscious meaning in such a way that "the drives are designated in the mind by representations and the affects that present it."[18] Through these ideational and affective representatives, the components of Freud's energetics, including the drives and instincts of life, are able to be felt and represented symbolically. And it is through this symbolics of unconscious forces and drives that the deeper truth of the subject can be discerned.

This brief overview of Ricoeur's reading of Freud leads directly to Henry's main critical question—namely, "which phenomenology accords with which psychoanalysis?"[19] For Henry the answer to this question is undeniably clear: it is only because Ricoeur situates them *within the same philosophical horizon, constituted by shared ontological presuppositions, that phenomenology and psychoanalysis can be perceived as the same: as a hermeneutic.*[20] Henry concedes that Ricoeur does offer an accurate interpretation of Freud, but this is precisely because Freud himself sometimes falls prey to the same traditional philosophical definition of consciousness. Both phenomenology and psychoanalysis define consciousness by the power of representation, and this leads them to understand their own endeavors in terms of the process of bringing something into the light of representation, into the light of consciousness. Under this influence, phenomenology and psychoanalysis ultimately reduce the unconscious to the hermeneutical recovery of conscious meaning.

Against this hermeneutic tendency, Henry goes on to raise the question of whether the unconscious might bring about a "radical calling into question of the metaphysics of representation and thus of the mode of phenomenality whose model is found in perception?"[21] Although Henry only raises this question in his article on Ricoeur, he does indicate that this latter option—which challenges the metaphysics of representation—could be developed by a different type of phenomenology and a different interpretation of psychoanalysis. Indeed, this other phenomenology and this other psychoanalysis is elaborated subsequently in his book *The Genealogy of Psychoanalysis*.

## A Material Phenomenology of the Unconscious: The Henryan Alternative

Henry's preface to the Italian translation of *The Genealogy of Psychoanalysis* affirms that "this book comes from phenomenology."[22] This assertion is especially significant in light of Ricoeur's attempt to reconcile phenomenology and psychoanalysis by assigning them a shared hermeneutic task. In contrast with Ricoeur, Henry's writings on psychoanalysis set out to provide a "new interpretation of the phenomenology/psychoanalysis relation."[23] Instead of going beyond phenomenology, Henry proposes a new conception of phenomenology and an even more rigorous phenomenological account of the unconscious than Freud himself offers.[24]

To understand Henry's conception of the phenomenology/psychoanalysis relation, it is helpful to begin with his contrast between the concept of consciousness in its ontic and ontological senses.[25] Ontically, phenomenology is the study of consciousness in terms of how objects are given to consciousness, and as such it studies the various modes of givenness by which something is presented to consciousness: really or imaginatively, fully or partially, and so forth. In its ontic sense, then, phenomenology discloses the contents of consciousness. But, in addition to studying what appears in consciousness, phenomenology can also inquire ontologically into the origin of appearing. In so doing, it reveals the power by which something initially comes to appear in consciousness. Here, the pure fact of appearing can be distinguished from the disclosure of what appears or is given in appearance. Just as the phenomenology of consciousness admits these two different perspectives, Henry contends that the unconscious can also be analyzed in terms of the distinction between its ontic and ontological senses.

The great breakthrough of Freudian psychoanalysis is the discovery of the unconscious. Ontically, the unconscious can be defined as a content that is not present in conscious. As such, it is defined primarily in negative terms—that is, as something that is absent or withdraws from the field of appearance and consciousness. But if the unconscious involves anything more than the sheer negation of consciousness, Henry insists that it is necessary to put forward an ontological understanding of the unconscious that discloses its own positive reality. This element is missing, however, from Freud's account of the unconscious.

The failure to provide an ontological determination of the unconscious, according to Henry, explains why and how Freud falls short of the significance of his own discovery. Because Freud continues to remain under the influence of the history of Western philosophy in which consciousness is conceived in terms of representation, he is able to define the unconsciousness only ontically—that is, in terms of contents that are not yet represented. Understood as such, the unconscious would not differ ontologically from consciousness. Accordingly, it would be possible to translate the one directly into the other, such that "every unconscious content can take the opposite quality of consciousness and enter the light; every conscious content is destined to leave it and return to the unconscious."[26] To go beyond the Freudian (and Ricoeurian, for that matter) account of the unconscious, Henry contends that it is necessary to carry out a "radical critique of psychoanalysis—a philosophical determination of the concept of the unconscious."[27]

Henry's ontological—or positive—determination of the unconscious is developed phenomenologically. Henry explains the contrast between the ontic and ontological conceptions of the unconscious in the following way: "the unconscious has two wholly different meanings, depending on whether it refers to the inevitable obscurity of all mental content once it quits the 'present' of intuition and self-evidence and becomes a mere virtual representation or whether it refers to life itself, which necessarily escapes the light of ek-stasis."[28] Whereas the ontic account treats the unconscious simply as a hidden content that does not happen to appear, the ontological conception of the unconscious establishes its meaning on its own terms, with its own reality and its own distinctive mode of appearing. The positive reality of the unconscious resides in the affective realm of life. This domain escapes consciousness because it does not reveal itself in the light of the world or the transcendent mode of appearing. Instead, the unconscious reveals itself exclusively in the immanent mode of appearing that is characteristic of life: it reveals itself in and through the auto-affective experience of life.

To explicate this auto-affective dimension of the unconscious, Henry offers a reinterpretation of Freud's "energetics" in the 1895 "Project."[29] There, Freud defines affects as "the qualitative expression of the quantity of instinctual energy of its fluctuations" and then distinguishes between two different types of excitations: exogenous excitations (the *phi*-system) and endogenous excitations (the *psi*-system). Setting aside Freud's own pretenses to establish a science of the unconscious that treats it quantitatively, Henry recasts these two types of excitations in the context of his own material phenomenology. From that perspective, they can be described as two different modes of affectivity: hetero-affection and auto-affection. The exogenous excitations correlate with a hetero-affection in which the body is stimulated by external sources; in response to exogenous stimuli, one can respond through either pursuit or flight. Endogenous excitations, in contrast, correspond with an auto-affection that arises within oneself and whose impetus is life. Insofar as these stimuli emerge entirely within oneself, there is no option to flee the influence of these instincts and drives. The auto-affection of life is a continuous active presence within oneself: "Because, in its auto-affection, affect is radically passive with regard to oneself and is weighed down with its own being up to the unsupportability of this charge, it aspires to discharge it, it is the movement itself of the drive, which Freud calls the endogenous excitation that never ceases and in other words, auto-affection as constitutive of the essence of absolute subjectivity and of life."[30] The unconscious, understood as the auto-affection of life, serves as the basis for a new principle of constancy that takes the place of a substantial self. The life of the unconscious is a continual active reality. It does not cease to influence consciousness and cannot be dismissed by it because life continually expresses itself in the form of action, force, drives, and energy.

By defining the unconscious ontologically in terms of the auto-affectivity of life, Henry transforms the relation between consciousness and the unconscious in at least three ways. First of all, consciousness and the unconscious are established as two irreducibly different modes of appearing: there is a light of the world and a light of life (to borrow the words of the Gospel of John). Whereas the world conforms to the transcendent mode of appearing and thus admits conscious representation, the appearing of life withdraws from representation and expresses itself according to the immanent mode of appearing that is characteristic of energies, drives, and forces. Second, this sharp phenomenological divide between two irreducible modes of appearing— the transcendent appearing of the world versus the immanent appearing of life—helps to explain why the unconscious resists representation. To bring the unconscious into the light of consciousness is to alter and distort its proper mode of appearing.[31] The unconscious thus resists consciousness precisely because its own mode of appearing cannot be translated into the realm of consciousness. Lastly, this phenomenological distinction gives rise to a new understanding of the ontological dependence that exists between consciousness and the unconscious. The unconscious, instead of simply being the negation of conscious, is called by "the name of life."[32] Identified in its positive reality as life, Henry asserts, the life of the unconscious is the source of all conscious appearing: "Life, as a transcendental power of appearing, reveals the dependence of the intellect upon the emotional life."[33] But if the unconscious is granted primacy as the source of all appearing, then the puzzle that Henry leaves unanswered is: How can this source of appearing be made intelligible without a relapse into the realm of conscious representation?

It is worth noting that the actual Henry-Ricoeur debate is conducted entirely as a one-sided affair. Henry accuses Ricoeur (and Freud, no less) of reducing psychoanalysis to a hermeneutics of meaning, but Ricoeur does not ever respond to this critique, nor to Henry's own interpretation of Freud in *The Genealogy of Psychoanalysis*. Nonetheless, it is possible to lend voice to a Ricoeurian reply, *avant la lettre*, by returning to some earlier remarks on psychoanalysis in Ricoeur's *Freedom and Nature*. There, it becomes clear that Ricoeur cannot endorse Henry's pursuit of a direct path to the unconscious because it is an approach that he himself adopted at an earlier time (and later rejected). This is evident, for example, in his assertion that "psychoanalysis is only a hyletics of consciousness."[34] By associating the unconscious with the hyletic material of consciousness, the early Ricoeur identifies the unconscious with the prereflective, affective dimension of conscious life.[35] The hyletic matter of needs, emotions, and drives exposes thought to another dynamism—an affective realm—whose materials are inaccessible to consciousness and remain out of its control.[36] To the extent that this early approach to the unconscious closely resembles Henry's own material phenomenology, Ricoeur's later book on Freud offers not only a self-critique of that earlier position but also a response to the Henryan interpretation almost three decades before its publication.

Let me briefly explain how Ricoeur's *Freud and Philosophy* critiques his earlier position. The whole problem of Freudian epistemology for Ricoeur boils down to a question concerning the interaction between consciousness and the unconscious: "how can the economic explanation be *involved* in an interpretation dealing with meaning; and conversely, how can interpretation be an *aspect* of the economic explanation?"[37] The unconscious, on the one hand, is "id and nothing but id."[38] This thought-independent reality justifies the naturalistic traits of Freud's topography and his economics of the unconscious that describe the cathexis of desire.[39] Through the processes of investment in and withdrawal from objects, the economy of desire operates on its own terms and signifies desire purely as desire.[40] And this justifies the drawing of a dividing line between "the reality of the id and the reality of meaning."[41] But, on the other hand, there is also a drive toward expression and a search for intelligibility. That explains why Freudian psychoanalysis must be more than just a hyletics. The acknowledgment of this search for meaning leads Freud to adopt a "double epistemology"—or a mixed discourse—that is situated at the crossroads between an "energetics" of force and a "hermeneutics" of meaning.[42]

The disagreement between Henry and Ricoeur about the prospects of this passage from the discourse of force (energetics) to the discourse of meaning (symbolics), and vice versa, becomes especially evident in comparing their views regarding the Lacanian slogan that the unconscious is "structured like a language."[43] Henry rejects this view outright because for him, to bring life—the world of affects, forces, drives, energy—into language is to bring a nonlinguistic reality into the ideality of language. By conveying life in a discourse that is not suited to it, the translation of the unconscious into language inevitably betrays the original material reality of life. Although Ricoeur also acknowledges the limitations of the Lacanian claim that the unconscious is structured like a language, he develops a more nuanced understanding of the likeness between the two.

When it is said that "the unconscious is structured like a language," Ricoeur notes that "the problem is to assign an appropriate meaning to the word 'like.'"[44] To say that the unconscious is *like* a language is to say neither that it is nor that it is not linguistic. As such, the bar that separates the law of conscious representation from the law of life is not simply "a barrier that separates the systems" but also "a relating that ties together the relations of signifier to signified."[45] This twofold dynamic of language—operating as both a barrier and a bridge—leads Ricoeur to conclude that the economic explanation guarantees that desire "is not a phenomenon of language" and at the same time that "there is no economic process to which there cannot be found a corresponding linguistic aspect."[46] This more nuanced reading shows how Ricoeur could reply to Henry's accusation that he reduces the unconscious to consciousness. Ricoeur accepts that there is a distinct language of life and that it can indeed serve as a barrier that preserves and maintains the irreducibility of the unconscious to consciousness.[47] But the language of life is not only a barrier to consciousness, according to Ricoeur. It can also be a bridge that allows the unconscious and the affective realm to express itself in the language of consciousness. This bridge function—which links phenomenology and psychoanalysis to a hermeneutics of meaning—remains underdeveloped in Henry's account of the unconscious.

## Henry's Immanent Teleology of Desire

Thus far, the Henry-Ricoeur debate has shed light on two possible ways of mapping the relation between psychoanalysis and phenomenology: the Ricoeurian approach that links them through a shared hermeneutics of meaning versus the Henryan approach that links them through a material phenomenology of affective life. But we have not yet considered their implications for the central topic of this chapter: desire. In addition to its discovery of the unconscious, Freudian psychoanalysis provides a nontraditional account of desire. Instead of being channeled toward natural aims, Freud emphasizes the plasticity and malleability of desire that open it to many possible aims. But the difficult question for the Freudian account of desire becomes: what is the true source of desire, and what does it seek? A significant divide opens up between Henry and Ricoeur in their treatment of this issue: Henry posits that desire is guided by an immanent teleology established by the laws and aims of life while Ricoeur emphasizes the mixture of natural and cultural influences on desire.

Henry's immanent teleology of desire is guided by two fundamental laws: (1) the law of preservation; (2) the law of growth.[48] The first law of desire, according to Henry, is that *life seeks to persevere in its own being*. This law is clearly influenced by Spinoza's notion of the *conatus*, which refers to the fact that "each thing, as far as it can by its own power, strives to persevere in its own being."[49] But its full meaning can be unpacked only by following the logic of the immanent self-differentiation of life. As such, the first law of desire can be examined from two perspectives: that of the living individual and that of Life. From the former perspective, it affirms that living individuals seek their own self-preservation. This law draws support from the many different conscious activities in which living individuals engage for the sake of promoting their effort to continue to live (nourishment, shelter, self-protection, etc.). While this perspective locates the *conatus essendi* in consciousness, it does not explain why individual survival itself is a good. That question can be answered only when desire is traced back to a more primary, unconscious origin in Life. From the perspective of Life, the law of preservation refers to Life's own desire to continue its own existence. This perspective explains why the living individual comes to have desires in the first place. Life brings the living individual into existence because it seeks to persevere in its own existence and because it can continue to do so only through living individuals. From that perspective, the law of preservation is an active force, a drive, that operates on its own and according to its own motives. Outside the scope of consciousness or deliberation, Life implants the desire within the living individual to survive and continue its own existence. Based on this logic of the immanent self-differentiation of life, the first law of desire is thus an intersection between these two perspectives: from the perspective of the *ratio cognoscendi*, the living individual desires to persevere in its own existence while from the perspective of the *ratio essendi*, Life implants its own desire to persevere in its own existence into the unconscious.

These two perspectives reveal a mutual bond between Life and the living individual. Life, on the one hand, is dependent on the individual for its existence; it can exist only in and through living individuals. But, on the other hand, the living individual is also dependent on Life in the sense that it comes from life and is preserved in its own being by life, which enters into the self at each point of its being, according to Henry.[50] The ceaseless activity of life—its continual flow into the individual—provides a principle of self-constancy that takes the place of consciousness as a constant. The desires of Life and of the living individual depend on one another for the furtherance of their aims. The law of perseverance is fulfilled when the living individual seeks to preserve its own life, but it is violated when the living individual turns against Life and seeks its destruction. This is how the first law becomes a normative principle in Henry's practical philosophy.

The second law of desire—the law of growth—can also be analyzed through the logic of the self-differentiation of life. The second law establishes that *life seeks more life*. This means that life is more than a state of entropy; it strives for "a free reign, to deploy its being and to let it grow."[51] From the perspective of the living individual, this law of growth means that the living individual seeks to expand its energies and powers, such that each living individual seeks "the self-growth of the absolute subjectivity of life."[52] Just as the eye always wants to see more, so too desire always seeks to live more, to experience more, and to do more. For a living individual, self-realization or self-fulfillment is tantamount to the movement of self-growth: it signifies the continual desire to see more, to feel more, to love more, and so forth. To be clear, this growth is not measured quantitatively but qualitatively in terms of the intensification of life.[53] Each living individual grows by living more intensely—that is, by seeing, feeling, or loving more intensely. But why, one might ask, does the living individual seek to intensify its own feeling of life in the first place? The answer comes from the adoption of the perspective of Life as a ratio essendi.

Life, too, is governed by the law of growth: Life always seeks more life. This means that Life does not simply seek to continue to exist for a longer time but also seeks its own growth and intensification. If the living individual desires to live more intensely, this is because Life itself continually seeks its own expansion and intensification. It accomplishes this in and through the living individual. Its own striving is expressed through the unconscious drives and forces of life that are placed in the living individual. These unconscious drives and forces push the living individual to accomplish the goals of Life as such. Based on these two overlapping perspectives, the law of self-growth can be described as follows: while the conscious desire of the living individual is to seek the intensification of its own life, the unconscious drive to live intensely originates from Life itself. This law is fulfilled when the individual engages in activities or forms of life that enable one to live more intensely, but it is violated when the living individual turns against Life and seeks to mask it or flee from it. The law of growth thus establishes a second normative principle in Henry's practical philosophy.

As a corollary to these two laws of desire, it could be added that life always seeks to overcome suffering.[54] To be clear, the pathos of suffering is an essential feature of the phenomenological structure of life: "all life is a passion," as Henry says.[55] The passion of life stems from this undergoing of a radical passivity with regard to one's own being. The individual comes into life from life and, Henry adds, continues to live only to the extent that life continues to enter into it. This pathos of life is rooted in the continual, relentless, and unescapable entrance of life into the living individual. Life accumulates and weighs on the living individual, and in this sense, the pathos of life introduces a burden and a suffering of life. The immanent teleology of life, however, calls for the transformation of suffering into satisfaction and joy. Henry describes the passage from suffering to joy as follows: "According to the immanent teleology of life, need is satisfied in the activity into which it changes itself spontaneously. Such is the movement of life, its auto-movement, according to the elementary subjective sequence: Suffering-Effort-Enjoyment. Since the immemorial dawn of humanity, this elementary sequence—objectively called need-work-consumption—has been invested in the material, that is subjective, production of indispensable goods, in the 'real process of production.'"[56] The affective sequence that passes from suffering to effort and then to enjoyment can be illustrated by the process of satisfying a need: the suffering of a lack leads one to do something in order to fulfill what is lacking and enjoy this fulfillment. Henry's immanent teleology emphasizes that the satisfaction of need is not exclusively or even primarily an empirical or natural process; it is not about what actually is needed or what actually is done. Instead of focusing on the actual objects of need, Henry describes this process subjectively—that is, as a process of affective transformation. The satisfaction of need is entirely about the affective dimension of a process that leads from suffering to effort and then from effort to joy.

But without this reference to the objects of need, Henry's account gives rise to the question: why does the individual experience a lack and seek to overcome it in the first place? The answer, again, can be discerned by shifting from the individual's experience and adopting the perspective of Life as such. The living individual happens to find satisfaction and joy in particular goods only because they coincide with the strivings of Life as such. This overlapping of the joy of the individual with that of Life can be explained by invoking the two laws of desire again. First, the law of preservation establishes that Life is a principle of constancy. Life is continually experienced as the suffering of a pathos: one undergoes the constant influx of life and the weight of its pressure on the self: "The thrust of the drive coming from suffering pushes it to change itself.... This is the original union between the affect and action. The principle of this union resides in the tireless activity through which life works to transform the sickness of unsatisfied need into the well-being of satisfaction."[57] The weight and pressure of life gives rise to the effort to change oneself by engaging in various activities through which individuals try to find a release from the burdens of life.[58] Because life continually and relentlessly enters into the individual, it gives rise to a continual impulse to respond to the needs of life, to maintain itself, and to intensify its life. The joy of satisfaction, then, does not stem from anything external to life; it is defined solely in relation to Life's own search to continue and grow. The individual finds joy precisely when its own augmentation and intensification coincides with that of Life as such while the living individual experiences suffering when they do not coincide.

We have now identified three central features of Henry's immanent teleology of life: (1) the law of preservation; (2) the law of growth; (3) the transformation of suffering into joy. These laws of desire inform Henry's account of the psychoanalytic cure. Henry asks, "Does not the cure itself demonstrate that the representation of one's situation, its conflicts and their history, by analysis is useless so long as the precondition of that consciousness, a modification of life, does not occur?"[59] Henry answers that the cure of the patient does not take place in consciousness through a process of becoming aware of something new or forgotten. This would amount only to a change in the patient's representation of reality but not a change in reality as such. A true cure must produce a real change in the patient's life. It must produce a self-transformation of the patient.

This self-transformation is accomplished by the establishment of a new relationship to life. For example, imagine a patient who is suffering from melancholy or depression. The cure would not be attained by simply encouraging the patient to represent the world differently, for instance, by adopting a more positive attitude or mindset. Instead, the cure must be rooted in the patient's own relation to the laws of life and desire. This might require combatting the patient's escape mechanisms, perhaps through their abuse of drugs or alcohol. Instead of trying to flee the suffering of life through mind-numbing or self-destructive routines, the patient might find a new way to embrace the whole of life, suffering and all. This might occur through an embrace of new creative outlets that provide opportunities for self-growth and intensification of life. These life-affirming activities provide one indication, among many, of how the weight of a patient's suffering can be transformed into joy.[60]

While this provides only a very schematic account of more complex and challenging issues that arise in clinical settings with individual patients, a pair of philosophical questions need to be raised about Henry's overall account of the immanent teleology of desire. First, a question of completeness. Are two laws (plus a corollary) sufficient to account for the entire teleology of desire? In addition to preservation and growth, might other laws of life need to be introduced (e.g., social or moral laws) to explain the teleology of desire? Second, a question of normativity. From a normative perspective, the laws of life seem too simplistic. Can a desire or action be called good simply because it is more intense or bad simply for being less intense? Are there other values that are equally important but not measured by intense feelings? These questions, which are familiar in the context of contemporary debates about normative ethics, remain unexplored by Henry. While it is important to remain open-minded about the prospect of a Henryan response to these questions, it's equally possible that, if these questions were addressed seriously, the shortcomings of his immanent teleology of desire would be exposed.

## Ricoeur on the Limitations of Immanent Teleology

Possible limitations of Henry's account of desire begin to surface when it is compared to the teleology of desire developed by Ricoeur in *Freedom and Nature* as well as *Freud and Philosophy*. Ricoeur provides what might be called, purely for the sake of contrast with Henry, a transcendent teleology of desire. That is simply to say that his account of desire emphasizes the external influences on desire (correlating with Freud's "exogenous excitations"). From *Freud and Philosophy*, I will call attention to the role of culture in shaping and cultivating the expression of desire while the biological influence of the vital realm will be drawn from *Freedom and Nature*. These external influences provide a compelling alternative to the above questions on which the immanent teleology of desires stumbles.

In examining the influence of culture on desire, it is worth noting, first of all, that Henry's reading of Ricoeur focuses exclusively on the first half of part III of Ricoeur's *Freud and Philosophy*—that is, on the two chapters dealing with the epistemological status of Freudian psychoanalysis and the archeology of the subject. But part III, which is entitled "Dialectic: A Philosophical Interpretation of Freud," is actually comprised of four chapters. While Henry's reading stops with the first two, Ricoeur's third chapter proceeds to link the archeology of the subject—which leads back to the unconscious—with an implicit teleology of Freudian psychoanalysis in which the subject seeks to become conscious of its own reality. Through this alignment of an archeology and a teleology of the self, the fourth chapter places two different types of hermeneutics—a critical hermeneutics and a constructive hermeneutics—into a dialectical relation. The selective nature of Henry's reading of Ricoeur, I will show, reveals the limitations of Henry's immanent teleology of desire.

At the outset of the chapter entitled "Dialectic: Archeology and Teleology," Ricoeur affirms that "in order to have an *arche* a subject must have a *telos*," a point he reiterates over the course of his career.[61] Within the psychoanalytic context, this means that the antecedent reality of the unconscious does not place the self entirely at its mercy. In addition to the archeological direction that shows the influence of the past on the present, Ricoeur invokes a Hegelian phenomenology of desire in which a vision of the future shapes the present. As a result of the dialectical relation between the archeology and teleology of desire, there turn out to be "two dispossessions of consciousness" that point in two opposite directions. The archeology of consciousness points toward an unconscious origin that precedes the present while the teleology of a future gives shape to the development of the present.[62]

One of the main preoccupations of Freudian thought, in fact, is "the theme of the prior, the anterior" in relation to consciousness.[63] Before the subject ever formulates its own perceptions and conceptions about "its own house," it is already immersed in life as a subject of desire. Conscious thoughts are the product of a prior inheritance of a given body, place, history, and language. This inheritance from the past takes hold of the subject before it can take its own seat and possess itself in consciousness. The archeology of the subject, as a result, reveals the prior presence of the "other of oneself within oneself."[64] But for Ricoeur, this archeology should not have the last word in defining desire, which is not simply traceable to an archaic past; it must be linked to a teleology pointed toward the future.

In his treatment of the teleological dimension of desire, Ricoeur turns to Hegel, who concedes that the Cartesian cogito's affirmation that *I am, I exist* is undeniably certain, but it is true only in a trivial or superficial sense. Due to the fundamental opacity of life, the immediate awareness of one's own living does not yet allow one to know oneself adequately or fully. Instead, it is a starting point from which one strives to know oneself better through the progressive deepening of self-consciousness. This striving is identified with what Hegel calls the "restlessness" [*Unruhigkeit*] of life. To say that life is restless is to say that it is always in development, so to speak, a work in progress. For Hegel, the movement of life is guided by the work of negation. This means that life does not seek what it already has but what it does not yet have and that it does not seek what already exists but what does not yet exist. This restless striving accounts for "the unsurpassable character of life and desire."[65] It means that the self always desires more: to become more than what it is, to acquire more than what it has, and to become what it is not yet. The source of this movement, as Ricoeur explains, can be traced back to the "ever-recurring otherness residing in life. It is life that becomes the other, in and through which the self ceaselessly achieves itself."[66]

The process of self-becoming does not occur arbitrarily, however. It is guided by culture, whose sway over natural desires is evident in education, for example.[67] Education, as a process of *Bildung*, reshapes and channels what is initially given by natural desire. It articulates a set of cultural values establishing what pursuits are desirable or not and how those values should be realized. Culture's influence on the teleology of desire sheds light on the meaning of Freud's famous remark that "where id was, the ego comes to be." It suggests that the natural desires of the id are guided by psychic processes such as identification and sublimation, which bring natural desire under the tutelage of cultural influences and orient it toward higher goals. This cultivation of desire informs the task of becoming a self; it presents a set of ideals and aspirations for the self to achieve.

By highlighting culture's influence on desire, the Ricoeurian account helps to pinpoint a significant limitation of Henry's immanent teleology of desire. The Henryan account suggests that desire—affective material of needs, drives, and forces—is self-guiding. It describes the internal features of the development of life without imposing any external constraints on what types of change ought to be desired or how they ought to be pursued. The teleology of desire is simply defined as the continuation and intensification of life. But are the pairs of pursuit-flight and increased-decreased intensity sufficient to guide the teleology of desire and the process of self-becoming? Without the influence of culture, the problem is that the Henryan account, so to speak, offers an id and an ego but no superego.

Ricoeur's account circumvents this problem by introducing an external standard—the representation of an ideal—to guide the process of self-becoming. While Ricoeur, like Henry, acknowledges that the self is guided by a desire and an effort to be, desire does not simply exist for the sake of its own continuation. Beyond the simple choices to either pursue or flee life, Ricoeur's teleology of desire posits ideals that exceed desire and orient it. These ideals are provided by culture. Guided by a teleological ideal, the process of self-becoming aims to narrow the gap that divides the self in its actuality (where the id was) and the self in its ideality (what the ego will be). By passing through the filter of cultural representations and ideals, the Ricoeurian account thus provides better criteria to assess choices between an array of multiple and sometimes conflicting goods. This array of possibilities can be assessed in terms of which goods best promote the development of an ideal self.

In addition to the cultural influence on desire, another external feature that is excluded from Henry's immanent teleology is the influence of organic life. Recall that Freud rejects naturalistic accounts of desire that would reduce desire to the accomplishment of natural goals. The Freudian self is able to put up resistances against purportedly natural impulses or goals, but that does not imply that organic life has no influence whatsoever on desire, either. To echo a question first raised by Emmanuel Falque, is it really possible to speak about a desire without a body?[68] Even if a purely naturalistic account of desire is dismissed, can desire be wholly uprooted from the organic body, and can it forego all consideration of the metabolic processes of vital life?

The answer for Ricoeur is clearly negative. Desire does not simply emerge from a pure field of logical possibilities; its possibilities are anchored to the concrete reality of an organic body. "My body," as Ricoeur observes in *Freedom and Nature*, "is the most basic source of motives and reveals a primordial layer of values: the organic values [*valeurs vitales*]."[69] To have a body is to have needs and to value things on the basis of those needs. I find joy in bread or water because my body needs nourishment. Things are enjoyable or satisfying in relation to the specific conditions of my body. For example, drinking a glass of water might be desirable under certain conditions, but it is not always enjoyable. Once my body's thirst is quenched, drinking more water becomes undesirable and may even run up against the practical limits of how much water my body can hold. It makes little sense to speak of what is valued or desired without reference to these natural circumstances. Insofar as the organic body is a source both of value and of limitation, it defines the scope and boundaries of the desirable.

Although desire is linked to the organic body, the psychoanalytic account of desire holds that biological desires do not trigger automatic or instinctive reactions. Instead, they retain a plasticity that allows them to be deferred, suspended, or overcome by other motives. Following Ricoeur, it might be said that desires "incline without compelling."[70] While my bodily needs might incline me toward something of value, their presence does not automatically determine my pursuit of them. The plasticity of desire is evident, for instance, in acts of sacrifice where competing desires enter into conflict. Due to hunger, I cannot help but to value the piece of bread and to be drawn toward it. The bread would satiate my hunger. But due to another conflicting value—say, loyalty to a friend or a cause—I might refuse the bread and choose to remain hungry if it were offered as a bribe. But if these two options were simply laid out as pure possibilities without any reference to the values of the organic body, would the act of sacrifice have any meaning anymore? Of course, I could choose to pursue one or the other. However, the point is that the worth of the act of sacrifice as well as the temptation of betrayal acquire meaning only in reference to bodily need and the experience of hunger. Without any reference to the reality of an organic body, Henry's immanent teleology seems unable to account for acts of sacrifice and other related experiences in which different values enter into conflict.

## Conclusion

This treatment of the Henry-Ricoeur debate over Freud has focused on two main issues: their rival interpretations of the unconscious and of the teleology of desire. With respect to the unconscious, the chapter began with the observation that psychoanalysis challenges the classical phenomenology of consciousness by introducing a split between consciousness and meaning. Henry and Ricoeur both accept the value of this psychoanalytic insight and advocate for a rapprochement between phenomenology and psychoanalysis. For Ricoeur, these two discourses can be reconciled through a hermeneutics of meaning. In response to that approach, Henry asks, "Isn't the originality of a thought of life lost?"[71] From his perspective, the reconciliation of phenomenology and psychoanalysis can be accomplished only by grounding the unconscious—with its affects, forces, and drives—in a material phenomenology of life. These differences are characteristic of the methodological differences that we have identified between their two rival approaches to the phenomenology of life.

This study of the teleology of desire, likewise, is consistent with the duality of the pathos (as affect) and praxis (as force) of life that has been articulated in previous chapters.[72] Henry establishes a link between affect and force through an immanent teleology of desire in which an affective sequence unfolds from suffering to effort to enjoyment [*souffrance-effort-jouissance*]. Desire arises, first of all, from the pathos of life. Life brings the individual into life and continually preserves it in life at each point of its existence. This continual influx of life, which Henry associates with the "endogenous excitations" described by Freud, accumulates as an increasing weight on the self. This suffering of the weight of life motivates the effort to act in order to reduce or discharge it.

The self exerts its own force—its power to act—by engaging in various activities that seek to alleviate its own suffering. In so doing, this sequence culminates with the affective transfer from suffering to enjoyment, which is found in activities that promote the continuation and intensification of one's own life as well as of Life as such.

This chapter questions whether an immanent teleology can provide a sufficient account of desire. Through a comparison with Ricoeur's emphasis on the external influences that shape desire, there is good reason to believe that desire cannot be entirely contained in the immanent experience of life. Cultural influences guide desire toward socially approved activities and goals in a given cultural context while biological factors define the scope of what can be desirable for an organic body in a given life situation. The influence of these external factors helps to show why a purely immanent account of desire remains just as inadequate as a purely external account offered by a natural teleology of desire. The phenomenology of desire helps to show why both the immanent and the transcendent modes of appearing are necessary.

This critique of Henry's immanent teleology links back to an issue mentioned in the introduction to this book, concerning the foundationalist tendency in Henry's phenomenology of life. Practicing a maximalist approach to phenomenology, Henry continually questions back to the origin or first starting point of all appearing. This leads him to posit a founding relation between the two modes of appearing, such that immanence founds the possibility and meaning of transcendence. The consequences of this founding relation extend to his phenomenology of desire. Henry questions back to the arche or origin of desire and locates this in the immanent appearing of life. To maintain its privileged role, his analysis minimizes all the external factors that could possibly influence desire and focuses solely on the development of a teleology that is entirely immanent to life. But the limitations of this account offer a clear indication that Henry's thesis concerning the foundational role of the immanent mode of appearing should be replaced by a both-and strategy that acknowledges the interplay between the internal (immanent) and external (transcendent) influences on desire.

# 5

## Praxis

### The Henry-Ricoeur Debate over Marx

KARL MARX STANDS ALONGSIDE FREUD as one of the so-called masters of suspicion who challenge the phenomenology of consciousness by separating meaning from consciousness.[1] Marx's critique of ideology and his elevation of praxis over theory is the focus of the other actual confrontation between Henry and Ricoeur. On the one hand, Henry's massive two-volume 1976 study, *Marx*, offers a humanistic interpretation of Marx that challenges the prevailing antihumanist orthodoxy in France at the time.[2] Henry summed up some of the key elements of his book in a presentation entitled "La Rationalité selon Marx," to which a panel comprised of Ricoeur, Mikkel Dufrenne, and R. P. Dubarle responded. Following this exchange, Ricoeur published an extended book review of Henry's *Marx* in 1978.[3] Ricoeur, on the other hand, makes references to Marx throughout his career but never develops an equally extensive treatment of Marx. His most detailed discussion occurs in his *Lectures on Ideology and Utopia*, which were delivered in fall 1975 at the University of Chicago.[4] Toward the end of his sixth lecture—which is his second of two lectures on *The German Ideology*—Ricoeur has a paragraph describing Henry's new (but not yet published) book on Marx.[5] While that lone paragraph might give the impression that Henry didn't really impact his thinking, closer inspection of the content of his two lectures on Marx's *The German Ideology* reveals that Henry actually exerts a greater influence on Ricoeur's interpretation of Marx than he admits. Together, these various engagements display a period in the mid-1970s during which both Henry and Ricoeur are deeply engaged with Marx as well as the interpretative differences that set them apart from one another.[6]

The core of their dispute comes to the surface most clearly in the exchange that followed Henry's presentation "La Rationalité selon Marx."[7] There, Ricoeur expresses his immense esteem for Henry's accomplishment but suggests that his reading of Marx commits an interpretive violence. To be precise, it steers Marx's thought toward the philosophical view articulated previously in Henry's *The Essence of Manifestation*.[8] This perhaps explains why Henry introduces a sharp divide between a praxis that is rooted wholly in the subjective experience of one's own body and an economic realm that is entirely objective. Henry goes too far, according to Ricoeur, in advancing the claim that one side of this division—namely, the subjective dimension of praxis—is the ultimate foundation for all of Marx's thought. This leads Henry to unduly diminish the unchosen circumstances [*Umstände*] that shape praxis. As an alternative, Ricoeur proposes that what is fundamental is precisely the interaction between the subject and the world, where the "acting individual is put into situations that it did not posit."[9] In response to this objection, Henry concedes that Ricoeur is touching on an issue that is "absolutely fundamental" but also difficult[10]; he observes that, in *The German Ideology*, Marx says that living individuals do not only act but also create the circumstances themselves in which they act.[11] This implies that living individuals are the source not only of their actions but also of the background conditions in which they act.[12]

This debate amounts to more than a mere technical dispute over the proper interpretation of Marx; it addresses a fundamental question concerning the nature of human action. This question is at once methodological and epistemological: Can praxis be understood directly, without the filter of ideology, through a phenomenology of subjective lived experience alone? Or does praxis always require mediation through some form of ideology and consideration of the broader set of circumstances in which one lives and acts?[13] In their efforts to grapple with this question, a familiar pattern unfolds. Henry's reading of Marx is thoroughly Biranian in the sense that it traces all actions as well as their circumstances back to their subjective origin in living individuals, whereas Ricoeur's critique emphasizes the external circumstances (biological, historical, linguistic, etc.) that shape the lives of living individuals. As this contrast between their respective readings of Marx unfolds, it becomes increasingly clear that the debate over Marx serves as a proxy for articulating their rival approaches to the phenomenology of life.

## From a Phenomenology of Consciousness to a Phenomenology of Life

During the preparation of his Marx book, Henry contributed an essay—"The Phenomenology of Consciousness, the Phenomenology of Life"—to a 1975 collection in honor of Ricoeur.[14] Quite curiously in that context, Henry's essay never explicitly mentions Ricoeur's name and never cites any of his work. The latter half of this essay resurfaces almost verbatim in Henry's book on Marx, and so one might wonder whether it belongs in the collection at all.[15] With a little interpretive effort, however, it becomes possible to tease out a Marxian critique of the prospects of a hermeneutic phenomenology. The essay, as its title indicates, distinguishes between two orientations: a phenomenology of consciousness and a phenomenology of life. Henry insinuates that Ricoeur's hermeneutic phenomenology, along with other developments in existential philosophy, remain tethered to a phenomenology of consciousness even when they purport to go beyond it.

Henry's account of the phenomenology of consciousness follows the contours of his critique of Husserlian phenomenology already described in chapter 1 of this book. For Husserl, consciousness is defined primarily in terms of intentionality; it is directed outside itself toward objects of meaning. In the act of representation, being comes to be defined as an object for itself, and the meaning of this object is conferred by the activity of thought, by a *Sinngebung*. The phenomenology of consciousness thus stands in the lineage of the Western philosophical tradition that has restricted appearing to the transcendent mode of appearing—that is, to a relation between consciousness and something external to it. By contrast, Henry's phenomenology of life challenges this tradition and reveals an entirely different mode of appearing. The appearing of life is not given by a representation or some type of *theoria*; instead, it is revealed in an entirely immanent mode of appearing. Life reveals itself in the immediacy of the embrace of life that is directly felt but cannot be detached or put at a distance from oneself.

To chart the passage from a phenomenology of consciousness to a phenomenology of life, Henry draws inspiration from Marx's critique of ideology and, in particular, his critique of Max Stirner. In *The Ego and Its Own*, Stirner advocates for the absolute freedom of consciousness and gives it the power to determine all meaning, including the meaning of the holy,[16] which, from this perspective, "is the product of a givenness of sense which takes place in consciousness understood as the radical origin of this sense."[17] The important lesson here pertains to the function of ideology. As Henry explains, ideology is extended to "*the whole of the representations of human consciousness in the sense of mere representations.*"[18] The decisive function of ideology consists of its replacement of the reality of life with a representational substitute, an irreality. There are thus two crucial steps in Marx's critique of ideology, according to Henry: first, it exposes this substitution as a form of mystification carried out by ideology; second, it shows that a change in one's ideological conception of reality does not change anything about the reality of life itself.[19] As a result, the critique of ideology establishes that ideology offers only a representation of life and does not provide access to life in its reality.

Henry extends Marx's critique of ideology to Sartrean existentialism, specifically to Sartre's famous analysis of the voyeur in *Being and Nothingness*.[20] The voyeur peers through the keyhole without being noticed and delights in the power of his gaze to control and objectify the people who appear through the keyhole. But all of a sudden, he discovers that he himself, in turn, is being watched by someone else down the hallway. With this discovery, the voyeur experiences a dramatic transformation of his own being. His gaze sought to trap the other as an object of consciousness, but in discovering that he is seen by the other, he finds that his own being has been stolen away—he has become an object for the other. Sartre's account of this struggle of two gazes, according to Henry, is a prime example of an interpretation of Hegel's master-slave dialectic that is defined solely in representational terms. It is reduced to a struggle that takes place between two consciousnesses—that is, a struggle over how each is represented and appropriated in the consciousness of the other. But if this ideological struggle is all that is at stake, it does not touch in any way the real clashes and conflicts that occur between living individuals.[21] Hence, the Sartrean account of recognition remains within the confines of a traditional philosophy of consciousness.

It is also plain to see how the same critique of ideology could be extended to the hermeneutic work of interpretation, even though Henry does not explicitly make that connection. Hermeneutics seeks to resolve the conflict of interpretations. That is to say that it arbitrates between different perspectives on a given phenomenon by evaluating and balancing them; occasionally it even proposes a new interpretation that can resolve the conflict through a broader point of view. But for Marx's critique of ideology, a change of consciousness alone—a change of interpretation—does not amount to a change of reality. This only reaffirms Marx's oft-cited eleventh thesis that "philosophers have only interpreted the world in various ways."[22] The problem with hermeneutics, like Sartrean existentialism, is that it remains tethered to a philosophy of consciousness and is thereby unable to produce real change in the actual lives of living individuals.

Henry's challenge of existential philosophy and hermeneutics is unmistakably clear: both discourses continue to operate within the very same framework of the traditional phenomenology of consciousness—the realm of representation—that they criticize and claim to surpass. As a result, they are unable to realize the true aim of Marx's critique of ideology, which, according to Henry, is to provide direct access to life.[23] This leads Henry to conclude that Marx's thought leads us to the profound question: What is life?[24] Without passing through the filter of ideologies or hermeneutic detours, Marx's critique of ideology returns to the materiality of life and describes it purely on its own terms. Marx shows that life is revealed in praxis and that praxis has its own internal structure that is irreducible to theory.[25]

Quite interestingly, Marx's recovery of the materiality of life does not go unnoticed by Ricoeur, either. In fact, Ricoeur's essay "L'originaire et la question-en-retour dans la *Krisis* de Husserl"—which was originally presented as part of a Festschrift to honor Emmanuel Levinas in 1980—directly compares the critique of ideology to the performance of the "phenomenological epoche."[26] Insofar as both discourses perform a bracketing operation—whether of ideology or of straightforward consciousness—both Marx and Husserl are engaged in a process of questioning back [*question-en-retour*] to the origins of consciousness.[27] This process begins with what is explicit or present in consciousness, a set of naïvely accepted representations and constructions of the world. Questioning back from what is explicit, it seeks to recover what is implicit and the underlying source of consciousness—namely, the lifeworld.[28] This rapprochement between Marx and Husserlian phenomenology might be construed as Ricoeur's tacit reply to Henry's criticism. Its implications, at any rate, are quite clear. Whereas Henry defines Marx's critique of ideology in sharp contrast with Husserlian phenomenology, Ricoeur suggests that Husserlian phenomenology and Marx's critique of ideology are not opposed. Quite the contrary, they are united by a shared hermeneutical aim to recover and restore a deeper contact with the lifeworld. This reopens the prospect of a phenomenology of praxis that develops along different lines from Henry, a path that will be explored later when this chapter returns to Ricoeur's own account of ideology.

## Henry's Marx

First, let's establish the central argument of Henry's careful two-volume study *Marx*, which aims to provide both an interpretation and a surpassing of Marx's thought. In this sense, the book is not simply an exposition of what Marx meant; it also serves as a gateway to Henry's own philosophy of life.[29] This explains why Ricoeur is not mistaken to identify two voices in Henry's book as well as the reason why Henry is willing to concede this point.[30] Indeed, it is possible to make the same point about each of Henry's studies of individual thinkers, whether it is Descartes, Freud, Husserl, or even Kandinsky. In each case, Henry offers a reading of the thinker that at the same time provides a point of entry into his own phenomenology of life. But if Henry's reading is not innocent, these two voices contain the possibility for the originality of Henry's reading as well as the possibility of an interpretive violence against Marx.[31]

Bearing this in mind, note that Henry's primary aim is to restore "the voice of Marx" against Marxism. In fact, he understands Marxism as a total distortion of Marx's own philosophy and defines it precisely as "the interrelated set of misinterpretations that have been given concerning Marx."[32] Marxism completely stands Marx's thought on its head. The fundamental flaw of Marxism, according to Henry, is that it has been constructed out of secondary notions—such as the concepts of productive forces, social classes, and so forth—that are actually rooted in more fundamental concepts whose reality it either ignores or denies, such as the living individual and praxis.[33] The Marxist emphasis on abstract notions leads to the neglect of what is truly fundamental for Marx: the living individual. This oversight perhaps also explains the failure of political regimes that have been constructed on Marxism, as Henry elaborates in *Barbarism* and *From Communism to Capitalism*. To restore the voice of Marx's original intuitions and insights, it is therefore necessary to perform a sort of epoche of the Marxist legacy of misinterpretation and to recover the philosophy of living reality that emerges in the writings of the young Marx. The first volume thus focuses on Marx's theory of reality developed prior to *Capital* whereas the second volume utilizes these founding concepts to reconstitute the philosophical meaning of the economy. This way of organizing Marx's thought provides a direct counter to Marxist readings that see *Capital* as the culmination of Marx's thought; for Henry, *Capital* is only the elaboration of a more fundamental philosophy of the living human being that is already developed in Marx's early writings.

Henry contends that Marx's true discovery is the development of a new philosophical conception of the human being. Whereas Western philosophy promotes an abstract conception that defines the human in terms of intellectual activity, Marx's account of praxis marks an unprecedented development of a radical and radically new sense of subjectivity.[34] Marx defines the human being primarily in terms of its practical activities and abilities. In Marx's own words, "it is not consciousness that determines life, but life that determines consciousness."[35] To be clear, the point is not that life provides the content or the material for conscious representations. Instead, to say that life "determines consciousness" means that the reality of the living individual is the ground, the origin, of consciousness. Henry explains:

> This reality is what Marx calls 'praxis,' 'subjective' praxis in 1845—'non-organic subjectivity', 'the subjective force of labor', 'the force of labor', 'subjective labor', 'living labor', 'the living present', 'the body of the worker', etc. in the manuscripts and so-called economic texts which compose the essence of the prior work. In the context of the analyses in which they are inscribed, these expressions disclose an essential connection: *Force = Subjectivity = Life*. The fact that subjectivity is life challenges the classical concept of subjectivity which identifies it with 'consciousness' in the sense of a 'consciousness of something,' a consciousness of the object, of a representation.[36]

According to Henry, then, Marx's philosophical discovery of the living individual as the original ground of representation shapes the trajectory of his entire thought. It entails that the praxis of the living individual is the first premise of any understanding of society, history, and economics.[37]

Henry sheds additional light on the meaning of praxis by introducing the distinction (which was already treated in the discussion of Biran in chap. 3) between two basic aspects of any action: inner and outer. To recall this distinction, the outer aspect of praxis could be described as the *what* of the action; in other words, it refers to what is done, the *pragma*. Consider the activity of moving some object. Defined in terms of what is done, this action can be represented as a movement from one location to another. As a result, the outer aspect of an action can be observed, measured, and quantified. One can determine, for example, where it was moved, how far it was moved, how fast it was moved, and so forth. Yet, this representation of the movement does not exhaust the scope of its meaning, insofar as every action is also accompanied by an inner aspect that excludes the external perspective entirely. Praxis, as

Pierre Adler says, is neither consciousness nor matter but a living bodily activity.[38] In describing praxis as a living bodily activity, the Henryan account emphasizes the subjective experience of the individual who performs the action:

> Praxis designates the internal structure of action as it excludes from itself the objectification process, all distancing, all transcendence in general. What is held to be real, consequently, will be whatever excludes from itself this distancing, whatever is subjective in a radically immanent sense, whatever experiences itself immediately without being able to separate itself from itself, to take the slightest distance with regard to itself, in short, whatever cannot be represented or understood in any way at all. What is real, therefore, is need, hunger, suffering, labor too—everything that consists in this inner and insurmountable experience of the self. To the radical immanence of this subjectivity, which now constitutes reality for him, Marx gave the name appropriate to it: life.[39]

The internal aspect of praxis is revealed by the auto-affective experience of one's own activity. In the process of moving an object, for instance, I am aware not only of the thing moved but also of my own movement itself—that is, of my effort to move the object, of this effort being easy or difficult, and so forth. This subjective aspect of action is self-revelatory: in short, I know it simply by experiencing it or living through it. From this point, we could go on to retrace the steps of earlier chapters that have shown how praxis can be anchored in the self's possession of its own powers and trace the source of these powers back to the pathos of life from which these powers originate. In short, that is how Henry links Marx's philosophy of praxis back to his own phenomenology of life.

The distinction between the outer and inner aspects of praxis, according to Henry, serves as the basis for Marx's critique of wage labor. The outer dimension of labor—the work done—can be measured objectively in terms of the time spent or the amount of work completed. This external representation of labor becomes the basis for the determination of the wage, which is based on the amount of time spent laboring or the amount of labor done. But, as Henry helps to show, wage labor is alienating precisely because wages are based solely on an external measure of labor. They are detached entirely from the inner aspect of praxis—that is, from the subjective experience of the one who does the work. This inner aspect of praxis is the basis for the determination of specific tasks as hard or easy, skilled or unskilled: in short, it determines how labor is really experienced. Wage labor, consequently, is not simply alienating due to the actual wage that is paid. If that were the case, alienation could be overcome by an increase in wages. Instead, Henry's analysis confirms Marx's claim that wage labor is inherently alienating: it tries to substitute the inner aspect of praxis with an outer representation of a wholly different kind. Alienation arises for ontological reasons: the wage—as an external equivalent—destroys and offers a false substitute for the inner essence of labor as living work.[40] This gives rise to a separation between one's feelings about oneself and one's feelings about work, such that one feels like oneself only outside of work, and in one's work one feels only outside oneself.[41]

But one might wonder whether Henry's sharp division between the inner and outer aspects of praxis can be maintained. Is the affective experience of praxis exclusively subjective and one's own? Without denying the subjective dimension of praxis, might the meaning of praxis emerge at least partially in relation to a set of external influences? To raise this question is to open the prospect that the subjective dimension of praxis is malleable and adaptive to external circumstances in the same way as desires were shown to be in the previous chapter. As such, the affective dimension of praxis would not be guided entirely by its own laws. Instead, it would be informed by the specific circumstances in which one lives and would be adaptable to those life circumstances. Education, socialization, and culture—in short, an ideology—would thus exert some influence over the contours of praxis. And if this were the case, it would be necessary to reopen the broader question concerning the role of ideology: is ideology inherently dissimulating to the extent that it covers over our auto-affective experiences, or might it also have an integrative function that regulates a balance between oneself and the world as well as between oneself and others? While Henry interprets ideology solely in terms of its dissimulating function and regards it as a source of alienation and falsification of life, the Ricoeurian interpretation of Marx will open the prospect that ideology also serves an integrative function and thereby might play a role in overcoming alienation from the world and others.

## The Ricoeurian Critique of Henry's Marx

Ricoeur responds to Henry's reading of Marx in a panel discussion following Henry's presentation of "La rationalité selon Marx" and then goes on to develop those remarks in a lengthy book review of *Marx* that was originally published in 1978 in the journal *Esprit*. Ricoeur's review raises the central question of whether one hears more of Henry's own voice than Marx's in this book. As we have seen, Henry finds a deep kinship between his own philosophy of life and Marx's philosophy of praxis, insofar as the essence of praxis is identified with its inner aspect as an affective experience of living activity.[42] To be sure, Ricoeur agrees with Henry that the living individual is the fundamental reality for Marx, but he suggests that there may be a greater distance between Marx's understanding of practical activity and the suffering of life's pathos than Henry suggests.[43]

This point becomes evident in how Henry interprets the relation between "the individual and conditions" in Marx's *German Ideology*. For Henry, social and economic conditions are nothing other than the products of individual life. Consequently, they can be traced back to *"a single origin, a single creative principle* [naturans] *that produces the conditions of production, classes and ideas."*[44] In tracing the meaning of all praxis back to this single origin in the living individual, Ricoeur suggests that Henry "introduces, in his encounter with practical reality in Marx, a philosophy of the pathos of reality, which perhaps secretly differs from it."[45] Instead of defining praxis in wholly subjective terms and the economy in wholly objective terms, Ricoeur proposes that what truly matters is their intersection in *"the acting individual entering into determinations that it has not posited."*[46] In defining the fundamental situation of praxis in these terms, Ricoeur's reading emphasizes two keywords in Marx—*Voraussetzung* (presupposition) and *Umstände* (circumstances)—that lend greater weight to the nonvoluntary conditions that shape praxis.[47] To develop this key point of contention between Henry and Ricoeur, let me highlight three overarching themes from Ricoeur's book review: (1) representation; (2) history; (3) ideology.

Henry asserts that Marx's *The German Ideology* is based entirely on the distinction between representation and reality. Henry's most important contribution, according to Ricoeur, is the insight that idealization is not the opposite of sense experience for Marx, as is often supposed by traditional philosophy. Both theory and sense experience are grounded in the transcendent mode of appearing of the external world; they are both representational. But a representation is only ever a mere representation and remains separate from the reality of what it represents. This sets the stage for Henry's equation of the distinction between representation and reality with the distinction between theory and praxis. Clearly, to act is not to represent an object, and likewise to know how to act does not require one to represent one's actions as an object. Praxis, as a result, excludes representation and is defined solely by its own immanent determinations. Henry concludes that "what is real, therefore, is need, hunger, suffering, labor—everything that consists in this inner and insurmountable experience of the self."[48]

Although Ricoeur does not reject this distinction between theory and praxis, his question concerns whether it is possible or desirable to maintain this strict heterogeneity that separates the immanence of praxis from the transcendence of representation.[49] After all, if the reality of praxis is anchored entirely in the radical immanence of a pathos of life that is self-enclosed, how would it ever be able to pass into representation? It is precisely in response to this question concerning the relation between living reality and representation that a gap opens up between the voices of Marx and Henry, respectively. In contrast with Henry's insistence on the subjective aspect of praxis, Ricoeur asserts that "life cannot be radically immanent to itself and be human."[50] Praxis, instead of being purely subjective, is both determining and determined; in other words, it involves both life and its representations. This is why Marx always situates praxis within a set of circumstances to which it responds. To show the implications of this link between praxis and representations, Ricoeur invokes the historical circumstances that guide action as well as the symbolic order of society that illuminates its meaning.

Ricoeur asserts that the ultimate sense of history, in Henry's thought, is based on a phenomenological conception of life that is heterogenous with history.[51] Henry rightly rejects the view that would hypostasize history and treat it as a reality that exists on its own and develops with its own independent aims. Instead, history is always dependent on the living individuals who comprise it. Drawing from Marx's claim that individuals are the first premises of history, Henry asserts "there is no history; there are only historical individuals."[52] Although individuals are the topic of history and constitute its meaning, this doesn't mean that history is simply the product of individuals. Instead, for Henry, living individuals are able to act in history only because they have already entered into life. Life is a continual presence at each and every instant. As a result, life has a dual sense: (1) it enters into history through living individuals; (2) it remains outside of history as an ahistorical ground of living individuals and their history. Henry describes the latter relation between life and history in the following way: "Only a philosophy which from the start makes a place for the positivity of life can account for both the possibility and the positivity of history, a philosophy which recognizes that which is at the origin is not a project but a hunger, need, life as it is experienced in the actuality of the living present, in affectivity. Only that which is affective can have and, above all, can actually found a history. There is no history of the object; there is no history of the mind."[53] Here, we find that Henry anchors the meaning of history in the affective experiences of living individuals; they are the stuff of history. But the suffering of needs and desires themselves remains ahistorical and does not have any historical features.[54]

This wedge between the facts of history and the ahistorical features of life leads Ricoeur to suspect that Henry's account of the immanence of suffering conceals at least as much about Marx's thought as it reveals.[55] Henry unduly downplays the influence of involuntary circumstances [*Umstände*] on individual actions in Marx's anthropology.[56] Affective experiences, such as the suffering of hunger or cold, do not have a purely ahistorical meaning that can be separated from the historical circumstances in which they arise. These affective experiences, as we have said, belong to the real life of individuals who must respond to real life circumstances. Whereas the affective experience of suffering can explain the source or motive for action, the alleviation of suffering requires action in response to a given set of historical circumstance. For Ricoeur, this mediation between the internal realm of affective experience and the external circumstances of the world indicates something important about the pathos of suffering: affect and historical circumstance are necessarily conjoined.

Just as the pathos of suffering is always intertwined with historical circumstances, praxis is inscribed within the context of a given symbolic order that allows human action to be made intelligible. The symbolic order of a given society, as Marx understands it, can be traced back to its underlying class divisions; it is the expression of class interests. But Henry interprets the notion of a class in precisely the same way as a historical circumstance. That is to say that he treats class as a secondary reality, a hypostasis, that is dependent on the true reality of the living individual. This living reality, in contrast with the symbolic order, is posited as a nonsymbolic and nonideological reality. But, according to Ricoeur, this leaves Henry's analysis unable to explain *why* individual conditions do become expressed in general terms and *why* these conditions do come to be shared with others. While Ricoeur would agree that individuals are not causally determined by class relations, he also suggests that the notion of social class is not merely the result of the objectivist illusion. Instead, the individual is situated in relation to a set of social relations that really exist and shape how one can act on them. In this way, Ricoeur observes, "The status of class as an objective relation seems to escape from the alternatives presented by Michel Henry between conditions experienced as determinations of life and an objectivity that would only be maintained in representation. Between the pure objectivity of representation—which is ideology—and the radical passivity of existence—which is phenomenology, it seems to me that Marx conceived a type of receptivity to circumstances, to social conditions through which acting differs precisely from suffering."[57] Another name for this "receptivity to circumstances" is the reception of the symbolic order of society. If, as Henry suggests, this symbolic order is not co-substantial with human action, then how or why would it ever come to be added to praxis in the first place? How would it ever give rise to the concept of a class?

Here, we discover a fundamental difficulty with Henry's sharp contrast between praxis as reality and ideology as irreality. Ricoeur expresses doubt about whether it is possible to provide a nonsymbolic or nonideological account of the reality of praxis. Although one can speak legitimately about the need to remove ideological distortions of reality, it is quite another matter to argue in favor of the elimination of ideology—or the symbolic order—altogether. Indeed, Ricoeur does not believe that it is possible to imagine any "modality of action that would not be articulated originally by rules, norms, models or symbols."[58] This suggests that praxis can be accessed only through the filter of some ideology or represented in some kind of symbolic structure.[59] Like the representatives that bring the unconscious drives into consciousness, the symbolic order of society is what makes the reality of praxis intelligible. For Ricoeur, it follows that ideology and praxis are inevitably entangled with one another.

## Ricoeur's Lectures on Ideology and Utopia

To pursue the question of the relation between ideology and praxis more deeply, it can be instructive to examine Ricoeur's most extensive treatment of Marx: his published lectures on *Ideology and Utopia*. Interestingly, Ricoeur explicitly mentions that he has been influenced by Henry's "important work," which reorganizes Marx's texts around the notion of concrete bodily effort.[60] Although Henry's work is mentioned in only one paragraph of the lectures, close inspection of Ricoeur's two lectures on Marx's *German Ideology* points to a much deeper influence on Ricoeur's reading of this text.[61]

At the outset of his lecture on *The German Ideology*, Ricoeur distinguishes between two competing interpretations of the text: the structuralist reading versus the humanist reading.[62] The structuralist reading of Marx is associated primarily with the work of Louis Althusser,[63] who asserts that Marx breaks free from the traditional philosophy of consciousness in this text, such that individuals are no longer fundamental. The focus of Marx's thought shifts accordingly to anonymous structures such as class and the forces of production. In place of the living individual, the structuralist reading emphasizes the distinction between base and superstructure. By contrast, the second perspective is the humanist reading whose proponent goes unnamed. It considers objective notions like class and history to be mere abstractions that are based on the more fundamental reality of living individuals. Clearly, this humanist perspective can be traced to the Henryan reading of Marx. Depending on which of the two readings is followed—the structuralist promotion of class or the humanist defense of the individual—a corresponding shift occurs in the role of ideology. It leads to either the distortion of science or a distortion of the real life of individuals. Through a careful reading of *The German Ideology*, Ricoeur seeks to mediate these two alternatives and establish a position that stands somewhere between them, insisting that "the great discovery of Marx here is of the individual under definite conditions."[64]

It is important to note that Ricoeur's lecture pursues many of the same topics as his book review of Henry, including the notions of representation, history, class, and so on. While it can be illuminating to read the two texts side by side, there is no need to cover themes that have already been discussed earlier in this chapter. For that reason, my focus will be primarily on his discussion of the role of ideology.[65] In Marx's work, ideology is always depicted in a negative manner. It describes the world of representation that is opposed to the realm of real life. Ideology produces an inversion through which ideas come to be regarded as reality. Ricoeur observes that the conceptual alternative to ideology for the early Marx "is not science but reality, reality as praxis."[66] The critique of ideological distortion thus derives from a kind of realism of life, a materiality of praxis.[67] But at the core of Ricoeur's reading is the question about the nature of ideology that we raised earlier: Does ideology play only a negative dissimulating role, or is it possible to identify a positive function of ideology?

This search for a positive ideology opens the question, Ricoeur says, of "whether there could be a language of real life which would be the first ideology, the most simple ideology."[68] Ricoeur detects a "language of real life" in Marx that is fundamental to his analysis: "The production of ideas, of conceptions, of consciousness, is at first directly interwoven with the material activity and the material intercourse of men, the language of real life. Conceiving, thinking, the mental intercourse of men at this stage still appear as the direct efflux of their material behavior. The same applies to mental production as expressed in the language of the politics, laws, morality, religion, metaphysics, etc., of a people."[69] This language of real life opens the possibility of overcoming the sharp opposition between ideology and reality. In this respect, the language of real life provides a "symbolic structure of action of action that is absolutely primitive and ineluctable."[70] This establishes a key point: our ideas, our conscious representations, are not simply imposed onto praxis and real life from the outside. Instead, the language of real life suggests that praxis has its own symbolic structure, its own language, from the outset. This language is the expression of living reality itself, from itself and by itself.

Marx's notion of the language of real life paves the way for thinking about the positive function of ideology. Ricoeur uses it to answer Mannheim's paradox, which raises the question of whether it is possible to escape ideology.[71] Even if one is carrying out a critique of ideology as Marx does, Mannheim's paradox suggests that one can do so only from the perspective of some ideology. There is no pure, unfiltered access to reality. And if everything is ideological, then this raises the deeper puzzle: how can there even be a theory of ideology that is not itself the product of ideology? Marx's critique of ideology, like any other critique, is developed from the perspective of an ideology. In this respect, the critique of ideology would call for a critique of itself. This would lead to an infinite regress because that critique, in turn, would call for a critique and so on ad infinitum. In his book review, Ricoeur raises this point with respect to Henry's account of praxis: "The objections that one can make against every genealogy of true thinking on the basis of life seems ... to be addressed equally to the Marx of *German Ideology* and to Michel Henry. These objections concern, ultimately, the possibility of defining praxis itself before or without a symbolic space in which it might be articulated. In short, can one distinguish between individuals 'such as they can appear in their own representation or in that of the other' and individuals 'such as they are really, that is to say acting and materially producing'?"[72] Like Mannheim, Ricoeur is denying Henry's claim to gain direct access to praxis without the filter of an ideology. Every attempt to describe praxis, including Henry's, is accomplished through some ideology. And as a result, it cannot free itself from the critique of ideology; instead, the tools of ideology critique must also be turned against it, and so on ad infinitum.

To resolve this paradox, Ricoeur contends that it is necessary to surpass the opposition between ideology and praxis. Ricoeur's answer to Mannheim's paradox proceeds in a couple steps. First, it involves the abandonment of the view that one can attain an immediate nonlinguistic, nonsymbolic meaning of praxis. To support this view, Ricoeur draws from the work of the anthropologist Clifford Geertz, who, along with others, suggests that symbolic systems are inextricable from social life.[73] Symbolic systems make it possible to identify praxis as praxis in the first place. After establishing that praxis is always symbolically mediated, the next step is to show that a nondistorting concept of ideology is possible. This is accomplished by showing that, between ideology and praxis, there is "an inner *connection* between the two terms."[74] This inner connection is produced by what we have called the language of life, which opens the possibility of an authentic language or theory that gives expression to life.

In addition to overcoming Mannheim's paradox, this establishes the basis for a plausible reply to Henry's earlier criticism that identified Ricoeur's hermeneutics with the phenomenology of consciousness. To recall, Henry asserted that hermeneutics reduces the social conflicts between actual individuals to conflicts of interpretation that exist only on the level of conscious representations. However, Ricoeur would respond by asking, "How can people live these conflicts—about work, property, money, and so on—if they do not already possess some symbolic systems to help them interpret the conflicts? Is not the process of interpretation so primitive that in fact it is constitutive of the dimension of praxis?"[75] Ricoeur's point is that ideology plays more than a distorting role in relation to praxis. The symbolic order of society is intrinsic to the recognition of what counts as praxis, and it also plays a necessary role in resolving the real-life conflicts between individuals. In advocating for this inner connection between ideology and praxis, Ricoeur's claim is that ideology has an integrative function in constituting and legitimating social reality. Without the symbolic structure of life, human action would be unintelligible to others. Ideology allows human actions to be situated within a social context that makes them intelligible for other members of society. It is only on the basis of this positive function of ideology that integrates a shared social reality that it then becomes possible to speak about the distortive function of ideology.

Perhaps the mistake on Henry's part is to assume that external influences—especially the social influence that comes from others—are necessarily alienating. To be sure, ideology can distort my relation to myself and lead me to misunderstand myself. But at the same time, it would be hard to deny that my own affective responses, in turn, can sometimes be misguided or wrong. In such cases, an ideology or symbolic order can play a positive role in establishing the correct affective response and helping me to recalibrate the relation between my affective experiences and social circumstances. This positive role of ideology suggests that the realm of affect is not purely self-enclosed in the immanence of life but instead is the product of a complex process of symbolic mediation between the individual and the social world. The appreciation of this complex formative role of ideology is perhaps Ricoeur's most important contribution to the interpretation of Marx.

## Conclusion

While Marx's claim that praxis determines thought poses a challenge to the phenomenology of consciousness, both Henry and Ricoeur recognize it as a significant philosophical breakthrough that can be incorporated into a phenomenology of life. Their readings of Marx call attention to the practical realm in which living individuals strive to satisfy the various needs and wishes that define a human life. But the differences that emerge in their debate over Marx are emblematic of the deep differences between a maximalist versus a minimalist approach to the phenomenology of life.

Henry's interpretation of praxis is rooted in his distinction between the transcendent and immanent modes of appearing. In the transcendent mode of appearing, praxis is disclosed in terms of what is done, the *pragma*. The outer aspect of an action can be observed, measured, and quantified, but for Henry, this does not define the whole of praxis. In addition, praxis can be revealed through its immanent mode of appearing. The inner aspect of praxis refers to the auto-affective experience of one's own activity—that is to say, the feeling of one's effort and of this effort as easy or difficult, and so forth. This auto-affection of praxis does not rely on the external mode of appearing at all; it can be accessed directly simply by living through it. Consistent with the radicality of his phenomenology, Henry contends that this subjective aspect of praxis signifies the true meaning of praxis and serves as the ground of all transcendent determinations of praxis.

Although Henry considers the subjective dimension of praxis to be fundamental, it is important to be clear that this does not imply that praxis is defined entirely by the free activity of living individuals. The subjective dimension of praxis is rooted in life, and previous chapters have shown that life has a dual sense that includes both pathos and praxis. To make sense of this duality, Henry's account of praxis can be analyzed by the two forms of evidence that govern the Cartesian circle. From the perspective of the ratio cognoscendi, the living individual engages in praxis through its personal effort to act in order to satisfy the real needs of life. The efforts of living individuals produce actual social circumstances and have actual historical effects. Although living activity can freely produce the circumstances in which individuals live, the living individual does not create the real needs of life themselves or the labor power through which it responds to them. Adopting the perspective of the ratio essendi of life, Henry traces the praxis of the living individual back to a more original pathos of life. One can enter into possession of oneself and one's own labor only in and through the original pathos that grants these powers to oneself. Living individuals are able to act in circumstances only because they have already received the power to act from life, a continual presence that acts on the individual at each and every instant but itself remains ahistorical. This means that the needs, desires, and aims of life as such remain ahistorical and are accessible to all living individuals regardless of circumstance. Viewed from these two perspectives, it follows that the total subjective reality of life includes both praxis and the pathos of life.

Yet, this chapter has shown that Ricoeur conceptualizes the given circumstances of life quite differently from Henry. While Henry's maximalist phenomenology traces the meaning of praxis and pathos back to the immanence of life, Ricoeur's hermeneutic approach to the phenomenology of life denies any direct or immediate access to the subjective reality of praxis. This is part and parcel of his rejection of the foundationalist aims of Henry's maximalism. Rejecting every attempt to privilege the immanent mode of appearing, Ricoeur's critique of Henry shows the necessary connection between immanence and transcendence in determining the meaning of praxis. The subjective aspect of praxis, Ricoeur insists, cannot be detached from the external factors that influence it. This chapter has examined two key points in support of this claim. First, Ricoeur shows that the meaning of praxis is always filtered through the lens of an ideology. In addition to its distorting function, ideology also has an important integrative function that helps to make actions intelligible. Second, Ricoeur shows that the actions of an individual must be situated in a specific sociohistoric context. The meaning of praxis is context-sensitive, which is to say that it depends on the particular context to which it responds. As a result of the influence of these two external factors, Ricoeur contends that a full understanding of praxis requires a focus on the interaction between immanence and transcendence; in his words, it must focus on the living individual who acts within an unchosen set of circumstances.

The Henry-Ricoeur debate on Marx's account of praxis interestingly reveals a difference between two rival conceptions of pathos. While Henry emphasizes the pathos of life that reveals itself within the subjective experience of the living individual, Ricoeur highlights the individual's exposure to an external set of life circumstances.

Despite this difference between their conceptions of pathos, are these two readings necessarily incompatible? Perhaps not. After all, it is noteworthy that Henry, like Ricoeur, references the passage in which Marx mentions the "language of real life" and likewise considers this language of real life to be the origin of ideology.[76] This suggests that Henry's critique of ideology might not entail the outright rejection of all ideology; more narrowly, it is targeted against a specific type of ideology—namely, one that introduces a separation between consciousness and the individual's life. In its positive meaning, however, Henry observes that it is possible for ideology to overcome this separation and introduce "a set of representations rooted in life, which is its 'expression,' its 'language.'"[77] When ideology is rooted in the principles of life, the necessity it displays on the level of thought becomes inseparable from the necessity of life itself.[78] Does this mean that Henry's own phenomenology of life could be defined as an ideology in this positive sense? Perhaps. Henry's embrace of the language of life suggests that the differences between Henry and Ricoeur may not be insurmountable. But what exactly is the language of life? And what is its role in the development of a phenomenology of life that seeks to integrate the pathos and praxis of life?

# 6

## Language

*Words of Life and the Living Word*

BOTH HENRY AND RICOEUR EMBRACE Marx's reference to the "language of real life," yet it remains unclear exactly what they take this expression to mean. Accordingly, this chapter takes up the question: what is the language of life, and what is its precise role in a phenomenology of life? The question of language is pursued to different degrees and with different means by Henry and Ricoeur, respectively. While Henry's work rarely discusses the topic of language and utilizes a rather unsophisticated theory of language, Ricoeur writes extensively about the topic of language and engages contemporary developments in the Anglo-American philosophy of language. This chapter will show how these more sophisticated tools in Ricoeur's work can be leveraged to improve Henry's phenomenology of language and provide greater insight into the language of real life.

Language is the focal point of only one of Henry's essays: "Material Phenomenology and Language" (1996). Literary and other artistic forms of language are discussed in the interview "Narrer le pathos" (1991) while religious language is taken up in the essay "Speech and Religion: The Word of God" (1991) and in Henry's final book, *Words of Life* (2002). These texts, though relatively few in number, are important nonetheless. They show that even though Henry distinguishes life from the language of the world, he does not relegate life to a silent extralinguistic reality. There is a language of life, and, as Henry notes in his reading of Marx, it communicates the pathos of life.[1] Instead of being a silent or mute experience, the pathos of life expresses an individual's suffering of real pain, real toil, and so forth in a universal language that is accessible to all living individuals and communicable across all linguistic differences. To counter the widespread neglect and misunderstanding of Henry's views on the language of life, the first part of this chapter will carefully identify its key features, its mode of access, and its phenomenological grounding.

Yet, the limitations of the Henryan account of language should not be ignored either. The first limitation results from Henry's sharp dichotomy between immanence and transcendence or between the internal realm of affect and the external biological and cultural world in which one lives. With respect to language, Henry distinguishes between the representational language of the world and the affective language of life. But this distinction is unable to explain how these two discourses could ever intersect productively to infuse life into the world and bring life to language. The second limitation is symptomatic of Henry's phenomenological maximalism that continually seeks a first principle, or ground, of all meaning. Henry identifies the origin of all language with the language of life, which is experienced as the pathos of receiving an original call. Through a close reading of Henry's account of the call of life, which is developed in his debate with Jean-Luc Marion, we will show that Henry's phenomenological maximalism leaves him ill-equipped to explain the concrete activities of actual speakers in ordinary discursive contexts.

These two limitations of the Henryan account of language can be overcome, as this chapter will show, by drawing from the more sophisticated tools of Ricoeur's philosophy of language. In contrast with Henry, Ricoeur writes extensively on the topic of language. During his so-called linguistic turn in the 1960s–'80s, Ricoeur devotes countless articles and books to the philosophy of language. This difference in quantity also translates into a difference in the quality and depth of Ricoeur's analyses. In contrast with Henry's adoption of a rudimentary theory of language, Ricoeur—primarily due to his engagement with twentieth-century Anglo-American philosophy of language[2]—provides a more sophisticated account of language that overcomes the limitations of Henry's phenomenology of language.

The first limitation of the Henryan account—its inability to link the language of life productively with the language of the world—will be addressed by examining Ricoeur's 1975 book, *The Rule of Metaphor* (though the same could made with Ricoeur's theory of narrative). The French title, *La Métaphore vive*—literally, *Live Metaphor*—suggests that language is more than a set of dead metaphors that have ossified into the system of our language.[3] It also includes living metaphors that are able to produce new meanings; in this way, they bring language to life or, perhaps better, bring new life to language. But what exactly does it mean to say that a metaphor is alive? And if the living metaphor brings new meaning into language, what is the impetus of this novelty? Does it arise from an extralinguistic source that precedes and somehow remains outside of language, or is it already contained within the resources of language itself? Ricoeur's answer to these questions—through his theory of metaphor and of language, more broadly—indicates that a poetics of life can tap into language's generative potential to enhance life.

In addressing the second limitation of the Henryan account, Ricoeur's engagement with the pragmatics of language is especially relevant. Henry's maximalist approach leads him to trace the language of life back to the original givenness of the call of life and the pathos of receiving that call. But this has little to do with the day-to-day life of ordinary speakers who use a language. By focusing on actual utterances made by actual speakers in discursive contexts, the pragmatics of language can correct the first limitation of the Henryan account. Pragmatics shows how the language of life can be anchored to the concrete reality of individual speakers in everyday life and thereby offers a more compelling account of the language of real life.

## Henry's Phenomenology of Language

In his essay "Material Phenomenology and Language (or, Pathos and Language)," Henry distinguishes between two types of language: the language of the world and the language of life. His account of the language of the world resembles a traditional view that conceptualizes language in terms of *apophansis*—that is, as statements that say something about something. In its referential function, language represents the world. The word *table*, for example, is a name that stands for the physical object to which it refers; it functions like a label attached to a physical object and stands for it in either its presence or absence. Likewise, an apophantic statement like *the cat is on the mat* depicts a state of affairs that can be either true or false. The statement is true when this depiction corresponds with an actual state of affairs in the world and false when it does not. But this familiar picture of the representational function of language, according to Henry, relies on a set of unexamined assumptions not only about language itself but also about the world's own manner of appearing.

The standard view of language as reference presupposes a particular type of appearing—that is, the appearing of the world. It correlates with what Henry calls the transcendent mode of appearing and thus can be characterized in terms of three key features.[4] First, in the transcendent mode of appearing, the world is *different* from the object that appears within it; for example, the "table" is different from the surrounding context in which it appears. From this difference between the object and the world, it follows that the disclosure of an object is distinguishable from the world in which it is disclosed. Second, just as the sun shines down on all things equally, the appearing of the world is *indifferent* to the particular objects disclosed within it. The table, the cat, and the mat all appear indifferently within the world, which is to say that they are simply there. That is why each of these objects can be presented in the impersonal, third person manner of the "there is" (the "*il y a*"), for example, "there is a table"; "there is a cat," etc. Third, and perhaps most importantly, Henry asserts that the appearing of the world is *not self-generating*. It does not bring the objects that appear in the world into existence, instead it only allows them to be seen. Building on this analysis of the world's mode of appearing, Henry extends them to what he calls "the language of the world."

The language of the world, as Henry describes it, possesses three corresponding characteristics. First, the word is *different* from the object that it represents; the object "table" remains external to the word "table" which refers to it. This provides the basis for the distinction between the signifier and the signified, between the word and its object. Second, just as the appearing of the world is indifferent to the objects disclosed within it (like a light which shines on all things equally), it can also be said that the language of the world is *indifferent* to its referent. Any particular word could in principle be attached to any particular object. Without any necessary connection between the word and its object, it follows that the connection between a particular word and a particular object is arbitrary and purely a matter of convention. Third, and perhaps most importantly, the language of the world is *not creative*. Words do not create or posit the objects in the world to which they refer. Instead, they only represent a reality that is already there and given. The language of the world can thus be associated with three characteristics: 1) the *distance* that separates experience from its contents; 2) its *neutrality* or impersonality with respect to these contents; 3) its *powerlessness* to create its contents.

Yet, the language of the world encounters limits. Its scope is restricted to the appearing of the world. Consequently, it is unable to access another wholly different type of appearing—the appearing of life—which Henry characterizes as an immanent mode of appearing. It is the polar opposite of the appearing of the world: life appears without any distance, in the auto-affectivity through which one experiences oneself, and with the creative power to generate its own appearing. The key point, in the present context, is that the language of the world can only obscure or falsify the appearing of life. For this reason, Henry calls for another type of language—the language of life—that is suited to the appearing of life. Henry describes the language of life as an exact counterpoint to the language of the world: 1) it is not different from life but identical with it; 2) it is not based on convention but is universal; 3) it is not dependent on the world but independent and self-generative. Let me briefly elaborate each of these three features.

The first feature of the language of life affirms the identity between the word and life. Life reveals itself *kath'auto*, which is to say from itself and by itself. In the self-revelation of life, there is no distance or gap between what reveals (the word of life) and what is revealed (life). This means that life does not speak about anything but itself and does not refer to anything outside itself. This direct self-expression of life itself is exemplified by the pathos of the cry: "The cry belongs to the immanence of life as one of its modalities in the same way as the suffering which the cry bears within itself is one of life's modalities. It is true that its belonging to life can be recognized only if the cry is grasped in its subjective utterance, as a phonic act of the living body possessing the phenomenological status of life, and not as a behavior of the objective body uncovering itself to us in the world."[5] The cry of life does not refer to a behavior or gesture that would be observed from the outside. Instead, as the self-revelation of life, it reveals the pathos of life, the pure suffering of life, in its immanence—that is, as a pure auto-affection. This means that life is both the form and the content, the subject and the object, the sender and the recipient of the cry of life.

Second, each living individual is acquainted with this language of life despite the hundreds of different languages spoken across the globe. The language of life is neither ambiguous nor hidden. It is given in a clear and direct manner to each and every living self through the pathos of joy and suffering, and it does not have or need to have any recourse beyond the experience of this pathos alone. Because life reveals itself *kath'auto* [in and through itself], there is no need for a hermeneutic detour through the external world or the text. Each living individual has direct access to this language through the pathos of the experience of life or, more precisely, through the auto-affection of one's own suffering and joy. Even though each living individual has their own auto-affective experience of this pathos, the necessary connection between the language and pathos of life ensures that this experience is communicable to all. My own experience of this pathos is the same as the pathos that is experienced by others. The language of life—exemplified by Henry's very Rousseauian analysis of the cry of life—thus secures an affective bond among the living. It is addressed to every living being and intelligible to all living individuals.

Third, the language of life is the self-generating origin of language. Whereas the language of the world is powerless to create reality, the language of life generates the reality about which it speaks. In fact, as Henry observes, the language of life "reveals simultaneously the reality of life and the Self without which no life is living. The unthought of our ultimate, phenomenological condition, that of being living beings in life, consists in this double revelation."[6] It follows that the language of life is self-generative in a dual sense that resembles the birth of the self: it generates both itself and the self to whom life reveals itself. That is to say, first of all, that the language of life expresses itself without depending on anything outside itself; it reveals itself entirely from itself. This perhaps explains why Henry characterizes the language of life as the "noise of my birth."[7] Independent from the words and conventions of any ordinary language, it communicates itself purely through the affective dimension of life. In addition, it generates the addressee to whom it speaks. This ensures that the living individual is capable of receiving its message, delivered directly from life to the living individual, without any iintermediary that would disrupt the relation between the sender and its recipient.

For all its clarity, Henry's sharp dichotomy between the language of life and that of the world gives rise to a difficult dilemma. On the one hand, if the language of life abandons all the characteristics of the language of the world, how would it be able to speak about the world—or indeed, about anything other than itself—at all? But, on the other hand, if the language of life does inevitably resort to the language of the world, how could this representational language provide access to a wholly different kind of reality in turn? As a result, it seems that Henry's account is caught in a dilemma of whether to speak or not to speak: either not to speak about a form of appearing that is inexpressible through the language of the world[8] or else to speak with the language of the world about a form of appearing that forever eludes it.

Jean Greisch, playing the role of a self-described "hermeneutic evil genius," touches on one side of this dilemma when he observes that Henry's description of life as a pathos of pure suffering, entirely immersed in itself, submerged by itself, and so forth, actually utilizes metaphors that are borrowed from the natural world (for example, of bathing in water).[9] Greisch raises the suspicion that Henry's own description of life, instead of being detachable from metaphor, is itself metaphorical. To describe the language of life, he suggests, it would always be necessary to draw from the language of the world: the world of natural elements, of growth and decay, of vital activities, and so forth. For Greisch, it follows that Henry's purported distinction between the language of life and the language of the world is untenable. The language of life is always entangled in the general metaphoricity of the language of the world.

In response to Greisch, Henry offers a telling concession: "What could be more natural and more true than the fact that the language that speaks about suffering carries within it the metaphors of the world (of its appearing, the source of all metaphors)? But what could be more false than the notion that the word that expresses suffering, that the word of Life—that Life is in itself a metaphor?"[10] To make sense of this mixed response, note that Henry contrasts between the descriptive language that speaks about suffering (from an objective third-person standpoint) and the expressive language that reveals suffering (from a subjective first-person standpoint). When suffering is spoken about through the use of descriptive language, it utilizes metaphors drawn from the language of the world. In this respect, Henry readily concedes Greisch's point that metaphor can be used appropriately to describe the suffering of life. But when it comes to the other aspect of language—the language that expresses suffering—Henry insists that it is nonmetaphorical and must remain so. Instead of standing for something else or resembling something else, this language reveals life directly in and through life itself. Henry's response to Greisch thus provides a helpful clarification of his stance: whereas the language *about* life does fall under the rule of metaphor, the language *of* life necessarily escapes it. The language of life, purified of all metaphors, offers a direct, immediate, nonmetaphorical expression of life.

## Metaphor: Wanted Dead or Alive?

With the previous exchange in mind, I want to resituate Greisch's question about the metaphoricity of the language of life in the context of Ricoeur's theory of metaphor and press his criticism a bit further.[11] The linkage between language and life in Ricoeur's thought gets obscured by the English translation of the title of *The Rule of Metaphor* [*La Métaphore Vive*], even though the use of the term *live* [*vive*] does figure importantly in the argument developed there. Specifically, it signals Ricoeur's rejection of the view that language would consist only of dead metaphors that have come to be sedimented in language to such a degree that we are no longer able to perceive their original status as metaphors at all. Contrary to that view, Ricoeur holds that language is alive and that living metaphors give life to language. This notion of a living metaphor emphasizes the metaphorical process over and above its results. The metaphorical process is one of the ways in which language is able to create new meanings or, to echo Humboldt's words, make an "infinite use of finite means."[12] Living metaphors allow language to grow, pushing the boundaries of the expressed further into the unexpressed.[13] This growth and expansion of a language is potentially limitless in the sense that it is always possible to say something more or to say something differently.

The clearest account of the metaphorical process emerges in Study 7, "Metaphor and Reference," where Ricoeur endorses the tension theory of metaphor. The tension theory, first proposed by I. A. Richards in *The Philosophy of Rhetoric* (1936),[14] seeks to avoid two extremes that would slacken the tension between a metaphor's two terms: the tenor and the vehicle. On the one pole, there is what Ricoeur calls ontological naiveté (a pure *is* that forgets metaphor and mistakes it for reality). Thinkers like Turbayne and Wheelwright, respectively, focus on cases in which metaphors are taken literally and sediment into actual beliefs about reality. On the other pole, there is the realm of mythic metaphor (a pure *as if* that forgets reality entirely and relegates metaphor to the realm of pure possibility). Thinkers like Northrop Frye relegate metaphor to an exploration of the realm of pure possibility without any reference to the actual world. Despite the obvious differences between them, Ricoeur notes that these two approaches share an important assumption: the positivist conception of truth. By restricting the scope of truth to empirical verification, the figurative meanings invoked by metaphor no longer have a place in the objective world. They are relegated to a purely subjective realm of pure possibility with no bearing on the world.[15] And if these figurative meanings were to find expression in the world, they could be construed only as the result of some error or misconception about the world as it truly is.

The tension theory of metaphor, in contrast, holds the subjective and objective realms together in a more encompassing conception of truth.[16] To illustrate this conception of metaphorical truth, Ricoeur draws from the work of Douglas Berggren, who, in his words, has gone further than anyone "in the direction of the concept of metaphorical truth."[17] According to Berggren, metaphors keep their primary and secondary referents in view with a stereoscopic vision that encompasses them both. Berggren distinguishes between two different kinds of tensive relation in metaphors: "poetic schemata," which pertain to the inner life, and "poetic textures," which pertain to the external world. I consider these two tensive relations to be important, insofar as they disclose a productive connection between the two different types of language that Henry insists on keeping apart.

To elaborate, the poetic schematization of inner life is described by Berggren as a centripetal process that offers "a visualizable phenomenon, whether actually observable or merely imagined, [that] serves as a vehicle for expressing something about the inner life of man, or non-spatial reality in general."[18] This type of metaphor provides a schematic image of some aspect of reality that remains invisible or unobservable. For example, when Dante's *Inferno* depicts Satan trapped in a lake of ice, the lake serves as a visual schema that portrays the invisible—that is, the inner life of Satan that we cannot see. It makes the invisible visible. But in so doing, the poetic schema of the metaphor does not make any claim about its literal truth, nor does it merely assert itself as a pure logical possibility. Instead, there is a productive tension that binds the literal image of a lake of ice to the presented reality of a certain type of inner life (not to mention the tension with a common representation of hell as a pit of fire rather than an icy lake). Held together, this metaphorical tension includes both sameness and difference: the soul is not literally a block of ice, but the metaphor lets us see how its qualities resemble a block of ice. By revealing something about the inner life of a soul, this poetic schema leads from the external world to an inner life that we would not be able to access otherwise.

But metaphors are not restricted to the depiction of inner subjective life, according to the tension theory. They can also disclose the truth of the external world by conveying what Berggren calls the poetic texture of the world. Formally, this resembles the poetic schemata of the inner life, although the metaphorical process of poetic textures moves in the opposite direction—it passes centrifugally from the inner life to the external world. For example, when Hölderlin describes the "joyous undulation" of waves, this image transfers the feeling of joy from our inner life to the external world—namely, the movements of the waves on a lake. The point is not to say naively that the waves really do experience the feeling of joy, nor is it simply to describe a purely imaginative possibility of a world in which waves would have feelings. Instead, the metaphor ascribes a poetic texture to the waves that opens a new way of seeing and of relating to them; one might say that it helps us to locate our own feeling of joy in the movement of the waves. Through poetic schemas and poetic textures, living metaphors are able to produce a metamorphosis of our inner experience of life as well as our experience of the external world.[19]

This metaphorical tension accounts for the distinctive contrast between the "truth" of metaphor and a positivist conception of truth. To illustrate this point concerning metaphorical truth, Ricoeur observes that "When the poet [Baudelaire] says that 'nature is a temple where living columns . . .' the verb 'to be' does not just connect the predicate 'temple' to the subject 'nature.' The copula is not only relational."[20] That is to say that the metaphorical *is* functions in a twofold manner: on the one hand, the copula affirms a relation of likeness (is) between the subject (nature) and predicate (temple), but on the other hand, it also maintains a difference between them in the sense that the subject (nature) is not the predicate (temple). Metaphorical truth thus includes both sameness and difference, such that two things are shown to be similar in spite of their difference and different in spite of their sameness.[21] The living metaphor holds this duality in a living tension.

The main takeaway from this discussion is that Ricoeur's conception of metaphorical truth is wholly absent from the Henryan account of language, and this omission prevents Henry from making any significant linkage between the language of the world and the language of life. This can be traced back to the fact that Henry, like other theorists of metaphor whom Ricoeur criticizes, adopts a positivist conception of truth concerning the world. Accordingly, Henry conceives the language of the world solely in terms of its representational function; it either does or does not correspond with the world. By relegating the metaphorical function to the language of the world, the metaphorical *as* is measured solely in literal terms—namely, whether it accurately discloses objects within the horizon of the world. While Henry concedes to Greisch that metaphors of the world can help to describe life, he cannot fathom how metaphor could ever produce the appearing of life. In contrast with Henry's insistence on the nonmetaphorical access to life, Ricoeur's conception of the living metaphor provides a valuable alternative. The metaphorical schemas and textures show how it is possible for these two different types of discourse—the language of life and the language of the world—to pass into one another in a way that not only returns to life but also brings life to the world.

Ricoeur's discussion of Aristotle's "Rhetoric" in the first study of *The Rule of Metaphor* adds insight to the generative power of metaphor.[22] Aristotle observes that metaphor has the power to grasp active reality and that the poet Homer is said to represent "everything as moving and living."[23] On this point, Ricoeur comments that we moderns believe that we understand the Greek notion of *phusis* when it is translated as "nature." But the Greeks didn't understand nature as an inert or inanimate given like we commonly do; they understood nature as being alive. Ricoeur speculates that this might explain how Aristotle can say that "mimesis can 'represent things as in a state of activity' and characters as 'acting and doing.'"[24] Indeed, for Aristotle, metaphor can even turn inanimate objects into living beings.[25] By displaying the inanimate by means of the animate, the living metaphor presents inanimate things *as if* they were active and *as if* they were alive. But the living metaphor doesn't simply explore this as a pure possibility in the imaginary realm of the *as if*. It brings forth a truth about the world itself as an active reality. The living metaphor, in other words, brings the world to life as a living cosmos.[26]

## Phenomenology of the Call: The Henry-Marion Debate

While the previous section addressed a problem resulting from Henry's sharp distinction between two types of language by embracing a more sophisticated account of the metaphorical transfer of meaning, this section will address a problem that stems from Henry's maximalist approach to language. Not only does Henry distinguish between the language of the world and the language of life; additionally, he claims that the language of life is the origin of all language. Due to the foundational role of the language of life, it follows that the language of the world is ontologically dependent on the language of life. In other words, without the language of life, there would be no language of the world whatsoever. This view is characteristic of Henry's foundationalist aim to establish life as a ground or first principle of all phenomenological appearing. After showing how this maximalist approach informs the famous debate between Henry and Marion concerning the phenomenological givenness of the call, I will challenge Henry's aim to establish the language of life—specifically, the call of life—as the principle and origin of all language whatsoever. Henry's focus on the passive reception of the original call of life—the call that comes from life itself—neglects the role of the active dimension of the call that is brought to the fore in Ricoeur's philosophy of language.

In 1991, Henry published a critical essay entitled "Four Principles of Phenomenology" in response to Jean-Luc Marion's book *Reduction and Givenness* (1989). There, Henry credits Marion with the discovery of a new phenomenological principle: "so much reduction, so much givenness." Henry interprets this principle as a radicalization and surpassing of its three predecessors: (1) the Kantian principle "so much appearing, so much Being"; (2) Husserl's "principle of principles" defined in §24 of *Ideas I*; (3) phenomenology's motto "back to the things themselves." In agreement with Marion's view that each of these three principles has defined appearing in a way that unduly narrows the scope of appearing, Henry acknowledges that Marion's fourth principle ("so much reduction, so much givenness") marks an important breakthrough and broadening of the scope of appearing. No longer restricted to the field of possible objects nor to the horizon of being, Marion's phenomenology yields the possibility of a pure, unrestricted givenness. "Far from limiting, restricting, omitting, and thus from 'reducing,'" Henry observes, "the reduction opens and gives. And what does it give? Givenness."[27] The reduction, in other words, does not restrict appearing at all; instead, it restores appearing by leading back [*reconduit*] to the origins of appearing and by allowing appearing to show itself unconditionally. The fourth principle thus yields a phenomenologically pure givenness.

What Henry cannot accept, however, is Marion's account of the results of this fourth principle. For Marion, by bracketing the appearing of beings as well as the horizon of being, the most radical form of phenomenological reduction provides access to what gives itself otherwise than being: the pure form of the call [*Anspruch*]. When the other speaks, the call is addressed to me in a way that is unconditional: its arrival is neither anticipated nor controlled in any way by me. But Henry responds that Marion's description of the call does not fully escape the narrowing of appearing that takes place in his predecessors. To be precise, it continues to replicate the structure, if not the content, of the ek-static mode of appearing that is presupposed by traditional phenomenology. Henry explains, "The pair Call/Response is substituted for the classic dichotomy of Subject/Object.... It only reverses a relation conceived in both cases as constitutive of phenomenality, as preserving it. Far from escaping from the call of Being and from its implicit phenomenology, the structure of the call refers to Being and receives its own 'structure' from it: the opposition of Ek-stasis."[28] Insofar as it retains the ek-stasis that divides the sender from the addressee, Marion's account of the call imposes the very same restriction on appearing that has blocked access to the phenomenality of life all along. The call structure imposes a difference—a gap—between the sender and the addressee, the speaker and the hearer. For this reason, Henry believes that it is necessary to contrast between "two phenomenalities and thus two phenomenologies" and that this contrast will demonstrate "a hierarchy of appearing" between the call of being and what conditions it.[29]

In contrast with Marion's account of the pure form of the call, Henry's material phenomenology shows that the call of Life has an altogether different phenomenological structure from the transcendent mode of appearing. Henry explains:

> The other call, the call of life, stands beyond every call, for it does not put forth the proposition of whether to live or not to live. The call of life has already thrown us into life itself, crushing us against it and against ourselves, in the suffering and joy of an invincible pathos. The call has already made us alive at the moment we hear it. Its sound is nothing other than the noise of life, its rustling in us, the embrace in which it gives itself to itself and gives us to ourselves in one and the same givenness.[30]

This point of contrast can be summed up as follows. In the pure form of the call posited by Marion, there is a distance introduced between the addresser who calls and the addressee who is called, due not only to the physical separation between the two but also to the temporal delay between the call and its reception. By contrast, the call of life admits no such distance; it has already been received when we hear it; life has already embraced us when we are aware of it. The call of life, in its immediacy, signifies the original givenness that conditions and precedes every other ordinary instantiation of a call-response structure. It is the origin—the first starting point—of all givenness whatsoever.

To make further sense of this contrast, it might be helpful to recall the distinction between the formal and the material levels of phenomenological analysis. Considered formally, it could be said that the pure form of the call describes an ek-static relation; it is always possible to distinguish formally between the addresser and the addressee or between the call and the response. But Henry's material phenomenology leads this formal structure back to the materiality of life. Considered materially as the call of life, there is no longer any gap that would separate the caller and the one who is called, or, in other words, Life and the living individual. The call of life, as Henry observes in the passage cited above, both "gives itself to itself and gives us to ourselves" and belongs to "one and the same givenness."[31] Life as the sender and the living being as the addressee belong to one and the same reality: they are both in life. For this reason, the call of life occurs, without any distance, in the immanence of life itself. This leads Henry to redescribe the fourth principle in the following terms: "'So much reduction': this final and radical dismissal, issued to being and all that is, to all that comes from it or goes with it, speaks and calls in its name—in the name of the world. 'So much givenness': that which, in the absence of this being and its call, in the absence of ek-static appearing, gives nonetheless, gives everything—self-givenness, Life, and in it all those who live [*tous les vivants*], and the cosmos itself."[32] The implication of this formulation is quite clear. Against Marion's suggestion to the contrary,[33] Henry does not reject the fourth principle of phenomenology at all. What he rejects is Marion's description of what it gives—namely, the pure form of the call. In place of a formal account, Henry's material phenomenology analyzes the call concretely as the call of life and from that perspective finds that the fourth principle entails the radical immanence of this call.

Henry's debate with Marion provides important insight into the phenomenological structure of the language of life, but Henry is not willing to end simply with a description of this phenomenological structure. He goes a step further to make a foundational claim that the language of the world is dependent on the call of life: "we can say that every linguistic intentionality, which intends a transcendent meaning, can relate itself to that meaning only on the condition of having already entered into the possession of itself in the self-donation of the pathos which turns it into a life. Thus, at the same time as it presupposes the making-see which defines this linguistic intentionality, it presupposes this originary revelation in which there is neither intentionality nor seeing, in which nothing is ever seen."[34] For Henry, the language of the world depends on the prior revelation of the language of life. The call of life thus signifies the origin—the arche, the first principle—that allows for the phenomenalization of all phenomena. With this discovery of the self-revelation of the call, phenomenology arrives at its true starting point, its true foundation.

Setting aside the question of whether this foundational claim is true, the problem is that Henry focuses so much effort on establishing the language of life as the origin of all language that he ignores the mundane, everyday reality of language. This gives rise to a question: how can the language of life be returned to the lived experience of actual speakers of language? The search for an answer in Henry's work quickly goes cold. Aside from his description of the cry of life or the call of life, Henry has very little, almost nothing, to say about the actual features of living languages or about the actual discursive situations in which language is spoken. This is a glaring (and potentially devastating) gap in his analysis. A minimalist approach that sheds this foundationalist baggage can be beneficial in that regard, because it reconnects with the actual features of discourse between actual speakers of a language.

## Ricoeur's Minimalist Alternative

Whereas Henry never engages the contemporary philosophy of language, Ricoeur focuses extensively on developments in twentieth-century Anglo-American philosophy of language. As a consequence of his many years of teaching at the University of Chicago and continuous speaking engagements across the United States, Ricoeur became acquainted with the tools of language analysis and weighed in on a number of debates in Anglo-American philosophy of language. As a result, his work is much more attuned to the real-life contexts in which actual speakers communicate with one another. Although Ricoeur's writing on language covers a wide array of topics, here I will isolate a few key themes that are directly relevant to remapping the distinction between the language of the world and the language of life in a more concrete and compelling manner.

Ricoeur's most basic formulation defines discourse as "saying something about something to someone." This definition can be broken down into two basic components: (1) the referential function: saying something about something; (2) the interlocutionary function: saying something to someone. These two components of the definition correspond roughly with two broad areas in the philosophy of language: semantics and pragmatics. Whereas semantics is concerned with language as reference, pragmatics is the field that is concerned with how language is used in actual discursive contexts. I propose that the division between these two areas of study can be aligned with the Henryan contrast between the language of the world and the language of life. Of most relevance here is Ricoeur's discussion of pragmatics, an area of which Henry seems to be wholly unaware. In particular, I will suggest that the pragmatics of language provides important insight into the language of life by locating it concretely in the voice of a speaker and in the speech acts of a speaking subject.

Ricoeur develops his theory of discourse (a term he prefers over the French term *parole*) in response to the structuralist movements fashionable in the 1960s and '70s in France. In particular, he rejects the view that language can be treated as a code or a closed system of signs. Saussurean linguistics, for instance, introduces a distinction between language [*langue*] and speech [*parole*].[35] It sets aside the domain of speech—or discourse—altogether on the ground that only language as a system could be the object of a single science. The establishment of structuralist linguistics thereby relies on "bracketing the message for the sake of the code, the event for the sake of the system, the intention for the sake of the structure, and the arbitrariness of the act for the systematicity of combinations within synchronous systems."[36] But this move displays a key limitation of the structuralist account: it closes language off from any relation to the outside. Ricoeur challenges the structuralist account by asking, "If language were not fundamentally referential, would or could it be meaningful? How could we know that a sign stands for something if it did not receive its direction towards something for which it stands from its use in discourse?"[37] As an alternative, he turns to the field of semantics, which studies the referential function of language as well as the pragmatics of discourse in which real-life speakers communicate with one another.[38]

This distinction between semantics and pragmatics parallels Henry's distinction between the language of the world and the language of life. The language of the world, on the one hand, is associated with the said. It involves what is spoken about, or the content of the utterance. In virtue of the ideality of meaning, the content of discourse—the message—is able to outlive the transience of the words of spoken discourse. On the other hand, the language of life is associated with saying, or, in other words, the act of speaking. It is expressed through the voice and the living discourse of a speaking subject. The voice delivers the speaker as a living individual who says something to someone in a specific discursive context; the interlocutor, likewise, is addressed as a self in flesh and blood who is capable of a response. If this parallel marks the first step in a minimalist approach to Henry's account of language, what is clearly most important is to show how the pragmatics of discourse can shed light on the language of life.

While I cannot go into the full details of Ricoeur's engagement with the fields of semantics or pragmatics here, it is important to isolate two features of utterances that are central to his discussion of pragmatics: (1) utterances are always attached to an utterer, or a subject of utterance; (2) utterances are interlocutionary acts, or, in other words, they are always addressed to a recipient or hearer.[39] Concerning the former point, Ricoeur's description of the link between the utterance and the utterer is of considerable interest. He notes that statements do not refer; speakers do. Obviously, the speaker's voice is a material condition for the production of an utterance. Speaking is a physical act in which the voice is "proffered outside by breath and articulated by phonics and gesticulation."[40] The physical act of speaking anchors the utterance in the personal body of a speaker. That is to say that the utterance is not simply reducible to what is said because the utterance is tied to someone. The voice of the utterer—the I who speaks—marks the speaker's personal presence in an utterance.

In addition, Ricoeur emphasizes that utterances take place as interlocution. That is to say that the utterance has a destination; it is addressed to someone who receives it. In the full discourse situation, the individuality and personal presence of the addressee is just as important as that of the speaker. Consider, for instance, statements of the form "I command that . . ." or "I promise that . . ." These utterances do not simply refer to something to be done in the future. They signal, on the one hand, something about the utterer. They identify me as the one who is issuing a command or making a promise. Likewise, depending on their specific content, they may commit me personally to performing certain actions in the future—for example, to enforce the command or to fulfill the promise. Promises and commands, for example, also signal something about the addressee of the utterance. They are issued to a recipient—you—who is just as much a living individual as the utterer. For example, if I command you to do something, it doesn't simply matter that this order is fulfilled by someone or that this promise is fulfilled for someone. It is tied to a specific addressee—a personal you; it sets an expectation that the addressee would carry out the command personally. This implies that the interlocutors—the speaker and the addressee—are nonsubstitutable in the discourse situation and essential to the meaning of an actual utterance. In this respect, the pragmatics of language preserves what Henry would call the ipseity of the self and the other; their uniqueness as living individuals is implicated in the discourse situation.

This feature of the pragmatics of language signals the first of two missed opportunities for Henry to anchor the language of life in the ordinary use of language. Henry could have focused on the fact that utterances are produced by the living voice of an incarnate speaking subject. The voice is, of course, an instrument for producing sound. It produces sound through the emission of air and its passage through the lungs, vocal cords, and mouth. This material production of living speech [*parole*] is set aside, for example, by structuralist accounts of language. In a quasi-Galilean manner, language is no longer spoken and heard between individuals; it is reduced to a system of phonemes and signs that no longer have anything to do with actual sounds or actual speakers.

Much more work would need to be done, of course, to map the specific trajectory that such an analysis would follow. After fleshing out a critique of the treatment of language as a system, Henry could go on to add that the living voice of a speaking subject is more than just an instrument. The voice is not simply a set of audible sounds. It brings life to language. Building from the personal presence of the speaker's voice, one could then imagine the subsequent steps by which Henry would trace this voice back to the language of life.

To be charitable, Henry does offer a few suggestive remarks that point in this direction. The interview "Narrer le pathos" offers a discussion of Henry's novels and his own artistic process. At one point, the discussion turns to a statement that he made in an earlier interview to the effect that "language does not exist." He explains that what he meant to say is that ordinary language is transparent; we pass straight through it to arrive at the things to which it refers. But in contrast with this referential function of language, he tries to clarify the role of language in the creative process: "In fact, I have been occupied with language, but otherwise, at another level. Thus, when I compose, I remake each sentence until it gives me satisfaction and coincides with my respiration, but more profoundly when it is animated by the pathos that I am seeking. Language is perhaps a window but what it allows to see is ultimately not the dog that barks and that I am mocking desperately: it is pathos."[41] What is most fascinating here is the proposed connection between respiration and language. As a writer, Henry attests that he seeks to make each sentence coincide with his own respiration. The goal of his creative language, instead of representing the world accurately, is to align with a desired pathos. His literary language, in other words, aims to find the right voice or the right pattern of speech to convey the pathos of life. While it is unfortunate that Henry does not add further detail to this point, it provides at least a rudimentary indication of how future scholarly work might attempt to embody the language of life in the living voice of a speaker.

In addition to the lack of a phenomenology of the living voice, a second missed opportunity arises with respect to speech act theory. Ricoeur's discussion of speech acts always defers to the theory first proposed in J. L. Austin's book *How to Do Things with Words*. Austin recognizes that language does not only consist of declarative statements that make claims about the world that are either true or false; in addition, some types of statements—performatives— actually *do* something. Oaths, christenings, orders, warnings: these are some common examples of performative statements. To utter them is not to make a statement about the world; instead, performatives aim to make something happen. For example, if I issue the order to close the door, this utterance is telling someone to do something to make this happen. Instead of representing the world, performative statements aim to produce a particular state of affairs in the world. In short, they make things happen.

Austin's analysis of speech acts shows that they can be broken down into several different layers: the locutionary act (saying something), the illocutionary act (doing something in saying), and the perlocutionary act (the effects by saying). For example, imagine I say to you, "I am thirsty." The meaning of this statement doesn't simply raise the question of whether I truly am thirsty and whether this state of affairs is either true or false. In addition, this utterance has an illocutionary dimension that is not directly stated; for instance, it can function implicitly as a request for a glass of water. And the perlocutionary act here is that it brings about a particular course of action on the part of the addressee—for example, it might prompt you to bring me a glass of water. All of this is to say that the meaning of a performative statement includes more than what is asserted explicitly on the level of the locutionary act; its meaning is tied to the specific context in which it is uttered, to specific features of the utterer, and to how interlocutors are expected to act on what is said.

The theory of speech acts could have been another prime opportunity for Henry to link the language of life to actual discursive contexts. One could easily imagine an analysis of speech acts that would develop along the same lines as his other phenomenological investigations. Like movement and praxis, speech acts aim to make something happen in the world. Performatives cannot be reduced to what happens or what is done, however. From this starting point, Henry could then question back from the locutionary—the said—to the illocutionary dimension—the unsaid—of speech acts. Arriving at the illocutionary level of speech acts, he might even question Austin's account of illocutionary force. For Austin, an illocutionary act derives its force from a social power vested in a particular title or public role; the speaker's social role ensures the efficacy of the speech act (or the reverse). What if the true illocutionary force behind the speech act were not attributable to the social but instead were to be located in a deeper force still—that is, in the original language of life and its force? Conceivably, this is how Henry might have questioned back to life as the original source of the ability of speakers to communicate with one another and of the force to do things with words. While much more work would be needed to develop this analysis fully, the main point is simply to indicate how a minimalist phenomenology of language might tether the language of life to the concrete discursive contexts that Henry's maximalism neglects.

## Conclusion

This chapter has identified two limitations in Henry's account of the language of life and proposed that the use of Ricoeur's more sophisticated tools can put the language of life on a stronger footing. Let's tie these two threads of the argument together to arrive at a central insight.

First of all, we have challenged Henry's maximalist aim to establish the language of life as the foundation on which all other aspects of language depend. Henry articulates the phenomenological structure of the language of life through his analysis of the call of life. In contrast with the referential language of the world, the call of life reveals life purely and unconditionally. But Henry's maximalism leads him to focus solely on establishing the original pathos of the language of life through which one enters into language and to neglect other significant aspects of language. This narrowing of the scope of his phenomenology of language can be illustrated through the phenomenological structure of life as pathos and praxis.

The language of life can be made intelligible through the two different sources of evidence in the Cartesian circle: the *ordo essendi* and the *ordo cognoscendi*. As an ordo essendi, the call of Life is issued from Life itself. It is life's own revelation of itself and reveals itself through the language of life without any prior mediation or constraints. Life reveals itself to every individual in the language of life to every living individual in a universal language of pathos. Each living individual is an addressee of this call. As the recipient of this call, the living individual receives the call in a pure pathos, an absolute passivity that precedes any activity. But there is a gap in Henry's account of the language of life. To be precise, it ignores the active dimension of the language of life through which the living individual reveals its personal presence. In addition to the pure pathos of receiving the call of Life, the language of life can be articulated from the perspective of the ordo cognoscendi. This is made evident by a living individual who is capable of speaking and expressing itself. Borrowing the tools of Ricoeur's philosophy of language, we have located this self-revelation of the living individual in the pragmatics of language. The living voice and various speech acts of the speaking subject actively reveal the personal presence of the living individual. Through his focus on mundane discursive contexts, the Ricoeurian account of language thus delivers the second type of evidence needed to complete the Cartesian circle and thereby capture the full meaning of the language of life as both pathos and praxis.[42]

In addition to proposing a more complete account of the language of life as pathos and praxis, this chapter has challenged Henry's insistence on maintaining a sharp dichotomy between the language of life and the language of the world. Henry presumes that life is wholly absent from the language of the world and, as a result, that the language of life must remain separate from the language of the world. This implies that any attempt to weave these two types of language together would lead only to a falsification or distortion of the reality of the language of life. But this chapter has challenged the assumption that the language of the world does not admit life into it. What if, in place of Henry's contrast between a language of life that is alive and a language of the world that is lifeless, these two discourses were brought together in such a way that language would bring the world to life and thereby enliven the world?[43] The possibility of a mutual relation between these two languages is opened and explored by Ricoeur's notion of living metaphor.

The broad task of bringing the language of life into contact with the language of the world belongs to a poetics of life. Such a project, though it exceeds the bounds of this book, could take an initial cue from Aristotle's observation that "lively expression expresses existence as alive." Lively expression is evident, for instance, in the metaphorical schemas and textures of living metaphors where meaning circulates back and forth between life and the world. Of course, the domain of lively expression is not limited to metaphorical language; it also includes other modes of poiesis, such as fiction, poetry, and other creative art forms. These modes of expression draw from the language of the world to provide access to the language of life—indeed, this is precisely what Henry does in his own novels and rich phenomenological descriptions of life. Lively expression can deploy the language of life to make the world alive and convey it as a living cosmos. By opening the possibility to explore the generative intersections between the language of life and the language of the world, this chapter opens the door for a new poetics of life.

# 7

# Death

*Being-towards-Life and the "Life after Life"*

HENRY AND RICOEUR BOTH OPERATE against the grain of a philosophical tradition that has been preoccupied with death from Plato to Heidegger. In place of traditional philosophy's emphasis on death, the phenomenology of life affirms that life is more than the contrary of death and more than a mere preparation for death. We are not born to die but to live.[1] The need to think life on its own terms is endorsed boldly by Henry's claim about the inevitable "triumph of life over death"[2] as well as Ricoeur's effort to think about human finitude *sub specie vitae* rather than *sub specie mortis*.[3] By thinking about life independently and on its own terms, the two thinkers reframe Heidegger's existential analytic of Dasein by replacing the notion of being-towards-death with a more fundamental mode of being-towards-life.[4]

This affirmation of life over death immediately gives rise to important questions about the bounds of phenomenological reflection: Does thinking about life on its own terms imply that a phenomenology of life must remain within the boundaries of birth and death that define an individual lifespan and the scope of one's own lived experience? Or does it require crossing over the threshold of one's lifespan and positing a life beyond death?[5] If the latter were possible, how would the phenomenology of life square with traditional philosophical accounts of immortality and the afterlife? Drawing from various indications in the writings of Henry and Ricoeur, this chapter contends that it is possible to remain within the bounds of phenomenology and at the same time engage the question of life after death.[6]

On the surface, the very prospect of a phenomenology of the afterlife and immortality might seem like a contradiction in terms. After all, phenomenology purports to study the appearing of phenomena with regard to their various modes of givenness to consciousness. Phenomenology, in its rigor, is defined by the performance of the phenomenological epoche that brackets or suspends all explanatory schemes that stand outside of experience itself. And to be sure, metaphysical doctrines like that of the immortal soul or the afterlife would seem to count among the sorts of beliefs that are supposed to be put out of play and sidelined by the epoche, insofar as their source cannot be traced back to lived experience. After all, who among us has ever experienced their own death or a life after death? Just as Epicurus famously pronounced that death is "nothing to us," so too it would seem to follow that immortality and the afterlife can signify nothing to a rigorous phenomenology.[7]

Yet, it may not be too far-fetched to claim that immortality does have a legitimate phenomenological significance. After all, consider Alfred Schutz's famous anecdote about his final meeting with Husserl in December 1937, at which Husserl is reported to have said that "even though he, the mundane man, will have to die, the transcendental ego cannot perish."[8] This remark about the immortality of the transcendental ego is consistent, moreover, with an earlier observation made in the context of Husserl's writings on passive syntheses: "Even if the presently 'enduring' unitary object or event can cease, the process of the 'enduring' itself cannot come to a halt. The 'enduring' is immortal.... This implies that the process of living on, and the [pure] ego that lives on, are immortal.... Immortality is now given as the incapability of crossing out the present that is being ever newly fulfilled."[9] These statements, among numerous other examples, put a damper on any wholesale dismissal of the prospects of a phenomenology of immortality. Granted, many naïve beliefs about immortality and the afterlife rightly should be set aside by the epoche, but that does not entail that all such beliefs whatsoever must be set aside. Indeed, this chapter contends that the concepts of immortality and the afterlife can acquire a legitimate and profound phenomenological significance, if and when they are situated in the context of a being-towards-life that reveals the very precise meaning and significance of life as survival [*la vie comme survie*]. To be toward life, in a phenomenological sense, is to be directed toward what I call "living after."[10]

The meaning of *living after* will be elucidated in this chapter through a multistage progression. To set up the issue, the chapter begins with a brief outline of Heidegger's account of being-towards-death as well as his analysis of Dasein as a "thrown projection" [*geworfener Entwurf*]. Turning to Henry's phenomenology of life, it resituates the phenomenological structure of life as the duality of being-in-life and being-towards-life. While Henry describes Life as an eternal present that survives and continues to live after the death of the finite individual, his account of the survival of Life does not specify whether this survival includes the living individual or only Life as such. To explore this ambiguity, the chapter turns to Ricoeur's reflections on immortality and resurrection in *Living Up to Death*, where Ricoeur introduces a helpful distinction between two different senses of survival. The vertical sense of survival resembles Henry's claims about the eternity of Life, but for Ricoeur the metaphysical assumptions underlying survival in this sense make it more appropriate to a doctrine of faith. The horizontal sense of survival, by contrast, can be justified phenomenologically; it refers to the way in which an individual is oriented toward others who live after oneself. Unfortunately, Ricoeur did not have the time to fully develop that view. To unlock its potential phenomenological significance, the final step in this development will be to examine these questions: What role does the belief that life outlasts me and survives after my own death play within my own life? How does this belief orient my own sense of purpose and my own value commitments? Samuel Scheffler's recent work on death and the afterlife helps to clarify that belief in immortality and the afterlife is not simply about one's own desire for self-preservation. It extends the significance of one's own life beyond the care for oneself and links it to a horizontal survival, which is to say the survival of others and of Life in general. This horizontal conception of survival reveals the phenomenological meaning in one's own experience of a life that lives after oneself.

## To Be toward Death or Life?

The existential analytic, developed in *Being and Time*, establishes Dasein as a "thrown projection" [*geworfener Entwurf*]. This concept emphasizes the temporality of Dasein by pointing in two opposite directions: *thrownness* refers to the past and *projection* relates to the future. In this way, the phrase *thrown projection* establishes the intersection of the past and future in the present. To envision the role that this concept might play within a phenomenology of life, let me first situate it in the context of the broad outlines of Heidegger's existential analytic of Dasein.

The first part of Heidegger's existential analytic was already challenged by Henry's analysis of birth in chapter 2. For Heidegger, the notion of thrownness refers to the fact that the human being is always already found in the throes of the world. This is meaning of the *Da* ("there") in *Da-sein* (literally, "being there"). Heidegger goes on to describe this in terms of the structure of being in the world, which refers to Dasein's entanglement with the world that is already there and into which the self has arrived. But Henry rejects the applicability of the concept of thrownness to the human condition. Instead of being simply thrown into the world somehow, human beings are born. To be born is not to find oneself in the world but to find oneself in life. In place of the Heideggerian notion of being in the world, Henry's phenomenology of birth establishes Dasein as being in life, both as a living individual who has a life and has the task of leading a life.

The second part of the existential analytic, for Heidegger, begins with the observation that Dasein is not merely thrown into the world. It is not as if Dasein were entirely defined by a set of facts about the actual world into which it is thrown and as if those circumstances would predetermine the course of its development. Above and beyond its actual circumstances, Dasein is characterized by a set of possibilities it could become [*Seinkönnen*]. By taking hold of these possibilities and pursuing them, the living individual is able to surpass the actual circumstances that define its thrown condition. This is what Heidegger calls projection [*Entwurf*]. Through free projection, Dasein puts its free possibilities on display by actualizing them in the world.

The third part of this existential analytic introduces a limitation on the power of free projection through the encounter with death. Instead of signifying only the end of Dasein, Heidegger indicates that this encounter with death is the source of a fundamental self-realization. To project ourselves fully, in other words, requires us to project all the way to the horizon of our own death and try to find a deeper meaning in our being-towards-death. Heidegger identifies four important features that characterize being-towards-death: death is mine, certain, indefinite, and fundamental. First, to say that death is *mine* is to cut it off from all relations to others. It cannot be experienced through the deaths of others, only through my relation to my own death. Second, it is *certain* that I am going to die. Although one might try to evade or ignore that fact, my own life is finite and must come to an end at some point. Third, although it is certain that life will come to an end, we do not know exactly when it will happen. This makes the fact of death indefinite; it always arrives, in some sense, as a surprise. Fourth, to say that death is *fundamental* means that it prevails over all my projections of the future. This explains why Heidegger calls death the possibility of impossibility; it imposes an absolute limit—an impossibility—on the scope of my possibilities and my freedom. But this limit does not result in the defeat of the self; quite the contrary, it becomes the source of a fundamental self-awareness concerning one's own finitude.

This brief overview is not designed to provide a thorough reading of Heidegger's thought; instead, it simply provides a backdrop for a series of questions about the existential analytic from the perspective of a phenomenology of life.[11] In chapter 2, we already showed how Henry's phenomenology of birth challenges Heidegger's notion of thrownness and the related notion of being-in-the-world. The phenomenology of birth recasts the category of being-in as a more fundamental being-in-life. But additional questions can be raised about other Heidegger's analytic, in particular about the notions of projection and being-towards-death. What would result if the phenomenology of life, in parallel, were to reframe the concept of being-towards-death in terms of being-towards-life? How might this fundamental attunement to life contrast with the four key features of being-towards-death? Likewise, how would the notion of projection be altered if it were reoriented beyond one's own death and instead directed toward the future of a life after one's own life? Even more broadly, how might this reorientation toward life impact other related Heideggerian notions such as the temporality, care, and authenticity of Dasein? Under the rubric of being-towards-life, is it ultimately possible to establish a phenomenological ground for an eternal life?

Unfortunately, Henry's work does not provide direct answers to these interesting and important questions. This is symptomatic of his almost exclusive (verging on the obsessive) focus on questioning back to the thrownness of life—namely, what it means to have been born and find oneself in life. While Henry's phenomenology offers a detailed account of the significance of birth, it has very little to say about being-towards-life as a future-oriented projection of the living individual or about the significance of one's own death. Nonetheless, there are some scattered remarks in which Henry does speak about the eternity of life, which can be pieced together to form what I call a vertical account of immortality.[12]

## The Henryan Account of a Life after Life

The phenomenological structure of the relation between life and the living individual can be articulated by the two types of evidence in the Cartesian circle. From the perspective of a ratio cognoscendi, Henry questions back from the natural world and the organic functions of the body and returns to the original experience of life in a bodily cogito. The experience of one's own living flesh, as he shows, is an auto-affective experience whose meaning can be isolated from the natural body.[13] What I go through is simply the direct and immediate feeling of the life of my own flesh. This auto-affective experience of the flesh, according to Henry, is the origin and first principle of all lived experience. It anchors all the various capabilities that I exercise as a living subject and puts me in possession of their powers. Even if it is true to say that I am the source of these living powers *in one sense*, it is equally the case *in another sense* that I am not the source of my own life. From the perspective of an *ordo essendi*, Henry invokes Life with a capital *L* and indicates that Life is the generative source of the living individual and its powers.[14] The encounter with Life thus gives rise to an awareness of my own limits and limitations. I do not come into my flesh or my bodily powers through my own initiative; instead, I am born into them.[15] That is to say that I am brought into life by life itself. As a result, I undergo the pathos of life and find myself in life before anything that I might think, say, feel, or do.

The contrast between these two perspectives is the basis for Henry's distinction between a strong sense of auto-affection (that of Life) and a weak sense (that of the living ego). In the weak sense, auto-affection pertains to the living ego's experience of its own flesh.[16] In this simple feeling, the living ego both affects and is affected by itself, but it does not create itself. By contrast, the strong sense of auto-affection refers to Life's own power to affect itself. It too reveals itself and is revealed in the content of its own affection, but what sets it apart from the weak sense is the fact that it generates this content on its own. In other words, auto-affection in the strong sense engenders the self, and in so doing, places the self in the accusative position as a me rather than an I. The self is thus exposed to a radical passivity in the auto-affection of Life, which brings it into existence. This leads Henry to put forward a maximalist claim that a founding relation exists between these two different senses of auto-affection: "the self self-affects itself only inasmuch as absolute Life is self-affected in this Self."[17]

Within this context, we can now examine the relevance of these two senses of the auto-affection of life to the question of the immortality of the soul.[18] The strong sense of auto-affection correlates with the ordo essendi. As such, it reveals the self's ontological dependency on Life. I am not the source of my own life; instead, I am brought into life by Life itself. Life, as a generative source of the living individual, precedes intentional consciousness, the powers of the self, and even the passive modalities of one's own conscious experiences. Consequently, I find myself in life before anything else that I might think, say, do, or feel. This revelation of an absolute passivity with regard to one's own existence is well suited to a phenomenology of birth. But even if Henry's phenomenology describes a life that precedes and generates the living individual, it does not yet explain whether and how Life might also outlast me. In what sense, then, can it be said that Life continues to live after me?

To address this question, the first step is to note that Henry has a very distinctive account of birth, which is not simply an event that takes place in the past and then gets left behind. Instead of being an event that happens on just one day, birth is a permanent condition for Henry. That is to say that life carries out a "continuous creation" that brings the self into existence at each instant of our lives.[19] If this continuous birth into life were interrupted for even a single instant, Henry suggests, the ego would be destroyed. As a result, birth cannot be relegated simply to an event that occurs in the past; the birth of the cogito temporalizes itself and is carried along with the living present.[20] While this account of birth clarifies life's link to the past and present, it can also shed light on how Henry links the living present to the future.

In addition to being a continual source of the living present, Henry adds, Life engenders itself as an "eternal auto-affection."[21] Henry describes the eternity of Life in an extended passage from the first version of "The Phenomenology of Birth"[22]:

> Eternity designates the Ground of life understood as auto-affection, and thus as introduced by an essential dynamism, a pressure that does not cease. To say that the auto-affection of life is eternal means that it occurs as a movement, the movement of coming into the self, of crushing up against the self, of entering in possession of oneself and thus of the growth of the self, to be submerged by itself like always new content—always newly experienced, inasmuch as experience is the original temporalization immanent to the coming into self as subjectification of the absolute subjectivity, an arrival that does not cease, no more than that in which it comes and from which it grows and that is always given again. In this immanent temporalization that is radical in the sense that it excludes all ek-stasis, there is only what is experienced, always actually experienced, never past nor for that reason expected or to come, never marked by an irreality, never a being no longer or not yet experience but self-experienced as moving itself, a living present, that is, drawing its "present" from the lived experience

of life, not from the Time to come to the present of Time—being life itself, life that remains in itself in the auto-movement the process of its pathos-filled auto-affection. It is because the essence of its pathos grows on its own that life must be possible as life, as this eternal movement of coming into the self that is neither born nor perishes.[23]

This passage provides several important clues about how Life continues to live after the finitude of a finite life with a beginning and end. First of all, it asserts that Life is eternal in the sense that it "is neither born nor perishes" and thus cannot come into existence nor go out of existence. But this doesn't mean that life exists outside of time. Henry instead describes the eternity of life as a dynamic force, or a living eternity, that reveals itself in the active production of time. This means that Life is an unceasing source of the living present at each and every moment in time. The living present is alive because Life continually brings it to life. Just as time, for Plato, is "the moving image of eternity," it might be said that, for Henry, the individual's experience of time in the living present provides the moving image of the eternity of Life.[24] Consequently, even after the individual's loss of any experience of the present (through death), the living present itself persists because Life continues to be a source of the living present.[25]

To what conception of immortality, then, does Henry's phenomenology of life subscribe? The answer is now clearer. There is a fundamental distinction between the life of the living individual and the life of Life. Although the life of the living individual is finite and bounded by a beginning and end, the life of Life remains eternal and boundless. The life of Life is an active source of the life of the living individual. Life generates the individual, maintains its existence at every moment, and lives after the death of the individual. While the living individual is born and perishes, the life of Life is omnipresent, indestructible, and eternal.[26] But if this account of the eternity of Life is accurate, there is another important aspect of this question that still remains to be answered: what does the eternity of Life imply about the individual's own being-towards-life?

Let me propose an answer by way of a contrast with the Heideggerian account of finitude, or being-towards-death.[27] To recall, Heidegger characterizes death as mine, certain, indefinite, and fundamental. While death is something that each living individual must face inevitably, for Henry the attunement toward death is not what is fundamental. The survival of Life prevails over death; it outstrips death and continues to live after it. This more fundamental being-towards-life alters the nature of the confrontation with death. Regardless of whether I might personally survive after death, what is certain is the fact that Life itself will continue to live on. This certitude concerning Life's own survival might promote a different feeling: in place of the isolation of mineness, it introduces a sense of connection to the lives of others. From the perspective of being-towards-life, I experience myself as a member of a community of Life that precedes my own life and persists after it. Life's survival also promotes a felling of confidence in place of anxiety. The self has confidence that, come what may, the Life that embraces it and holds it in existence will continue to live on. While one's own personal survival may be indefinite and uncertain, there is certainty to be found in the fact that Life itself will continue to live on.

Authenticity, for Heidegger, involves a recognition of one's own finitude that results from a confrontation with death. But this goes only half the way for Henry. It remains within the confines of a self who is preoccupied with itself, with the question of its own existence or nonexistence, and who feels anxiety over the possibility of its nonexistence. But that can be only part of the story concerning one's being-towards-life. In addition to recognizing my own finitude through the possibility of my own nonexistence, the authentic self must also recognize the impossibility of Life's nonexistence. For Henry, authenticity entails a recognition of the finitude of one's own life and of the infinitude of Life.[28]

That said, Henry's account of the infinitude of Life might give rise to concerns from a phenomenological perspective.[29] Can Henry really make phenomenological claims about the infinitude and omnipresence of life from within the bounds of lived experience? It is one thing to say that life precedes my birth and survives my death. Claims of that sort are uncontroversial and easily verifiable, but it is quite another to thing to claim that Life is eternal and everlasting. What evidence can be found in lived experience that would support this detachment of Life from any particular living individual and this assertion of its own independent existence? Isn't this metaphysical speculation precisely the type of overreach that phenomenology sought to prevent? To press this point, the objection to Henry might go something like this. Henry's claims about the eternity of Life clearly outstrip what is given to lived experience. To the extent that phenomenology must remain within those bounds, it follows that Henry's claims about the eternity of Life and anything it might imply about immortality are irreconcilable with phenomenology.

Instead of trying to defend Henry against such objections here (though I think they could be defended), let's concede this objection for now but still leave open the prospect of a phenomenology of immortality. After all, it would be overhasty to dismiss this prospect wholesale based only on one specific formulation of it. There might be a lot of daylight between Henry's own claims about the eternity of Life on the one hand and a wholesale rejection of immortality on the other. Between these extremes, there is an opening, for example, to explore a minimalist alternative that conceives life as living after. This minimalist conception of living after differs from the Henryan account in one crucial respect: instead of positing the reality of an eternal Life that exists on its own and apart from living individuals, it advances only a minimal claim about the nonfinitude of a life that is unbound by the beginning or end of an individual life. The nonfinitude of Life simply acknowledges the fact that we are situated at neither the beginning nor the end of our own lives; in short, we find ourselves in life. But to be in life also implies that our own finite life here and now is inextricably connected to a life unbound by the constraints of the actual here and now—in short, being in life opens not only to a life that precedes us but also to a life after, that is, to a life that outlasts and survives oneself. Inasmuch as the horizon of life extends beyond the scope of the finite life of an individual, we will refer to this as a horizontal conception of immortality in contrast with the vertical account presented by Henry. And if this structure of living after is indeed phenomenologically justifiable, then the task will be to show its significance within our own lived experience.

### Ricoeur on Living Up to Death

To develop a minimalist alternative to the Henryan view, I turn to Ricoeur's reflections on living up to death. This concept first emerges in a set of 1994 interviews that were published the following year under the title *Critique and Conviction*. It comes up again in a set of working notes dating from the late 1990s and continuing up to the final year of his life; these fragments were collected and published posthumously in *Living Up to Death*. Ricoeur's treatment of this theme does not constitute anything resembling a complete or thorough account; instead, it comprises a series of rough outlines, preparatory sketches, and some very personal reflections from a philosopher who is in the process of dying and reflecting on the prospects of an afterlife. Despite their incomplete nature, these fragments turn out to be some of Ricoeur's most personal and poignant writings. They display his attempts to cope with the loss of loved ones as well as his own personal struggle to live while dying.[30]

Living up to death is Ricoeur's substitute for the Heideggerian notion of being-towards-death. In contrast with Heidegger's understanding of Dasein's relation to death, it expresses Ricoeur's view that birth and life signify more than an eventual path to death. With the notion of living up to death, Ricoeur insists that the self is never simply deathbound, as if the self were simply terminal and as if being terminal meant only being almost dead. More fundamentally, the self is always bound to Life: "No one is moribund when facing death; one is alive.... Life in facing death takes an upper-case L, that is the courage of living up to death."[31] Living up to death thus involves a certain type of living activity; it is a struggle for life and not simply against death. The living individual, including even the terminally ill patient who will die soon, is engaged in the effort to live, and this effort persists all the way up to death. Living up to death thus reconfigures dying as an act of life: it makes dying "immanent to life."[32]

This is a potentially valuable insight for caregivers that can lead them to see those who are dying in a different way. The terminally ill patient is not simply someone who is soon to die and who should be treated as almost dead or as good as dead. Instead, the patient should be seen as someone who is still living, holding on to life, and struggling for life. To see the patient in this way might lead them to be treated differently. It might lead caregivers to see their continued treatment as meaningful rather than a waste of time and resources. It might increase our compassion and concern for their well-being. It might even help us—the living—to better accompany the living individual who is dying and to suffer alongside them.[33]

Moreover, the notion of living up to death can offer valuable insight for the terminal patient who is preparing to die. It engages the patient in a task that is comparable to the classical techniques of askesis. What is at stake in this preparation for death is not so much a preoccupation with what will happen after death as "mobilizing the deepest resources of life to still affirm itself."[34] The ultimate goal of this process is to learn how to live with dying, which means both accepting the eventual reality of no longer existing and developing another hope besides the desire to continue existing. Ricoeur describes several techniques that can facilitate this shift of attitude, thus improving one's ability to cope with one's own mortality.

The process of askesis begins by acknowledging the limits of the imagination and removing many false images about the afterlife. We ought not follow the example of the Stoics, who would ask us to prepare for death by learning how to envision ourselves already as cadavers. We are unable to imagine ourselves dead, to imagine where we would be or what we would look like after death. Likewise, we should not seek to form images of others as dead. We cannot represent the dead and cannot imagine where they are or what they would look like. Moreover, Ricoeur rejects the anticipatory image that I might form of how others will remember me in the future. I cannot allow that anticipatory image to take the place of my confrontation with death here and now.

This process of detachment from representations and images of the dead and of the afterlife has a clarifying value: it shows that death is a confrontation with the unrepresentable and the unimaginable. The unfathomability of death is what makes it truly terrifying and explains the psychological appeal of illusory beliefs and images that offer false substitutes for the unknown. By combatting these false beliefs that arise out of fear of the unknown, this askesis of the imagination leads us to an agnostic position. The question of whether there is a life after remains an open question. But might this aporia, as Olivier Abel wonders, open the possibility for a new poetics?[35] Might it allow us to enter into a different type of relation with the afterlife?

In place of knowledge or the belief that something is the case, this different relation with death resembles what Ricoeur elsewhere calls attestation or belief in. To attest to something means first and foremost to express one's belief in something, to affirm one's credence and confidence in it. Such a relationship is built not so much on knowledge as on trust. This explains how it is possible to believe in the resurrection or life after death, even if its reality exceeds our power to know. The basis of this belief is grounded in trust and confidence in something or someone. Importantly, Ricoeur notes that there are two different ways in which this confidence can be expressed. It is possible to speak of confidence in either a vertical or a horizontal sense of resurrection: "resurrection is the fact that life is stronger than death in this twofold sense: that it is extended horizontally in the other, my survivor, and is transcended vertically in the 'memory of God.'"[36]

Ricoeur's notion of a vertical resurrection is inspired by Whitehead's process theology and signifies a way of belonging to the continuous presence of the eternal. It conceptualizes survival after death as a process of being taken up into "the memory of God." This phrase itself comes from the book of Psalms: "Who is the mortal whose memory you guard? The son of Adam about whom you are concerned?"[37] The biblical notion of memory, Ricoeur notes, means more than the remembrance of what has taken place in history or what I myself have done in the past; it also includes something like "care, solicitude, compassion" for the person I am.[38] This is an expression of a belief in a God who would know and remember me beyond my past deeds—indeed, beyond even the categories of time. Accordingly, such a God would remember me as someone who is no longer but once was and even somehow as more than what I once was. Here the profound challenge is to think about eternity without imagining a separate and parallel temporality of souls. This type of remembrance requires a full detachment and renunciation of the self. All that remains after this askesis is accomplished is a relation based on a confidence or hope entrusted in God and put in God's hands. How, then, should we express this hope in a vertical resurrection, to live on in the memory of God, without living anymore as a self? Ricoeur answers with total self-detachment: "Let God, at the time of my death, do what he wants with me. I don't claim anything; I don't claim any 'after.'"[39]

What we find in this notion of a vertical resurrection is a speculative gesture that is exceedingly rare in Ricoeur's oeuvre. Without doubt, it expresses his personal longing for eternity, a hope that he is not willing to give up. It expresses a belief in a type of survival of the self through a participation, or absorption, in an everlasting present. In the discussion of his "Biblical Readings and Reflections," Ricoeur sheds further light on this notion: "There is certainly a lot to say about life in a nonbiological sense, or in any case, more than a biological sense. In my current speculation, I am considering it [life], almost eschatologically, as disclosing itself to the dying. To the one who, for the spectator, is already more than deathbound, subsists still a living being in whom the last light of life shines. This light which breaks through the veils of the codes in which it is covered, during the time of empirical existence, is the fundamental."[40] Whether one will actually enter into the memory of God, Ricoeur concedes, is something that is left up to God, or at least to a hoped for God. Resurrection, in this vertical sense, is based entirely on an attestation to that possibility; in short, it is a question of faith.

Ricoeur's account of vertical resurrection could easily be transposed into Henry's account of Life. For Henry, Life brings the living individual into life and continues to enter into it ceaselessly at every point of its existence. Death marks the end of the finite living individual, but it does not touch Life as such. With the end of a finite life, the temporal reality of the living individual merges with the eternity of Life. It is carried into, to borrow Ricoeur's words, the memory of God and participates in the everlasting presence of life. Even if it is possible to link Ricoeur's account of vertical resurrection with Henry's account of eternal life, the fact is that both accounts are speculative and beyond the scope of what can be grounded in lived experience.[41] Regardless, neither this linkage with Henry nor its phenomenological limitations account for the real interest of Ricoeur's account of immortality. Instead, the phenomenological interest is to be found in the less speculative notion of a horizontal resurrection.

The horizontal sense of resurrection takes place on an empirical and historical level. It refers to the survival of others who live after me, including personal or close others as well as impersonal or distant others. With respect to the former type of survival, the horizontal sense of resurrection passes through one's friends, neighbors, and kin. Here, one often thinks about a will that bequeaths a personal inheritance to others in the form of wealth and possessions. But an inheritance is also transmitted in many other ways; it includes, for example, one's words and deeds that are held in the memories of others.[42] Just as a dying person must detach from their possessions, so too they must detach from the vanity of self-love and let go of the concern about how others will remember them. This self-attachment should be transferred to a love of others and concern for their lives: "I leave it to others, my survivors, the task of taking over my desire to be, my effort to exist, in the time of the living."[43]

This bequeath that transfers one's self-concerns to a concern for others is a good example of a pure or ultimate gift—a gift with no expectation of a return. For it implies that I give up all concerns about my own future and entrust the future entirely to others. Ricoeur puts it this way: "Because the only survival, on the empirical and historical plane, is the life of the survivors. With this theme of the survival of the other and in the other, we are still within the horizon of life. What do I do with my dead in my memory? This is a problem of the living with regard to those who are no longer."[44] Survival, then, is no longer about me; it becomes a question for the others to whom it has been entrusted. What should they do with all this stuff? What should they do with all these memories? What, ultimately, should they do with that past in this future? These are no longer questions for me; instead, they are questions that survivors have to bear in relation to those who are no longer.

But those who are near and dear are not the only ones implicated in the notion of a horizontal resurrection; it also extends to a relation to the anonymous or distant others I did not encounter in my own life or, at the most extreme, who were not even born in my lifetime. The difference between my relation to close and distant others is perhaps comparable to the difference between the spoken and the written word. Close others are those with whom I can speak and interact directly; distant others are more like the readers of a book with whom the author never enters into communication. The author must come to grips with the fact that their written work outlives the author—*überleben*—and acquires its own independent existence and meaning. Discussions of the so-called death of the author highlight the fact that the work enters into the hands of readers who will determine its meaning without the author coming to its assistance. In this sense, writing is a sort of preparation for death. One's own words (and increasingly one's own digital image) can be addressed to an immediate audience, but their impact can extend far beyond the context of the time and place in which they are said or written. To the extent that they can take on a life of their own, it is difficult to anticipate what future significance, if any at all, they will have. The dying person, like the author, must find a way to reconcile with a future in which one will exist, if at all, solely in the memory of others.

The relation to distant others requires an even greater degree of renunciation and detachment of the self than the relation to close others. In this case, the detachment from one's own works and deeds is at the same time a detachment from their impact on anyone in particular. They become anonymous, directed to an unknown other or to humanity in general. Ricoeur is not unaware of the difficulty of conceiving the future in these extremely impersonal terms and asks himself, "Can one go so far as to detach the idea of the future of humanity from that of the postmortem future of the person? That is a great question."[45] But he refuses to answer this challenging question about the limits of our ability to imagine a future without any trace of ourselves. Although the issue of how the horizontal resurrection might relate to the idea of a collective future of humanity remains an open question for Ricoeur, it is a question to which we will return momentarily through the recent work of Samuel Scheffler.

At any rate, the main takeaway point is that Ricoeur's notion of a horizontal resurrection opens a new pathway for phenomenological reflection on the question of immortality and the afterlife. Unlike the more speculative vertical account, it does not make any pretense to know whether Life itself is eternal or the soul immortal. For Ricoeur, those are issues that are better left to faith than phenomenology. Instead, the notion of a horizontal resurrection construes the afterlife as living after (or as *sur-vival* in the literal sense of *living on*). It is grounded in the finitude of living individuals who are born and die. This is part of what it means to say that we find ourselves in life. To be in life entails, first of all, that we are immersed in a life that precedes our own lived experience. In birth, I arrive after life in the sense that life is already there prior to my own awareness of it or of myself. But to be in life also includes the notion that life exceeds my own awareness in the sense that it continues to live on afterward. Following death, life continues to live after me. These two senses of living after—of a life that precedes me and outlasts me—untether the phenomenology of life from the phenomenology of consciousness and bring the living individual into relation with a Life that exceeds its bounds.

Presented in these very schematic terms, the Ricoeur's contrast between a vertical resurrection and a horizontal resurrection has become clear but its fruits might not yet be fully apparent. To develop a richer sense of what is to be gained from this notion of living after, the final step of this analysis turns to a discussion of the afterlife in a very different context: Samuel Scheffler's book *Death and the Afterlife*. Even though this is not his intended purpose, Scheffler's reflections on the afterlife help to elucidate and enrich the phenomenological significance of living after in its horizontal sense.

## Scheffler on Living After

To begin, it should be noted that Scheffler sets aside the traditional conception of the afterlife. This is the belief in what he calls a personal afterlife, where each individual would continue to exist personally in some form of nonbodily or spiritual life after their own biological death. This personal afterlife tracks with many popular and religious views about the afterlife as well as what Ricoeur labeled a vertical resurrection. In place of these common conceptions, Scheffler proposes a revised conception of the afterlife, understood in terms of what he calls a collective survival. This notion, as it so happens, aligns quite well with Ricoeur's notion of a horizontal resurrection described in the previous section. Scheffler's claim is that our belief in the collective survival of humans plays a significant—but largely overlooked—role in an individual life. The belief that other human beings will continue to live on after my own death shapes my perception of the value of many of my activities. Without this background belief, many, if not all, of the activities in which we are engaged in our own lives would come to lose their significance. In support of this claim about the importance of these beliefs in collective survival, Scheffler puts forward two hypothetical thought experiments in which it happens to disappear.

The first of these is a doomsday scenario that unfolds as follows. You will live a long and healthy life over a full human lifespan. But you and you alone discover that thirty days after your death, whenever that should happen, the entirety of the human race will be destroyed. We all know, of course, that the world will come to an end sometime after we die, and this knowledge doesn't affect the ordinary functioning of our day to day lives. But if we were to learn that the end of the world would be imminent in some more immediate way, then this would seem to have an impact on what matters to us. In this particular case, it is also noteworthy that the demise of humans would not be experienced personally by you. It happens only after you have died. So if death truly were, as Epicurus says, nothing to us, then it ought to follow that this doomsday scenario should mean nothing to you. You will not experience it, after all. Even though your personal survival is not at stake in this scenario, Scheffler suggests that few people would dismiss this imminent event with pure indifference. To the extent that we would be concerned with the very fact of the end of the world, the doomsday scenario poses a challenge to an experientialist account of value, which holds that actual experience is the sole basis for the values we hold.

Setting aside our concern about the suffering and loss of those who are near and dear to us that would result from the end of the world, it is equally noteworthy that many of our current projects would suddenly come to lose their value. Without confidence in the future survival of others, we would be less inclined, for instance, to pursue long-term projects that may not be completed within the scope of our own lifetime, such as the search for medical cures or the development of alternative sources of energy. Arguably, these endeavors, and many like them, would matter only to the extent that we believe that others will continue to live after us and carry these projects into the future. The doomsday scenario thus poses an interesting challenge to an egoistic theory of value: it suggests that some things are valued not only in relation to their consequences for ourselves; instead, our valuing of them extends beyond our own personal benefit and is tied to their survival and furtherance long after our own lives have come to an end.

The second thought experiment involves an infertility scenario that is borrowed from the P. D. James novel *The Children of Men*. The novel depicts a dystopian world that has suffered from an environmental crisis. The result of this crisis is that humans end up being unable to procreate. Those who are already born will continue to life long and healthy lives, but there will be no future generations to replace them, and so the human race will slowly die out. The characters in the story thus belong to the last generation of living human beings; indeed, there is even a character in the novel who is identified as the last human ever to be born. What is fascinating about James's thought experiment is that it suggests that our attachment to a future after our own is not simply reducible to our attachments to the other people we happen to know and love. Even if a doomsday scenario would lead us to be concerned about the loss of those we know and love, the infertility scenario suggests that our attachment to the future also includes an investment in the survival of humanity as such.

The novel explores what people would think and do, or not do, under such circumstances. How would people's motivations be altered if they were no longer acting under the belief that future generations would continue after their own lives? Would some activities come to lose their meaning? In the face of the end of humanity, would any activities retain meaning, or would we sink into a collective despair, as the James novel posits? Without going into all the interesting speculative questions concerning how this scenario might alter the motivational structure of an individual life, for our present purposes it should suffice simply to note that Scheffler takes the infertility scenario to show that we are actually invested in the notion of a collective afterlife more deeply than our own personal afterlife. If I were to discover that there is no such thing as a personal afterlife, there would still be plenty of reasons to value the activities of my ordinary life. But if I were to discover that there is no collective afterlife for humanity, Scheffler posits that this would lead to a general malaise and nihilism. To borrow in altered form Derek Parfit's well-known slogan, this thought experiment suggests that personal survival is not what matters. Indeed, our deep investment in the collective survival of life is one of the reasons why, Scheffler surmises, groups and traditions matter so much to us.

We often think of tradition in a backward-looking way that links us to our ancestors in the past, but Scheffler's observation serves as an important reminder that traditions and institutions also connect us to the future. They allow us to pass our own values down to others who will carry them into a future that is no longer our own. From this observation that values are not reducible to our own experience of them, Scheffler infers that another important feature of values is that they are inherently conservative, not in the political sense of the term but in something more akin to the physical sense of the term. That is to say that we do not only care for values as they pertain to our own lives; we also want them to be preserved and continue to live on. This desire to have our values persevere into the future plays a role in determining what matters to us here and now. It might lead us to join associations like churches or universities; it might lead us to devote our time and resources to causes that aim to preserve these values. In this respect, traditions and institutions are future-oriented; they are valued at least partly by their ability to carry the values that we hold dearly into the future.

While Scheffler himself takes his thought experiments to support a conception of values as "non-experientialist, non-consequentialist and conservative," the analyses of this chapter allows us to introduce an additional feature to this characterization.[46] Scheffler's discussion of the collective survival of life helps to clarify and elaborate Ricoeur's concept of a horizontal resurrection. In particular, it suggests that our commitment to the survival of a life after is not simply one belief among others. Instead, it is a fundamental attunement of the utmost importance. The values we attach to our lives depend on this underlying our attestation to their survival into the future. When our commitment and belief in them wavers or collapses, our values and sense of purpose are led adrift. Our own finite lives and the values we find in them, as a result, are deeply intertwined with a belief in a life after.[47] Instead of being contained in the bounds of its own finitude and preoccupied entirely with its own possible non-existence, the living individual is always in relation to the infinitude of life. This *in-finitude* exceeds the lifespan of a finite individual in two opposite directions: it extends back to the one's birth into the life that one has and reaches forward through a projection of living after beyond the life one leads. The latter defines the meaning and significance of the Ricoeurian notion of a horizontal resurrection.

## Conclusion

This chapter has advocated for a phenomenology of living after. Both Henry and Ricoeur seek to conceptualize life on its own terms, apart from a binary opposition with death. In place of Heidegger's account of being-towards-death, they seek to disclose a more fundamental being-towards-life. This results in a reframing of Heidegger's analysis of Dasein as a thrown projection [*geworfener Entwurf*] that goes beyond the anticipation of the end of one's own life and brings the living individual into relation with a life after.

To disclose the meaning of living after, this chapter has distinguished between two different senses of the survival of life: a vertical and a horizontal resurrection. The former notion can be detected in Henry's phenomenology of life, when Henry describes Life as an eternal present that survives and continues to live on, even after the death of the finite individual. But Henry does not specify whether this survival of Life includes the personal survival of the living individual or only the impersonal survival of Life as such. To explore this open question, the chapter turns to Ricoeur's late reflections on immortality and resurrection in *Living Up to Death*. Ricoeur's account of the vertical sense of survival, on the one hand, resembles Henry's claims about the eternity of life. It conveys the idea that one will survive death and continue to exist in some impersonal manner that is up to God. Ricoeur considers this sense of survival to be more appropriate to a doctrine of faith. But we have shown that the horizontal sense of survival, on the other hand, can be justified phenomenologically. The horizontal resurrection refers to the living individual's orientation to others who will continue to live on after oneself. To unlock the full phenomenological significance of this relation to a life after one's own, the chapter demonstrated the deep importance that belief in the horizontal survival of others and of Life in general has in relation to how we lead our own lives. This valuable insight shows that the infinitude of life does not only shape the life that we have but also shapes the life that we lead.

To elaborate, the phenomenology of living after extends the meaning of one's own life beyond the lifespan of the living individual. In being-towards-life, the self is oriented toward a future that is not its own. One's choices, activities, and goals are structured by a relation to the future survival of a life that continues to live after oneself. Indeed, without that background orientation toward the future, these activities would lose their significance here and now. This shows that the finite living individual is invested in a broader collective survival of life that resembles Dilthey's notion of the connectedness of life. To be connected to life means that in life we are never in it only for ourselves alone. We are connected to the living, not only to the dead after whom we have survived but also to those who will survive after our own death.[48] In this way, the notion of a life after life transforms the traditional meaning of immortality. While the desire for immortality is often associated with the longing for one's personal survival after death, the phenomenology of life suggests, to the contrary, that personal survival is not really what matters. Henry and Ricoeur, each in their own way, challenge the egocentric desire to make one's own life absolute. The notion of living after reorients and redirects this desire toward a collective sense of survival that promotes the furtherance of life as such. From this perspective, the longing for immortality is no longer about me and my personal survival; it becomes about life as such and its own survival.

To put a different spin on a familiar adage (that there is no *I* in the word *team*), the infinitude of life reminds us that there *is* an *I* in the word *life*, but this *I* stands neither at the beginning nor at the end of Life.

# 8

## For an Integrated Phenomenology of Life

THE PHENOMENOLOGY OF LIFE OFFERS a new path forward for phenomenology. As a phenomenology, it traces the fundamental question—what is life?—back to the I in life and poses this question precisely in terms of how life is given in one's own lived experience. This leads to the disclosure of the phenomenological structure of life's appearing and of its significance within the context of a human life. But what first motivates the development of a phenomenology of life?

While the classical phenomenology of consciousness emerges in response to an encounter of some epistemological stumbling block that calls into question naïve beliefs that have been taken for granted, I would say that the phenomenology of life is motivated by a different problem—namely, the feeling that one's connection to life has been lost somehow. This problem is expressed eloquently in the famous lines of the poet T. S. Eliot, who asks, "Where is the life we have lost in living? Where is the wisdom we have lost in knowledge? Where is the knowledge we have lost in information?"[1] Eliot's questioning is directed toward his own times but applies no less to ours (if not more so). These questions, as I read them, are not so much about how we are leading our lives as whether we are leading them at all. We find that our lives have become dispersed and somehow gone adrift. We are alive but feel that we are not really living.

Eliot's three questions identify a threefold cascade of loss: of knowledge, wisdom, and life itself. Each of these three losses can be traced back to a contemporary world in which philosophical and spiritual virtues have been replaced by false equivalents. Echoing this loss, Henry frequently cites the biologist François Jacob's observation that "life is no longer what is studied in laboratories."[2] In place of life, codes and data sets are the topic of study in biology today, and life itself is reduced to the processing of chemical and physical information. This reduction of life to information seeps into our everyday lives—for example, when individuals wear devices to collect information and feedback about their health and where health is defined by the measurement of a heart rate, calories burned, movement across distance, and so forth.

How, then, does the phenomenology of life answer the call to recover what has been lost through this reduction of life to information? It exposes the limitations of the attempt to know life externally through its transcendent mode of appearing. Observation, measurement, and data collection can provide external knowledge about life from the outside, but they cannot convey what it is like to be alive. In this way, the phenomenology of life is able to recover a dimension of life that has been concealed by our predominant modes of philosophizing and doing science. It restores our firsthand contact with life by investigating the immanent mode of appearing of life as it is experienced from the inside. In so doing, it provides new wisdom and insight into the living individual's own connection to life. While Eliot's question about what has been lost in our current way of living will be revisited later, let's first retrace some of the key milestones of this book's argument.

## The Argument for an Integrated Phenomenology of Life

This close study of the Henry-Ricoeur dialogue has exposed a contrast between two rival methodological approaches to a phenomenology of life: Henry's phenomenological maximalism versus Ricoeur's phenomenological minimalism. We have shown that Henry embraces the radicality of a maximalist approach that questions back from what is given in experience and discloses the origin of its appearing. Henry locates this origin of all appearing in the auto-affection of life. By returning to this original experience, the living individual regains a fundamental connection with life and is able to enjoy its embrace.[3] What is truly remarkable about Henry's thought is the originality of his philosophical breakthrough concerning an original affective experience of the pathos of life. This discovery opens an entirely new region of study—the experience of life in its immanent mode of appearing—that makes his work indispensable to any future phenomenology of life.

Drawing from Ricoeur, however, this book calls into question Henry's attempt to elevate his original discovery concerning the auto-affection of life to the rank of a phenomenological absolute. Methodologically, Ricoeur's minimalist approach calls into question Henry's commitment to the foundationalist enterprise of a maximalist phenomenology. In place of its radical search for an origin, Ricoeur focuses on mundane lived experiences and provides a careful hermeneutics that elucidates their significance. Substantively, this allows Ricoeur to uncover a questionable presupposition that guides Henry's phenomenological analyses: his sharp dichotomy between the immanent mode of appearing that is suited to life and the transcendent mode of appearing that pertains to the world. This turns out to be a pivotal point of contention between Henry and Ricoeur.

In their debates over Freud and Marx, Ricoeur challenges the sharp line of demarcation drawn between the immanent appearing of life and the transcendent appearing of the world in Henry's thought. Addressing the topic of desire in Freud's work, chapter 4 has shown how Ricoeur questions the purely immanent approach to drives and forces in Henry's work. As an alternative, Ricoeur calls attention to the external factors that shape desire, such as biological needs and cultural influences. These external factors show that the full meaning of desire requires the subjective experience of desire to be linked to the biological and cultural factors that shape it. A parallel argument is put forward in Ricoeur's reply to the Henryan reading of Marx. Chapter 5 presents Ricoeur's argument that the meaning of praxis cannot be reduced entirely to the subjective experience of effort; instead, its meaning must also pass through the filter of a given set of life circumstances and a social ideology. Instead of focusing solely on the subjective experience of the living individual, a full account of praxis, according to Ricoeur, should focus on the living individual who acts in a set of unchosen circumstances. Based on these two examples, it is clear that Ricoeur's substantive contribution to the phenomenology of life is his insistence on the necessary interplay between the subjective experience of life and the external circumstances of a life situation.

Moreover, this book challenges another important presupposition in Henry's phenomenology of life. Henry repeatedly describes the auto-affective experience of life as an immediate feeling of one's own living, which occurs without any distance or separation between the subject and object of this experience. This immediacy is attributed to the fact that life is both the subject and object, both the feeling and what is felt, in the auto-affection of life. But our analyses in chapter 2 have called the intelligibility of Henry's description into question by showing that his account of auto-affection actually operates with an implicit notion of internal difference between the living individual and life. This internal difference, which Henry was unable to articulate, can be characterized in terms of the logic of the double genitive. It introduces two different senses into a single expression such as the auto-affection of life, depending on whether the genitive is followed in an objective or subjective direction. As an objective genitive, the auto-affection of life signifies life's expression in the living individual and the pathos of being affected by a Life on which it depends as well. As a subjective genitive, the auto-affection of life refers to the living individual's feeling of its own force as a power to act and to lead a life of its own.[4] The key point, which extends to many other Henryan expressions, is that this single expression can accommodate both perspectives. Together, they reveal the duality of the pathos (affect) and praxis (force) of life.

These criticisms open a new set of questions about the path forward for a phenomenology of life: What would happen if this maximalist ambition to establish a first philosophy were abandoned? What would a phenomenology of life look like if life's immanent mode of appearing, instead of being treated as a radical origin of appearing, were placed alongside the transcendent mode of appearing as cofounding and mutually generating? This alternative has been explored in the main chapters of this book, which cover phenomenological themes such as birth, movement, desire, and so forth. In each case, our analyses make the case for a more comprehensive and integrated phenomenological framework that pairs the key insights of Henry's breakthrough with the minimalist approach advocated by Ricoeur. This alternative is offered by an integrated phenomenology of life, whose main features can be outlined as follows.

To show that the immanent appearing of life is structured by an internal difference between life and the living individual, our analyses have been guided by the formal structure of the Cartesian circle, which establishes two different sources of evidence: the ordo essendi and the ordo cognoscendi. From the perspective of the ordo essendi, life is the generative source of the living individual and its powers. Like Descartes's idea of the infinite, life is a reality that precedes the self and guarantees its being. It thus signals the self's ontological dependency on the prior reality of life, which places its stamp on the self before anything that I might think, say, feel, or do. As a result, I undergo the pathos of life and find myself in life prior to any initiative or anticipation. In this respect, life reveals the limitation or finitude of a living individual who is unable to create itself on its own. Yet, the full significance of life cannot be reduced to the suffering of this pathos. While the ordo essendi correlates with the evidence of life, there is another aspect of the experience of life—the ordo cognoscendi—that provides evidence from the perspective of the living individual's own experience. Like Descartes's cogito, the living cogito is a first starting point of all experience. One can acquire access to life only through first-person experience, and specifically, through the auto-affection of life. This feeling, in addition to providing evidence of one's passive exposure to life, puts the living individual in possession of itself, such that one is then able to exercise the various powers that enable one to lead a life of one's own. Together these two sources of evidence reveal an internal differentiation between life and the living individual that is implicit in the auto-affective experience of life.

How does this notion of an internal difference contribute to the advancement of our understanding of the immanence of life? While the notions of affect and force are mentioned often by Henry, their precise relation remains an unexplained black box in his work. Commentators, as a result, have generally followed Henry's own tendency to focus on the pathos of life without seeking to explain its linkage to his description of the force of life.[5] However, through the adoption of the logic of the Cartesian circle, this project removes that obscurity and sheds light on how these two notions can be linked in a way that is consistent with the thrust of Henry's work. Our analyses show that life is given experientially not only as a pathos that is given by life but also as a force through which I can lead a life. Life is both something that one receives and something that one leads. In this way, the integrated approach recalibrates Henry's own account of life's immanence to articulate the dual sense of life as a pathos *and* a praxis.[6]

This rereading of Henry also has implications for contemporary debates concerning the nature of the gift, most notably, for the work of Jean-Luc Marion. It suggests that the gift of life can be understood through the logic of the double genitive both as a given and as a giving. What does the givenness of the gift of life reveal through its pathos? According to the objective genitive, life reveals itself as a gift precisely because life is pregiven in advance of any particular lived experience. In its relation to life, the living individual is positioned as a passive recipient of a gift that is received without the recipient's prior knowledge or expectation of it.[7] Yet, the pathos of life does not exhaust the full meaning of the gift of life. After all, a gift is not something that one simply receives and then abandons (at least not if it is a good gift!). To receive a gift is to be empowered to do something with it—that is, to be able to use it in some way. According to the subjective genitive, to receive the gift of life is to receive the force that empowers the living individual to use the gift in order to lead its own life. This direct linkage between the pathos and the force of life as a gift through the double genitive suggests that the phenomenology of life does not merely contribute a new piece of knowledge about oneself: a rediscovery of the pathos of receiving the gift of life. This discovery, in turn, generates the possibility of doing something with it and includes the possibility of transforming one's own way of life. We will return to this very important point in our closing remarks.

Although this retooling of Henry's phenomenology of life marks an important advance that anchors pathos and praxis in the immanence of life, it is important to recognize that this contribution alone remains limited and incomplete. As Ricoeur's critique of the sharp dichotomy between the inner life and the external world shows, a full account of life must also include the external dimension of the relation between the pathos and praxis of life. For Ricoeur, the living individual always acts in the context of a set of unchosen circumstances. The pathos of life, in this sense, refers to the contingency of a given set of life circumstances, including the natural, historical, social, or linguistic contexts in which one lives. These background circumstances, in turn, are not simply a set of limitations that are passively imposed on oneself; they also are the conditions that enable one to lead a life and to give it a meaning.

Inasmuch as Henry and Ricoeur are speaking about pathos and praxis in two very different ways, it is not necessary to choose between either the internal difference articulated by Henry or the external difference developed by Ricoeur. Instead, it is possible to organize their contributions on two separate levels: (1) internally: in relation to the lived experience of life as lived; (2) externally: in relation to the socio-biological circumstances of life. Accordingly, Henry's phenomenology articulates the first level by conveying the internal difference of pathos and praxis within one's own subjective experience of life. In relation to life, I experience myself as the recipient of the life that I have but at the same time as endowed with a set of powers that belong to me and allow me to lead a life. However, Ricoeur's work supplements this account by recognizing the external factors that influence pathos and praxis on the second level. The living individual, for Ricoeur, does not act ex nihilo without the influence of its cultural surroundings and its biological reality; instead, one always acts in response to a given set of circumstances that one does not create. These life circumstances, which are given prior to any action, define the pathos of being given the life that I happen to have. They also provide the necessary background from which an individual can lead a life and in which their actions can be intelligible.

The integrated account embraces a both-and strategy that accommodates the full range of interactions between the pathos of having a life and the praxis of leading a life. As such, it maintains that the pathos of having a life includes the gift of life as well as the inheritance of a given life situation and that the praxis of leading a life involves the possession of a set of capabilities as well as a practical context that facilitates or inhibits their exercise. Instead of treating these as separate aspects of life, it explores how these elements combine, intersect, and mutually influence one another.

With this account of the integrated phenomenology of life now in clear view, let me conclude with a few more speculative remarks about its practical implications.

## The Interwovenness of Capabilities and Vulnerabilities

One compelling point in favor of the integrated account is that it coheres with our ordinary conceptions of the full range of human capacities and vulnerabilities. In this way, the integrated account is to be preferred over the accounts of life as pathos and praxis developed separately by Henry and Ricoeur. Each thinker, considered alone, captures only one aspect of our ordinary intuitions.

For Henry, the living individual is lifebound and put into life without a choice, but to be in life also means to be put in possession of the force of life. In using the notion of force, Henry is not referring to specific forceful behaviors or actions; instead, force should be taken in the sense of a *dunameis*, as a power to act. This refers to the various capacities—such as moving, desiring, speaking, and so forth—that define what a living individual can do. These capacities can be deployed or remain undeployed; they can be developed or remain undeveloped. Understood as a capacity, the force of life thus signifies a reserve beyond the actual, an array of practical possibilities that are not yet realized but could be. To identify life with these capacities is thus to emphasize life's potentiality over and above its actuality. It is to say that the possibilities of a life—of what a living individual can do or become—are always greater than its actuality.

Henry's account of the force of life is innovative precisely because it acknowledges its direct linkage to the pathos of life. Although I have a set of capabilities to act and can freely deploy them, they are first received as a gift of life. Similar to what we ordinarily call natural abilities, their gift structure entails that I do not create them or give them to myself. Given the specific content of the natural capacities that I receive, other natural limitations directly follow, such as the fact that I cannot regenerate my limbs, live underwater, and so forth. The pathos of life thus delineates a practical horizon for everything I can do; it defines the bounds of what is possible or impossible for me to do.

The Henryan account, though explicitly nonbiological, accords neatly with our ordinary conception of natural capacities (intellectual, physical, or sensory). While these capacities are received as a fact of birth, they are not always distributed equally. Some are advantaged or disadvantaged through no action of their own. This passive reception of our capabilities conveys an important part of our ordinary thinking about natural talents and abilities, but it does not tell the whole story. What this account misses are the various ways in which our interactions with the external world can also serve either to facilitate or impair an individual's power to act. Social structures, cultural values, and economic resources can all influence the degree to which one's natural capacities can be developed and realized. It is with respect to these sociohistorical factors that the Ricoeurian account proves to be especially insightful.

For Ricoeur, the autonomy of leading a life cannot be separated from the fragility of the life that we happen to have. Ricoeur, like Henry, anchors the ability to lead a life in human capabilities and the power to act. Ricoeur frequently mentions four specific capabilities: the power to speak, the power to act on a course of events, the power to gather one's own life into a narrative, and the power to impute actions to oneself as their author. Each of these powers is vulnerable to loss through changes of life circumstance such as illness, disease, aging, among other natural factors. But the last of the capacities on this list—imputation—is especially important because it highlights another type of influence that affects the ability to exercise one's capabilities. The ability to exercise a capability requires a reflexive ability to affirm one's possession of it and claim it as one's own. In the simplest terms, to exercise a capacity I must also recognize myself as someone who is capable to act and have confidence in my own abilities to exercise these capacities effectively. To believe that I can do something is already to be capable while believing that I can't do something is already to exclude myself from doing it. But how does one acquire the self-confidence that allows one to trust in one's own abilities? And conversely, how does one come to lack this confidence and doubt oneself?

Part of Ricoeur's answer comes from an acknowledgment of the influential role of the social world. Confidence in one's own ability to act develops in response to the approval that is received from others. Their encouragement and support can contribute to the growth of one's confidence, as commonly seen in the role of teaching or coaching. Training and reinforcement can boost one's capabilities, improving one's ability as well as one's level of confidence. While this displays the positive link between affirmation and accomplishment, the opposite dynamic can also take hold to shake or weaken our confidence. Suspicion and rejection can lead, in turn, to discouragement and doubt about our own abilities, weakening confidence to the point that one might not even try to do something. Confidence is fragile. Because confidence in our capacities to act is easily shaken, it turns out that autonomy—the ability to lead a life—is also fragile.

In addition to the social influence on our capabilities, Ricoeur recognizes a similar role played by legal, political, and cultural institutions. On the one hand, institutions can enable individuals to exercise their capabilities. They can ensure, for example, that everyone gets an opportunity to speak in public debate. But on the other hand, institutions can exercise a power over individuals that enforces an uneven distribution of such capabilities—for example, by allowing some to have more speech than others. Insofar as their role can be generative as well as repressive, institutions attest to the fragility of our capabilities.

Ricoeur's account of capabilities and vulnerabilities stands in clear contrast with the Henryan account. Henry does not address the complexity of the passage from having a capability to exercising it; everything seems to happen automatically through the fact of one's own will. In contrast, the Ricoeurian approach is attuned to the many ways in which social factors can amplify or impair our ability to lead a life. To be precise, his account identifies multiple dimensions of such influence: the psychological, the interpersonal, and the institutional. Each dimension can serve as either an enabling or inhabiting factor in relation to the capacity to act. My own self-confidence or lack thereof, the encouragement of others or lack thereof, and the recognition of institutions or lack thereof, all influence one's ability to lead a life. The pathos of life, for Ricoeur, arises from the gap that opens up between what the external world allows us to accomplish and what we ourselves aspire to do. This gap introduces a form of social suffering that arises when some impediment stands in the way of something I aspire to do or become.

The integrated account acknowledges the full spectrum of vulnerabilities ranging from those that occur naturally (such as the inability to speak) to those that are imposed socially (such as the prohibition of speaking) as well as their various degrees of interaction with our ability to act.

The natural factors, whether they come from life in a non-biological or biological sense, correspond with the notion that one receives certain traits, talents, and limitations simply as a fact of birth. These natural gifts are received without one's input. They incline us in one direction or another in life, even if they do not determine the precise course of an individual life. Our lives are also vulnerable to the sociohistoric circumstances into which we are born and live. Even the most gifted may achieve very little in harsh circumstances that thwart or impair their ability to act. Conversely, those who experience natural impairments can thrive and flourish in the context of a supportive and accommodating social environment. The point is that the realization of our natural gifts and talents, regardless of what they may be, requires a set of life circumstances that afford their cultivation and deployment. The power of the integrated account is evident in its ability to account for the full scope of this interaction between the life that I have and the life that I lead.

## The Pathos of Life and Meritocratic Thinking

There is a second way in which the integrated phenomenology of life can find practical relevance today. It challenges the rise of meritocratic thinking in contemporary culture and politics. Meritocratic thinking embraces the discourse of self-mastery.[8] A meritocratic society rewards individual accomplishment. There is something very appealing about the meritocratic ideal that individuals should get what they have earned. By awarding people for their talent, effort, and initiative, meritocracy offers an attractive picture of human freedom. It suggests that we are free to rise in society as far as our talent and hard work will take us. It puts success in our own hands and makes us masters of our own fate. But, in challenging the self-mastery of the ego, the phenomenology of life calls into question the sense of entitlement that often accompanies meritocratic thinking.

To elaborate, meritocratic thinking is especially tempting to the successful. It is psychologically appealing to interpret one's own success as a sign of one's superior talents, determination, and hard work. But can one truly say that one's own achievements are solely the result of one's own doing? The phenomenology of life calls this assumption into question by emphasizing the passive dimension of all our talents and abilities themselves. First of all, it points out that the so-called natural abilities are not at all the result of one's own doing; they are instead a gift of life received through the fortune of birth. In addition, the social circumstances into which one is born have a deep influence on our ability to lead a life, but the phenomenology of life assigns these circumstances to the unchosen dimension of the life one happens to have. As a result, much of what might initially pass as an individual's own doing can be traced back to the prior inheritance of life circumstances that are a matter of luck.

How does this awareness of the pathos of life change how one interprets the accomplishments in one's own life? In place of the self-congratulation of meritocratic thinking, seeing one's own life as a gift might lead one to give more credit to all the factors beyond one's control that have enabled one's success. Let me illustrate this point with an example. Consider the 100-meter dash in track. What makes this race exciting is the thin margin of error; at the highest levels of competition, the winner and losers of the race are separated by fractions of a second. In the midst of the race, anything can happen. A stumble out of the blocks or in the runner's stride can cost the favorite the race and open the door for others to win.

Given the individualistic nature of the sport, the extreme pressure, and the race's short duration, one would expect that the winners would claim their victory purely as a matter of their own doing: after all, they ran the race, and their superior performance produced the victory. But anyone who has ever watched track knows that postrace interviews often turn out differently. Few sprinters respond with the smugness of meritocratic thinking; instead, most respond with an appreciation of the gifts of fortune. For instance, they might give credit to their life circumstances, such as the coaches, partners, or parents who have helped them along the way to success. Some might even give credit to God for their natural talents and describe themselves as simply a vessel that expresses them. In any case, responses like these are noteworthy because these winners recognize themselves as the beneficiaries of good fortune. They give credit to the talent and ability that they have received through what we have called the pathos of life.

Perhaps it is the thin line between success and failure, the fragility of their success, that makes this reality salient to them. They recognize that the slightest change in health or the slightest mistake is capable of changing the outcome entirely. While the race crystallizes this vulnerability in the intensity of a short time span, it is also true in a less dramatic way for each of us in our day-to-day lives. If our own life circumstances had been otherwise, then our own achievements and successes could easily have turned out differently. The hubris of meritocratic thinking conveniently forgets about the vulnerability of our lives and their continual exposure to unchosen circumstances and potential misfortune. Like the sprinter, the phenomenology of life transforms how we see ourselves by calling attention to the gift structure of life. It reminds us that our own talents and abilities are a gift and that, if we do experience the joy of success, it is only because we are beneficiaries of the good fortune to exercise them in social circumstances that are conducive to our flourishing.

While much more could be said about this topic, the takeaway point here is that the integrated approach does not merely deliver a cognitive advance in the development of a phenomenology of life. To be sure, it provides an account of the intersection between one's vulnerability to the pathos of having a life with one's capacity to engage in the praxis of leading a life. In addition, it has a practical value. By changing how we understand our own relation to life, it has the potential to produce a real transformation in how we live.

\* \* \*

The conclusion opened with a reading of the famous lines in which T. S. Eliot laments the profound loss of our connection to life in the contemporary world. To recall, there are three cascading layers to Eliot's lament including the loss of life, the loss of knowledge, and the loss of wisdom. The phenomenology of life, likewise, is motivated by this feeling of loss. It challenges the distortion of life that has resulted from the reduction of life to information and the reduction of the knowledge of life to observation and measurement of the external world. The loss of connection to life alienates us from the wisdom of life. This is nowhere more evident than in today's research university, which measures the value of knowledge by the awarding of research dollars and the acquisition of commercial patents. The attainment of wisdom and increased self-understanding have little value under these metrics. This loss of connection to life is evident, likewise, in the distraction and waywardness that has overtaken our personal lives. This can be seen on our university campuses and in the streets, where all eyes are continually scrolling through screens and earphones block out all sounds. Each individual is more connected than ever to the world but less connected than ever to their immediate surroundings. This is how we are living, but must we live this way? What is the price of living this way?

In addition to seeking to recover and revitalize the individual's lived experience of life, the phenomenology of life should extend its focus to pursue questions like these—that is, questions about how we are living—that are so urgent today. In so doing, it might take an initial cue from Eliot's own diagnosis of how our lives have gone adrift. This is revealed later in the poem when Eliot reframes the question of what has been lost in our living by inserting a leading question: "What life have you if you have not life together?" His answer follows immediately: "There is no life that is not in community."[9] In the present context, perhaps this response generates more questions than answers. What exactly does a life lived in community mean? What does the relation between life and the living individual entail for the question of the community of life? How might the integrated account of life as pathos and praxis shed light on the nature of such a community? These unanswered questions concerning the nature and possibility of a community of life indicate a vital direction for future exploration in the phenomenology of life.

# NOTES

*Introduction*

1. Etymologically, the English word *life* derives from the proto-Indo-European word *leip*, meaning "to remain, persevere, and continue." Indeed, the present-day definition of life in biology remains remarkably close to these ancient roots. Life, according to one dictionary definition, is "a characteristic of a living organism . . . distinguished by the capacity to grow, metabolize, respond (to stimuli), adapt, and reproduce." See https://www.biologyonline.com/dictionary/life.

2. The MRS GREN list is a mnemonic device that helps students identify the essential functions of living organisms: movement, respiration, sensitivity, growth, reproduction, excretion, nutrition. I was reminded of this biology lesson by the biologist Paul Nurse, *What Is Life?*, 127. Nurse refines this list by reducing it to three features: evolution, cellular organization, and chemical, physical, and informational processing.

3. Henry, *I Am the Truth*, 47.

4. Interestingly, there is a rare condition known as Cotard's syndrome (named after the French physician Jules Cotard) in which individuals lose the sense of what it feels like to be alive without dying. They are alive but insist that they are actually dead. Recent studies have associated this syndrome with damage to the insular cortex of the brain. See Zimmer, *Life's Edge*, 16–17.

5. Haldane, *What Is Life?*, 58.

6. As a result, readers who might turn to Henry in search of an environmental philosophy or an ecological message are likely to be disappointed! Although it might on the surface seem like a focus on life would be conducive to environmentalism, the anthropocentric focus of his phenomenology of life may not offer strong support for an environmental ethic. This topic is explored in Lind, "Michel Henry's

Notion of *Bodily-Ownness* in the Context of the Ecological Crisis"; and Gschwandtner. "What about Non-Human Life?"

7. Kant's distinction between these two ways of knowing the human follows the divide between nature and culture. The integrated approach does not deny these two aspects of the "knowledge of the human." But instead of keeping them separate, the integrated approach emphasizes the reciprocal interaction between these two realms.

8. See Renaud Barbaras, *Introduction to a Phenomenology of Life*. For a clear statement of his disagreement with Henry, see chapter 1.1.

9. Etymologically, this linkage does find support. Both the early English word *lif* and the German terms *Leben* (for "life") and *Leib* ("flesh") descend from the same proto-Indo-European root word, *leip*. This shared etymology, when passing through German, supports the linkage between life and an organic body, which carries out processes related to the growth, maintenance, and survival of life.

10. Ovid, *Tristia*, book I, poem III, verse 12. I draw this phrase from the fascinating historical analysis of its use by Montaigne, Rousseau, and Biran by Anne Devarieux in "L'exil des affections pures," 139–58. Here, I am suggesting that this saying extends perfectly to Henry as well, even though Henry never mentions it.

11. See, for example, Johann Michel's account of the interpretive nature of human life in *Homo Interpretans*. Michel approaches Ricoeur's work precisely in terms of the anthropological question, asking, "In what way and to what extent can Ricœur's anthropology be described as hermeneutic or interpretive?" The answer, as the book's title indicates, is that Ricoeur understands the human precisely through the work of interpretation, such that interpretation is both the method by which we understand the human and the substance of what it means to be human.

12. Another pertinent discussion of Kant's anthropology occurs in Ricoeur's dialogue with Jean-Pierre Changeux in *What Makes us Think?*. There Ricoeur defends phenomenology against naturalism, precisely by citing Kant's discussion of these two perspectives toward the human. As an alternative to Changeux's naturalism, Ricoeur defends a phenomenological account of the mind which adheres to two different semantic registers of the human: the realm of meaning and the realm of objectivity.

13. The concept of the fault, which Ricoeur borrows from Jean Nabert, is developed by Ricoeur in *Fallible Man*.

14. The disproportion of life, as Ricoeur explains, gives rise to a tension between two perspectives toward the human. In contrast with Heidegger's interpretation of Kant, which identifies philosophical anthropology solely with finitude and takes finitude to be the defining feature of the human, for Ricoeur the experience of disproportion defines the human as an unreconciled division or noncoincidence of two poles: the finite and the infinite.

15. Due to the depth and complexity of the Henry-Ricoeur relationship, it has been necessary to bracket Barbaras's phenomenology of life from this project. However, this book's argument is engaged implicitly with Barbaras throughout.

16. There are many useful biographical resources for both thinkers that are available. For Henry's biography, consult Jean Leclercq, "Biographie de Michel Henry," 9–29. For an excellent overview of Henry's thought, see Frédéric Seyler's entry on Michel Henry in the *Stanford Encyclopedia of Philosophy*. For insight into Ricoeur's philosophical development, see Ricoeur's "Intellectual Autobiography" in Hahn, *The Philosophy of Paul Ricoeur*, 3–53. And for an excellent personal memoir, see Charles Reagan, *Paul Ricoeur*. For an excellent overview of Ricoeur's thought, see David Pellauer's entry on Paul Ricoeur in the *Stanford Encyclopedia of Philosophy* as well as his book *Ricoeur: A Guide for the Perplexed*.

17. The Phénoménologie de la vie series was initiated by Jean-Luc Marion and Paul Audi in 2003 and continued up to the publication of the fifth volume in 2015 by Presses Universitaires Françaises. The five volume series collects Henry's most important articles and interviews.

18. For a comprehensive listing, see Vandecasteele and Vansina, *Paul Ricoeur Bibliography*.

19. There is indeed one volume in French that has made initial progress in thinking about their relationship. Although I have benefited from that earlier collection of essays, it too is unable to cover the full scope of this relationship. Its lack of a systematic and comprehensive approach becomes evident in virtue of the fact that many themes highlighted in this book, such as birth, movement, language, and the afterlife, are not pursued there. See Hardy, Leclercq, and Sautereau, eds., *Paul Ricœur et Michel Henry*.

20. Ricoeur's expression of esteem occurs in the discussion that followed Henry's presentation of "Rationality According to Marx." This article, along with responses by Mikel Dufrenne, R. P. Dubarle, and Paul Ricoeur, is published in Henry, *Phénoménologie de la vie*, vol. III, 77–104.

21. Their most extensive important published exchanges are: Henry, "Ricoeur et Freud," 127–43; Ricoeur, "Le Marx de Michel Henry," 265–93; In addition, they refer to one another in the following passages: Henry, *The Genealogy of Psychoanalysis*, 349, note 62; Ricoeur, *Oneself as Another*, 320 ff.; Ricoeur, "L'attestation: entre phénoménologie et ontologie," 400.

22. Many of these early essays on Husserl are compiled in Ricoeur's English volume, *Husserl: An Analysis of His Phenomenology*.

23. For fascinating detail on this unique educational system and its legacy, see Schrift, *Twentieth-Century French Philosophy*.

24. Describing his education in an interview, Henry commented, "My training was derived from the philosophy that was taught in the high schools and preparatory

classes in Paris at the time of World War II. It involved the French reception, between 1870 and 1940, of Kantian thought by a series of philosophers like Lachelier, Lagneau, Boutroux, Alain, Nabert, Lachieze-Rey, etc. Despite the remarkable characteristics of their analyses, I perceived my disagreement with them from the outset. To me this often-Idealistic thought allowed the concrete to escape: what I am at the bottom of myself, my real life" (Henry, *Entretiens*, 87). Similarly, Ricoeur master's thesis on Lachelier and Langeau, entitled *Méthode réflexive appliquée au problème de Dieu chez Lachelier et Lagneau*, has recently been published in French.

25. This notion is drawn from Jean Wahl. See his "Preface to *Toward the Concrete*," 32–53.

26. This response is reprinted in Ricoeur, *Lectures 2: La contrée des philosophes*, 265–93. Ricoeur, of course, presented his own set of lectures on Marx at that time as well, which are published as *Lectures on Ideology and Utiopia*.

27. My English translation of this essay appears in *The Michel Henry Reader*. Henry, of course, was composing his own book on Freud at this time, *The Genealogy of Psychoanalysis*.

28. One brief expression of this view can be found in Dosse's biography *Paul Ricoeur: Les sens d'une vie*, 564–65.

29. Ricoeur, *Critique and Conviction*, 93.

30. Ibid. I take it that Ricoeur is referring to material that would eventually be published in his book *Memory, History, Forgetting*.

31. I have examined Ricoeur's early account of life presented in *Freedom and Nature* in "The Phenomenon of Life," 157–72.

32. See Worms, "Vivant jusqu'à la mort," 308.

33. Remark cited in Vandecasteele and Vansina, *Paul Ricoeur: Bibliographie primaire*," xxviii.

34. See Janicaud, "Toward a Minimalist Phenomenology," 89–106. For a reply to this account, see my essay "Is a Hermeneutic Phenomenology Wide Enough?," 315–26.

35. Henry, *The Genealogy of Psychoanalysis*, 325.

36. See the "Editors' Introduction" in Henry, *The Michel Henry Reader*, ix–xxviii.

37. It is worth noting that this is precisely the thesis that Renaud Barbaras rejects. Barbaras contends that, without any anchor to life in the biological sense, Henry's phenomenology of life consists only of metaphors and empty talk. Instead of generating transcendence, he holds that the pathos of life is ontologically dependent on it and derived from the world.

38. "Non-intentional phenomenology," in Henry, *Phénoménologie de la vie*, vol. I, 116.

39. For example, Rudolf Bernet rejects Henry's foundational claims and asserts that Henry is simply "wrong to consider this auto-manifestation [of life] as more

originary than the manifestation of mundane things and as somehow constituting the very essence of manifestation" (Bernet, *La vie du sujet*, 327).

40. This point of departure signals one of the self-imposed limits of this project. While phenomenology does not necessarily require the bracketing of religious experience or theology, this study will not thematize the religious and theological contributions of both thinkers, such as Henry's later Christian writings and Ricoeur's confessional writings.

41. Ricoeur, *Oneself as Another*, 320.

### 1. From a Phenomenology of Consciousness to a Phenomenology of Life

1. Due to the lack of paper in the prisoner of war camp, he inscribed his translation in miniscule handwriting in the margins of the book. This was one of the few items that he carried back home in his knapsack following the war, and today it is held in the Fonds Ricoeur in Paris. The details of this period of Ricoeur's life are chronicled in wonderful detail by Reagan, *Paul Ricoeur*.

2. Husserl, *Idées directrices pour une phénoménologie*.

3. These works are available in English as *A Key to Edmund Husserl's Ideas I* and *Husserl: An Analysis of His Phenomenology*. In his "Intellectual Autobiography," Ricoeur distinguishes between two rival interpretations of phenomenology: "According to the first, ratified by Max Scheler, Ingarden, and other phenomenologists of the time of the Logical Investigations, the reduction made the appearing as such of any phenomenon stand out more sharply; according to the second, adopted by Husserl himself and encouraged by Eugen Fink, the reduction made possible the quasi-Fichtean production of phenomenality by pure consciousness, which set itself as the source of all appearing" (Ricoeur, "Intellectual Autobiography," 11). It will become clear that Henry is aligned more closely with the latter interpretation of phenomenology whereas Ricoeur's affinities are closer to the former approach.

4. Among the most noteworthy treatments of this topic are the following two volumes devoted separately to Henry and Ricoeur: "Michel Henry's Radical Phenomenology," *Studia Phaenomenologica* vol. 9 (2009); "On the Proper Use of Phenomenology: Paul Ricoeur Centenary," *Studia Phaenomenologica* vol. 13 (2013).

5. Ricoeur, *À l'école de la phénoménologie*, 156. Elsewhere, Ricoeur observes that "in a broad sense phenomenology is both the sum of Husserl's work and the heresies issuing from it" (Ricoeur, *Husserl*, 4).

6. These claims about Husserl's Idealism themselves, of course, have been challenged in some recent Husserl scholarship. See, for example, Steinbock, *Home and Beyond*. More recently, see Neal DeRoo's excellent work in *The Political Logic of Experience*.

7. The influence of the phenomenological method on Ricoeur's early work is discussed, along with other influences on his work, in my introduction to *A Companion to Ricoeur's Freedom and Nature*.

8. This position is stated most clearly and forcefully in Henry's essay "Four Principles of Phenomenology" in *The Michel Henry Reader*.

9. These later developments in Ricoeur's thought—especially concerning the central role of language—will come into view in chapter 6.

10. For a more detailed discussion of Ricoeur's critique of Husserl, see my article "The Husserl Heretics," 209–29.

11. For a more detailed account of Husserl's own critique of naturalism, see Moran, "Husserl's Transcendental Philosophy," 401–25.

12. Ricoeur, *Freedom and Nature*, 4.

13. Yet, the phenomenological bracketing of naturalistic explanations cannot be equated with a rejection of their validity; it simply establishes two separate domains of inquiry or two separate perspectives: a naturalistic discourse of cause/effect and a phenomenological discourse of meaning. One important issue in Ricoeur's phenomenology of life, then, will concern the question of how, if at all, these two separate discourses should be understood to mix and intersect with one another. In a 1961 essay entitled "Nature et liberté," he puts forward the provocative notion that, while there is no such thing as "human nature," we can nonetheless speak about a "nature en l'homme" in which a mediation between these two discourses emerges.

14. Ricoeur, *Husserl*, 24.

15. Ricoeur, *Husserl*, 36.

16. Ricoeur, *Fallible Man*, 14.

17. Ricoeur, *Husserl*, 36.

18. Ricoeur, *Husserl*, 114.

19. Ricoeur, *Husserl*, 88.

20. Ricoeur, *Fallible Man*, 15.

21. Husserl, *Cartesian Meditations*, 102.

22. Reagan and Stewart, *The Philosophy of Paul Ricoeur*, 9; italics mine.

23. As an aside, let me note that in taking Husserl's analyses of perception to a new domain—the will—Ricoeur's project moves in a direction that was staked out earlier by Levinas's passage from theoretical to affective intentionality. It is interesting to note that Ricoeur echoes Levinas's criticism of the primacy granted to objectifying acts. Instead, he contends that all modes of intentionality should be taken as "equal and basic" (Ricoeur, *Husserl*, 222). This indicates that the intentionality of willing does not need to conform to the structure of perception any more than affectivity does for Levinas.

24. Ricoeur, *Freedom and Nature*, 4.

25. Ricoeur, *Freedom and Nature*, 17. Interestingly, Ricoeur does not mention Husserl's account of the lived body in *Ideas II* at this time. Perhaps he had not yet read those working notes yet. While *Freedom and Nature* was completed in 1948, Ricoeur did publish a two-part overview of *Ideas II* in 1951 and 1952. But the style of

the overview is mostly descriptive. As a result, it does not provide any clear indication of how he would perceive the similarities and differences between the Husserlian account of the body and his own.

26. Ricoeur, *Freedom and Nature*, 5.
27. Ricoeur, *Freedom and Nature*, 348.
28. Ricoeur, *Husserl*, 216.
29. Ricoeur, *Freedom and Nature*, 483.
30. Ricoeur, *Freedom and Nature*, 342.
31. Ricoeur, *Husserl*, 227.
32. Ricoeur, *Freedom and Nature*, 14.
33. I have written about Ricoeur's phenomenology of life in *Freedom and Nature* at greater length in the chapter "Life and Its Pathos."
34. Ricoeur, *Freedom and Nature*, 414.
35. Ricoeur, *Freedom and Nature*, 414
36. Ricoeur, *Freedom and Nature*, 415.
37. Ricoeur, *Freedom and Nature*, 418.
38. Ricoeur, *Freedom and Nature*, 428.
39. Ricoeur, *Freedom and Nature*, 432.
40. Ricoeur, *Freedom and Nature*, 435.
41. Ricoeur, *Freedom and Nature*, 436.
42. Ricoeur, *Freedom and Nature*, 417.
43. Ricoeur, *Freedom and Nature*, 486.
44. Ricoeur, *Husserl*, 228.
45. Henry, *Material Phenomenology*, 1.
46. Henry, *Material Phenomenology*, 2.
47. The classic formulation of these three ways comes from Kern, "The Three Ways," 126–49.
48. Henry, *Phénoménologie de la vie*, vol. 2, 89. In this context, it is also interesting to consult Claude Romano's challenge to this approach in the article "Must Phenomenology Remain Cartesian?"
49. Husserl, *The Idea of Phenomenology*, 23–24.
50. This is the first of the four phenomenological principles identified by Henry at the outset of his article "The Four Principles of Phenomenology."
51. Husserl, *The Idea of Phenomenology*, 37.
52. Henry, *The Essence of Manifestation*, 111.
53. This point is a central feature of Jean-Luc Marion's account of the Husserlian reduction's opening onto appearing. And it is a point on which Henry and Marion are in clear agreement. For more detail, see Marion, *Reduction and Givenness*, and Henry's critical appraisal in "The Four Principles of Phenomenology."
54. Henry, *Material Phenomenology*, 58.

55. Henry, *Material Phenomenology*, 65.

56. The significance of this text is treated extensively in chapter 1 of Henry's *The Genealogy of Psychoanalysis*.

57. Henry, *Phénménologie de la vie*, vol. 1, 118.

58. Descartes, AT, VII, 29: 14–15.

59. See Marion's essay "The Invisible and the Phenomenon" in *The Affects of Thought*.

60. But if the cogitatio is itself nonintentional and cannot be reached by way of intentionality, then this raises a question of method: how can we acquire a pure seeing of the cogitatio? (Henry, *Material Phenomenology*, 94).

61. Henry, *Material Phenomenology*, 41.

62. As Claudia Serban notes in "De l'hylétique à l'herméneutique," Ricoeur also detects this other potential within Husserlian phenomenology. Following the lead of Gérard Granel, Ricoeur proposes a contrast between a phenomenology of perception and a phenomenology of time. Through the development of a hyletics of time, Husserl promises to descend "into the obscure depths of the ultimate consciousness which constitutes all such temporality as belongs to mental processes" (Ricoeur, *Ideas I*, §85). For an anticipation of Henry's own move, see Ricoeur, *Time and Narrative*, 24 and 282, note 7. Also note that Henry thanks Ricoeur for sending the third volume of *Time and Narrative*, commenting "that it treats a subject that is so near to him that it is like it were for me a founding of my own research. For a long time I have been thinking about the living present, and on the trajectory that leads me toward this absolute, your own meditation will be for me an incomparable stimulation and encouragement" (Henry, "Lettre de Michel Henry," 19).

63. In his analyses of time, there is a recognition that the precondition for the consciousness of time is not intentionality itself but the prior givenness of the impression—that is, the Ur-impression that gives rise to the experience of time. Here, the impression would seem to be the pure phenomenon, the matter out of which intentional consciousness is able to occur. The study of this pure impressionality, indeed, does serve as the opening onto Henry's material phenomenology, but Henry carefully shows how Husserl's interpretation of impressional consciousness covers over this possibility and leads in the direction of the activity of constituting time. In place of the impression, "Husserlian phenomenology would recognize only its constituted being" (Henry, *Material Phenomenology*, 22).

64. Henry, *Material Phenomenology*, 17.

65. Henry, *Material Phenomenology*, 21.

66. Henry, *The Essence of Manifestation*, 279–80; translation mine.

67. Henry, *I Am the Truth*, 140.

68. Henry, *I Am the Truth*, 141; tr. modified.

69. Henry, *Barbarism*, 98.

70. It is thus surprising, given their efforts to develop a phenomenology of life, that they do not emphasize Husserl's way through the lifeworld, even though both thinkers were clearly aware of this aspect of his thought. My sense is that it would be possible, in following this way, to surmount most of their objections to Husserl's phenomenology.

71. Jacob, *The Logic of Life*, 299. The broader context of this citation is: "The processes that take place at the microscopic level in the molecules of living beings are completely indistinguishable from those investigated in inert systems by physics and chemistry. . . . In fact, since the appearance of thermodynamics, the operation value of the concept of life has continually dwindled and its power of abstraction declined. Biologists no longer study life today."

72. Eugen Fink echoes this potential of phenomenology in his essay "The Problem of the Phenomenology of Edmund Husserl," 51 ff.

73. Reagan and Stewart, *The Philosophy of Paul Ricoeur*, 66.

74. This effort to push Husserlian phenomenology to its limits is described as a common feature of the "Husserl heretics" in Sebbah, *Testing the Limits*. See also my review of the original French publication: Davidson, "Book Review: The Test of the Limit."

75. For an overview of the literature on embodied cognition, see Louis Shapiro's entry in the *Stanford Encyclopedia of Philosophy*. Enactivism constitutes one of the views contained under this umbrella term. See an interesting attempt to connect it to Ricoeur in Dierckxsens, "Imagination, Narrativity." Likewise, see a parallel attempt to link to Ricoeur by De Jaegher, "How We Affect Each Other."

76. The full context in which Ricoeur uses this phrase is as follows: "In a sharp-edged dialectic between praxis and pathos, one's own body [*le corps propre*] becomes the emblematic title of a vast inquiry which, beyond the simple mineness of one's own body, denotes the entire sphere of intimate passivity, and hence of otherness [*alterité*], for which it forms the center of gravity" (Ricoeur, *Oneself as Another*, 320).

77. The source of this splitting of the self, as we shall see in the chapters to follow, is located differently by Henry and Ricoeur, respectively. For Henry, it is clear that this split can be attributed to different orientations of the self: the transcendence that orients it toward the world in contrast with the immanence that is accomplished in its embrace of life. To heal this self-division, Henry's phenomenology seeks to restore the self's lost unity by leading back to the pure immanence of an original pathos of life. By contrast, this split has a different source and thus finds a different resolution in Ricoeur's work. Ricoeur is more wary about the prospects of a direct approach to the self. Influenced by the masters of suspicion, the direct approach can, at best, yield only a very abstract and formal access to oneself; it does not have the power to heal this division. Instead of being a work of restoration, the unity of the self must be produced in and through the mediation of the external world.

78. Ricoeur, *Freedom and Nature*, 13.

79. Cited by Devarieux, *L'interiorité réciproque*, 74, note 139. The reference points to Dosse, "Entretien avec l'auteur," 58–59, a source I have been unable to locate.

## 2. Birth

1. Cited by Devarieux, *L'interiorité réciproque*, 74, note 139.

2. This analogy is not quite perfect in the sense that, unlike the static One of Parmenides, Henry describes life as an active essence: "Life is not an immobile essence like an ideal archetype, such as a circle that is present in all circles, but instead an active essence, deploying itself with an invincible force, a source of power, a power of engendering that is immanent in everything that lives and does not cease to give it life" (*I Am the Truth*, 54; trans. mod.). That said, the main point stands. After all, how could one describe a continually active essence, an omnipresence, without ever making any reference to the gap of a temporal difference and distance that divides past, present, and future?

3. It is interesting to note that despite the fact that Emmanuel Levinas is most widely known for his use of Descartes's idea of the Infinite as a critique of Husserl's Idealism, it is noteworthy that Ricoeur offers the same diagnosis of Husserl's Cartesian Meditations, arguably even before Levinas. Chronologically, Levinas published his essay "Philosophy and the Idea of the Infinite" in 1957 while Ricoeur published his "A Study of Cartesian Meditations, I-IV" in 1954. Still, this point is anticipated in Levinas's essays in *Discovering Existence with Husserl* (1949). Either way, the salient point is to recognize that the same idea was emerging in both thinkers at roughly the same time.

4. Yet, it is also important to acknowledge that a more recent line of interpretation has recovered the emphasis on birth within the writings of Husserl and Heidegger. Recent Husserl scholarship, for instance, has uncovered a number of unpublished manuscripts devoted to fetal experience and the topic of birth. See Husserl's study of birth in *Grenzprobleme der Phänomenologie*.

5. Ricoeur, *Husserl*, 84.

6. Ricoeur, *Freedom and Nature*, 468.

7. For a broader discussion of the surimpression in Ricoeur's work, see Daniel Frey's chapter "Imagination and Religion: The Myth of Innocence in Fallible Man" in *A Companion to Ricoeur's Fallible Man*.

8. Ricoeur, *Husserl*, 222.

9. Ricoeur, *Husserl*, 103.

10. See, for example, Henry's assertion that one of the founding intuitions of Christianity is "the difference between Life and the living, that which separates the (absolute) self-affection of the former from the (relative) self-affection of the latter" (*I Am the Truth*, 194).

11. Janicaud's critique is developed in his reading of Henry in chapter "The Surprises of Immanence" in *Phenomenology and the "Theological Turn."*

12. Levinas, *Of God Who Comes to Mind*, 64.

13. Gendered assumptions about personal identity and the value of autonomy clearly feed into this oversight, and its underlying causes are discussed insightfully in the multiauthor volume *Birth, Death, and Femininity*, edited by Robin May Schott.

14. Henry, "The Phenomenology of Birth," 29–30.

15. Heidegger's account of natality may be more sophisticated than Henry admits or is aware of. For a thorough study of the theme of natality in Heidegger's work and a reflection on its broader implications, see Anne O'Byrne's book *Natality and Finitude*.

16. Heidegger, *Being and Time*, 46 [50].

17. Henry, "The Phenomenology of Birth," 33.

18. Henry, "The Phenomenology of Birth," 33.

19. Henry, "The Phenomenology of Birth," 35.

20. Henry, "The Phenomenology of Birth," 35.

21. Henry, "The Phenomenology of Birth," 36.

22. Henry, "The Phenomenology of Birth," 36.

23. Henry, "The Phenomenology of Birth," 37.

24. Henry, "The Phenomenology of Birth," 37.

25. Henry, "The Phenomenology of Birth," 44.

26. Henry, "The Phenomenology of Birth," 38.

27. I borrow this language from Arendt in order to highlight a linkage to Henry's description of the pathos of life in terms of suffering and joy (see Arendt, *The Human Condition*, 247).

28. While Henry does not use this term himself, I borrow this Derridean concept to describe the birth of the self. The entire debate between Derrida and Henry could be revisited and rethought fruitfully as a result of the adoption of the double genitive here.

29. Ricoeur, *Freedom and Nature*, 437.

30. Ricoeur, *Freedom and Nature*, 438.

31. This is just one instance in which Ricoeur's early work anticipates the hermeneutic turn that takes place later in his work. Note, for example, that the dialectic between understanding and explanation is already articulated but not yet fully developed in *Freedom and Nature*.

32. Here, Kohak translates the French term *filialité* as "sonship," but I prefer a more literal translation as "filiality." Henry's work also utilizes this term as well, which translators often render as "sonship" primarily because Henry unfortunately utilizes the condition of being a "son" [*fils*] in his description of filiality. However, as far as I can tell, there is nothing about the concept of filiality itself that warrants this gender assumption; the term derives from the Latin *filius* (son) and *filia* (daughter).

As a result, I would propose that the term *filial* should be taken to include all children and to apply to the parent-child relation more inclusively and that the entire analysis in Henry can be shifted accordingly.

33. This question is of much interest today due to the technological capacity to test genetic ancestry. While I cannot develop this theme fully here, Ricoeur's account might be helpful for unmasking some unwarranted assumptions made about the results of such tests. Just because my ancestry indicates that some part of my DNA can be traced back to some location, this does not mean that a corresponding part of myself is identical with the people of that location. The marketing of such tests, however, often presents the test in this way.

34. Ricoeur, *Freedom and Nature*, 435.

35. Ricoeur, *Freedom and Nature*, 438. Both Henry and Ricoeur make this equation between birth and engendering, though I find it difficult to discern their intended point. If *to engender* means to beget, to produce something or someone, then perhaps they are trying to emphasize that birth involves the production of a self through a filial relation. But to avoid possible confusion, it doesn't seem to me that they would use this terminology to make any claims about having a gender.

36. Ricoeur, *Freedom and Nature*, 39–40. In this way, Ricoeur's discussion anticipates later treatments of the significance of an umbilical self—for example, in the work of Jean-Luc Nancy. For a fascinating analysis of this theme, see Anne O'Byrne's chapter "Umbilicus" in Carnal Hermeneutics, 182–94.

37. Ricoeur, *Freedom and Nature*, 441.

38. Ricoeur, *Freedom and Nature*, 441–42.

39. Ricoeur, *Freedom and Nature*, 437.

40. For a more detailed discussion of carnal symbols, see the "Introduction" to Richard Kearney and Brian Treanor's book *Carnal Hermeneutics*.

41. It is, of course, possible to speak of reproduction as a way of returning this gift, but it would probably be more accurate to describe reproduction as regifting rather than as a gift return. Unlike a gift return, reproduction moves forward in time to the birth of another, rather than going back to the event of my birth. This is why the distinction between being born and giving birth remains irreducible; they cannot be converted to two sides of the same coin.

42. Henry asserts the convertibility of force and affect in the following passage from his essay "Phénoménologie et Psychanalyse," which I translate as follows:

> The Force/Affectivity connection is ... fundamental. ... Just as force is only possible on the basis of Affectivity, likewise Affectivity, which is to say Life, is necessarily force. ... To say that life in its affectivity experiences itself without any possible distance is to say that in the pathos of this experience that it continually has of itself, it is dealing with itself, with this content that it itself is, and from which it cannot escape. Thus life in its auto-revelation is an undergoing, a 'suffering of oneself' and thus

necessarily a 'bearing of oneself' that is stronger than any freedom and any possibility of putting it at a distance" (108; trans. mine).

I take this passage to be saying that the affect of life is the greatest force—the source of force—and that every force is thus an affect because that is how it finds itself as a force. This controvertibility of force and affect will be a central theme in the next two chapters.

### 3. Movement

1. A similar argument, which grounds the notion of causality in the experience of bodily force and effort, can be found in Jonas, *The Phenomenon of Life*, 22 ff.

2. For a detailed account of this distinction in Husserl's work, see Didier Franck's book *Flesh and Body: On the Phenomenology of Husserl*. If this claim is correct, it follows that the phenomenology of life in Henry and Ricoeur does not only surpass Husserl through a defense of passivity; it also goes beyond his analyses of the active dimension of the lived body.

3. Henry, "Un parcours philosophique," 61.

4. Henry, in a brief preface to the second edition in 1987, says retrospectively that his purpose at the time was "to establish against Idealism the concrete character of subjectivity and to do so by showing that it is identical with our own body [corps propre]" (Henry, *Philosophie et Phénoménologie du Corps*, v). As noted earlier, Ricoeur served as a member of Henry's dissertation committee and thus would have been familiar with this work, which was submitted along with *The Essence of Manifestation*.

5. Henry, *Philosophie et Phénoménologie du Corps*, 12. Additionally, it is worth recalling that in *Oneself as Another* Ricoeur praises Michel Henry's work as one of "the three great philosophies of one's own body [le corps propre]" (*Oneself as Another*, 322). The other two great philosophers of the body are Maurice Merleau-Ponty and Gabriel Marcel.

6. Henry, *Philosophie et Phénoménologie du Corps*, vi. Note that this brief "Avertissement à la Seconde Édition" is not included in the English translation of the book, which was published prior to the second edition.

7. See Henry, *Philosophie et Phénoménologie du Corps*, vi. For a more detailed study of this orientation in Henry's thought, see Jean, "Habitude, effort et résistance," 455–77.

8. See Ricoeur, *Oneself as Another*, 322.

9. Much more could be said about the mutual debt that Ricoeur and Henry owe to Jean Nabert, but that would be yet another story. For an expression of Henry's admiration of Nabert, see his note in *The Genealogy of Psychoanalysis*, 339, note 8. In addition to dedicating *Fallible Man* to Nabert, Ricoeur also wrote several important essays on his work that are surveyed in my essay "Jean Nabert: A Hidden Source of French Phenomenology."

10. Ricoeur's thesis has recently been published in France under the title *Méthode réflexive appliqué au problème de Dieu chez Lachelier et Lagneau*. It bears noting that Lagneau's reading of Maine de Biran is also treated extensively but critically in chapter 2 of Henry's *Philosophy and Phenomenology of the Body* and in §55 of *The Essence of Manifestation*.

11. For addition context about these influences, see the essays included in *A Companion to Ricoeur's* Freedom and Nature.

12. Nabert's influence on that period of Ricoeur's thought cannot be underestimated, even though it cannot be detailed here. In his *Intellectual Autobiography*, Ricoeur writes, "On the one hand, this tradition [of French reflexive philosophy] led back, through E. Boutroux and F. Ravaisson, to Maine de Biran; on the other hand, it tended toward Jean Nabert who, in 1924, had published L'expérience intérieure de la liberté.... Jean Nabert was to have a decisive influence on me in the 1950s and 1960s" (Hahn, ed., *The Philosophy of Paul Ricoeur*, 6).

13. Ricoeur, *From Text to Action*, II, 12 (trans. mod.).

14. The continued influence of reflexive philosophy is evident, for example, in the "Epilogue" of *Memory, History, Forgetting* (2002). In thinking about the difficulty of forgiveness, Ricoeur embraces the role of reflection and draws from Nabert's analysis of the fault and evil. See Ricoeur, *Memory, History, Forgetting*, 459–66.

15. Republished as "La Philosophie réflexive," in Jean Nabert, *L'expérience intérieure de la liberté et autres essais de philosophie morale*, 397–411. It is worth noting that Nabert's encyclopedia entry identifies Ricoeur's philosophy of the will as a joining of the phenomenological method with the reflexive method.

16. Nabert, "La Philosophie réflexive," 404.

17. Nabert, "La Philosophie réflexive," 406–07.

18. As Lagneau puts it, reflexive philosophy thus seeks "to rediscover thought even in the very least object." Cited by Ricoeur in his preface to Nabert, *L'experience interieure de la liberte et autres essais*, x.

19. In this way, they are precursors to recent developments in the field of embodied cognition that emerges with Varela, Thompson, and Rosch's book *Embodied Mind*.

20. Henry, "Un parcours philosophique," 161.

21. Indeed, Jean-Luc Marion says that Maine de Biran is Descartes's only successor with respect to the cogito. See Marion, "Descartes et la question de la technique," 285–301.

22. Henry, *The Philosophy and Phenomenology of the Body*, 5–6. In his preface to the English translation of this book, Henry explains that his study of Maine de Biran will provide "an application of the general theses—for which we argued in *The Essence of Manifestation*—to the problem of the body" (Henry, *The Philosophy and Phenomenology of the Body*, ix). It is worth noting that this linkage between the works remains

implicit to the extent that Maine de Biran is mentioned only once in *The Essence of Manifestation*, though the title of §35 is "The Coherence of the Internal Structure of Effort"—an obvious reference to Biran.

23. See, for example, Henry, *Incarnation*.

24. Henry, *The Philosophy and Phenomenology of the Body*, 8.

25. Henry, *The Philosophy and Phenomenology of the Body*, 8.

26. For an application of this thesis to the psychoanalytic context, see the recent work by Emmanuel Falque, *Ça n'a rien à voir: Lire Freud en philosophe*.

27. Henry glosses this type of reflection as the foundation for a transcendental phenomenology, seeing it as a shift from external perception to a transcendental self-experience.

28. Biran, *Essai sur les fondements de la psychologie*, 73.

29. Biran, *Essai sur les fondements de la psychologie*, 9.

30. Henry, *The Philosophy and Phenomenology of the Body*, 55. In support of this point, see Henry's observation that "the philosophy of Maine de Biran is not a philosophy of action in opposition to a philosophy of contemplation or of thought; it is an ontological theory of action and its originality, its depth ... consists in the affirmation that the being of this movement, of this action and of this power is precisely that of a cogito" (*The Philosophy and Phenomenology of the Body*, 54).

31. Biran, *Essai sur les fondements de la psychologie*, 3. Note that the Latin term *compos sui* (literally "self-control") also has a legal connotation. *Black's Law Dictionary* defines it as "having the use of one's limbs, or the power of bodily motion," and it serves as one ingredient in the determination of causal and legal responsibility.

32. Biran, *Essai sur les fondements de la psychologie*, 10.

33. It is not a coincidence that this dilemma reiterates the question posed to Henry's account of auto-affection in the previous chapter, where the question was raised as to whether auto-affection has a single or a double origin.

34. Biran, *Essai sur les fondements de la psychologie*, 575.

35. Biran, *Essai sur les fondements de la psychologie*, 220.

36. After discussing this passage, Renaud Barbaras challenges the conclusion drawn by Henry. He argues that Henry goes too far in saying that it implies a radical interiority. "All we can say is that the being of power is indeed availability ... and that in this sense it cannot be foreign to itself" (Barbaras, *The Affect of Thought*, 46).

37. These three theses are expressed in Henry's *Philosophy and Phenomenology of the Body*, 59–61. I draw these three propositions from the careful analysis of Devarieux, *L'intériorité réciproque*, 109.

38. But, in advocating that passivity should play a greater role in Biran's analysis, Henry is proposing an unorthodox interpretation of Biran. In fact, as Grégori Jean explains, Henry's criticism is a complete reversal of the standard critique put forward by Biran's successors in the reflexive tradition. The traditional critique argues that

Biran's analysis lacks an adequate ontology to deal with the active dimension of the subject and that this leads him to overlook the fact that there is subjective activity to be found even in the greatest degree of passivity. See this criticism, for example, in Ravaisson's book *On Habit*.

39. Henry, *The Philosophy and Phenomenology of the Body*, 159.

40. Henry, *The Philosophy and Phenomenology of the Body*, 155.

41. Henry, *The Philosophy and Phenomenology of the Body*, 156f.

42. This mixed psychology resembles the mixed discourse of the will that Ricoeur will introduce later in this chapter, but Henry construes it as a failure of the analysis to provide an ontological theory of passivity (Henry, *The Philosophy and Phenomenology of the Body*, 159). In this way, his critique of Biran also identifies a difference between Henry and Ricoeur over what it means to interpret the human being as a "homo duplex in humanitate."

43. Henry, *The Philosophy and Phenomenology of the Body*, 163 (Henry's italics). Whether Biran actually commits this oversight is debatable and would require a lengthy textual discussion. For one among many possible counterexamples, consider the following passage: "Observe that the cause that is the motor will and the effect that is the muscular sensation, or that of the movement itself produced in the body, are two homogenous elements of the same fact of consciousness, which are thus known, felt or perceived only in their relation of intimate connection" (Biran, XI-2, Appendice VIII, 285). This topic is examined in considerable detail in Anne Devarieux's book on Henry and Biran.

44. Pierre Maine de Biran, *The Influence of Habit on the Faculty of Thinking*, 56; cited by Derrida, *On Touching*, 150.

45. Henry, however, directly rejects this type of interpretation, stating that "the traditional interpretation of the Biranian opposition between the ego and the non-ego as being between effort and the real which resists it is unacceptable" (*The Philosophy and Phenomenology of the Body*, 37). His point is that the being of effort can be separated from this resistance of the external world and that its reality can be thought on its own without the opposition to the world.

46. And by extension, this argument could also apply to the two modes of appearing. If Derrida is right, this would undermine Henry's foundational claim that the transcendent mode of appearing is dependent on the immanent mode of appearing. To the contrary, it shows that the immanent mode of appearing depends on the transcendent mode of appearing. For this reason, it poses a deep challenge to the edifice of Henry's phenomenology of life.

47. In this respect, my reading of Ricoeur's relation to Biran will depart from the one recently developed by Eftichis Pirovolakis, who suggests that Ricoeur falls prey to Derrida's critique by offering a one-sided reading of Biran. Pirovolakis, in my view, doesn't see that Ricoeur is leveling a deeper critique that rejects the primacy of the

primitive fact as such. See his chapter "Volo ergo sum" in *A Companion to Freedom and Nature*.

48. Ricoeur, *Freedom and Nature*, 331–37.
49. Ricoeur, *Freedom and Nature*, 326.
50. Ricoeur, *Freedom and Nature*, 331.
51. Ricoeur, *Freedom and Nature*, 204–05.
52. Ricoeur, *Freedom and Nature*, 331.
53. Ricoeur, *Freedom and Nature*, 334.
54. Ricoeur, *Freedom and Nature*, 331; orig. italics.
55. Ricoeur, *Freedom and Nature*, 308.
56. Ricoeur, *Freedom and Nature*, 309.
57. Ricoeur, *Freedom and Nature*, 214.
58. Ricoeur, *Freedom and Nature*, 309. Of course, the notion of a docile body has come to be associated with Foucault's work in more recent times, and for Foucault it is inscribed within a social setting that seeks to produce a certain type of embodiment. And in response to the production of docile bodies, Foucault also makes interesting suggestions about the meaning of resistance within such social contexts. To be clear, this is not what Ricoeur is talking about. Yet, one interesting avenue would be to examine Ricoeur's account of the docile body as an ontological account of the body, which may undergird Foucault's account that operates on the social level.
59. Ricoeur, *Freedom and Nature*, 309.
60. Ricoeur, *Freedom and Nature*, 215.
61. Ricoeur, *Freedom and Nature*, 310.
62. Ricoeur, *Freedom and Nature*, 214.
63. Ricoeur, *Freedom and Nature*, 55.
64. It is worth noting that the notion of imputation is brought up again much later in Ricoeur's analyses of language and action in *Oneself as Another*.
65. Interestingly, research suggests that outcomes of actions play an important role in determining the extent to which we feel responsible for our actions. The more positive the outcome, the stronger is our feeling of the voluntary. Conversely, the more negative the outcome, the weaker our feeling of voluntariness.
66. As a sidenote, I would like to point out that the notion of imputation is brought into play later in Ricoeur's *Oneself as Another*. There, it is described as one of the four ways of inquiring into the being of the self: "Who is the moral subject of imputation?" (*Oneself as Another*, 16). And Ricoeur's treatment there is again based on the contrast between judgments made of an action and those that are made of a self. Imputability, Ricoeur says, "is the ascription of an action to its agent." Another person can ascribe an action to me and say, "It is you who," but I can also ascribe an action to myself in saying "it is I who." There again he will identify the limitations of

standard accounts by saying that they are only backward-looking and thus that they miss the forward-looking aspect of action.

67. Ricoeur, *Freedom and Nature*, 59.

68. Ricoeur, "The Unity of the Voluntary and the Involuntary," 5. Interestingly, the topic of the reflexive verb returns on the first page of Ricoeur's analyses in *Oneself as Another*, in the context of a discussion that connects the self [*soi*] to its use as a personal pronoun. This is set in contrast with the pronominal *se*, which designates the reflexive character of the personal pronouns. Interestingly, Ricoeur mentions the very same reflexive formulation as in *Freedom and Nature*: "*se decider soi-meme*" [loosely, "making up one's own mind"]. Ricoeur refers to "*se decider soi-meme*" as the "canonical form" of reflexivity. But it is also possible in language to nominalize *se* and convert it into the expression *decision de soi* [choosing oneself]. There is no problem with this linguistic shift as long as we recall that the nominalization of the *soi* was derived from the reflexive verb *se*. While Ricoeur doesn't directly pursue this analysis in further detail, it seems to me as if his previous analysis in *Freedom and Nature* is implied here—namely, the claim that the pre-reflexive relation to the self (in the active form)—its immanence—is prior to the objectification of the self as an object—its transcendence.

69. Ricoeur, *Freedom and Nature*, 60, tr. mod; cf. "The Unity of the Voluntary and the Involuntary," 5. This irreducibility of the reflexive relation to the self is actually captured best, I think, by Levinas's formulation that "*on n'est pas; on s'est*." For him, the fact that one is always riveted to oneself and that one cannot get rid of oneself gives rise to the pathos of being trapped.

70. Ricoeur, *Freedom and Nature*, 61.

71. In support of this connection with the docile body, one might find a similar point expressed by Henry in the following passage: "Such a sweetness where being comes to it without effort, is experienced in the passivity of suffering, in feeling, and enters everything that is. Consider the feeling of effort. What is given to it is the inner tension of existence that confronts the opposed-being and in this confrontation gives itself. It is effort but in the way in which effort is given to itself, in the feeling of effort, there is no effort. The being of effort, realizing itself in feeling, is its original passivity with regard to oneself, it being-given-to-oneself in suffering as suffering oneself, is its sweetness" (*Essence de la Manifestation*, 595; my translation).

72. Henry, *Essence de la Manifestation*, 595; my translation.

73. Henry considers that phrase to be one of the most laden with meaning that has been delivered by the philosophical tradition. See Henry, "Does the Concept 'Soul' Mean Anything?," 94–114.

74. We will return to this account of the subjective body when we turn to Henry's discussion of Marx. This account is extended to a theory of human action there. Living activity, or what Marx calls praxis, includes not only the objective measure of the work done but also the subjective effort that is put into it.

75. See, for example, the following passage: "Entering into possession of these powers, the ego is able to exercise them. A new capacity is conferred on it, no less extraordinary that that of being a self, even though it is a simple consequence of it. It is my capacity to be in possession of myself, to be one with it and with all that it carries within it, and they belong to it like the multiple components of its real being. Among these components there are the powers of the body, for example" (Henry, *I Am The Truth*, 136; translation modified).

76. In this regard, consider the reference to what precedes effort in the following passage: "But the movement by which life relentlessly comes into oneself . . . is not willed. It does not result from any effort, instead it precedes effort and makes it possible. It is total and radically passive being with oneself in which Being is given to itself in order to be what it is in conservation and growth—in order, eventually, to make an effort and act on this prior and pregiven Ground which is always presupposed" (Henry, *Barbarism*, 98).

77. Consider the following passage about the affective dimension of all power: "Here we are presented with a decisive connection between Affectivity and Power. If there is no power except that which is given to itself in Life's pathos-filled self-givenness, then every power is affective, not as the effect of circumstances that would be foreign to its own essence, but because it resides in this pathos-filled auto-affection that, by installing it in itself, gives it the ability to exert itself—to be the power that it is. Thus, the prior power of a transcendental Affectivity reigns in every power of our body" (Henry, *Incarnation*, 142).

78. See, for example, the essay "Phénoménologie et Psychanalyse," in *Phénoménologie de la vie*, vol. III.

79. Reagan and Stewart, *The Philosophy of Paul Ricoeur*, 61.

80. Ricoeur, *Méthode réflexive appliqué au problème de Dieu chez Lachelier et Lagneau*, 225.

81. Ricoeur, Méthode réflexive appliqué au problème de Dieu chez Lachelier et Lagneau, 31.

## 4. Desire

1. Ricoeur, *Freud and Philosophy*, 465

2. In addition to their published exchanges, there are several personal letters that Henry sent to Ricoeur between 1964 and 1984. These letters were kept on file by Ricoeur and attest to Henry's respect for Ricoeur's 1965 book. They have been published in *Revue Internationale Michel Henry* 1 (2011): 15–20. The first letter (March 19, 1964) was written in response to Henry's thesis defense, and Henry attests that "our conversations have been for me the opportunity for a true encounter" although they don't reveal much about the substance of their exchanges. Several more letters were sent between 1983 and 1984 while Henry was in the process of writing his book,

*The Genealogy of Psychoanalysis.* A February 23, 1983 letter relays that "I am planning in Easter to write a chapter on the unconscious and it is your admirable analysis of Freud's great essay on the unconscious that guides my own reflection" (16). Later the same year on June 19, Henry again expresses his "gratitude for the admirable commentary that [Ricoeur] offered of the 1915 article on the unconscious, a commentary that is at the heart of his own meditation" (17). Lastly, in a letter dated January 1, 1984, Henry writes that "he just completed . . . the revisions of his manuscript on the genesis of the unconscious in Western thought, where he expressed his intellectual gratitude [to Ricoeur] for his work and notably for his work on Freud whose lucidity helped him so much" (18).

3. Ricoeur's own interest in psychoanalysis, however, does not begin or end with that book. His initial interest was sparked by Roland Dalbiez, one of his high school teachers in Rennes. Dalbiez was the first French philosopher to publish a book on psychoanalysis, and his two-volume project on Freud turned out to be quite well-informed and influential. In fact, Henry also describes this project as "the first great French work on Freud" (*Genealogy of Psychoanalysis*, 290–92). Dalbiez's influence is most evident in Ricoeur's brief treatment of the unconscious in *Freedom and Nature*, where Ricoeur takes aim at certain aspects of Dalbiez's realist interpretation of Freud. Ricoeur also continued to write articles on psychoanalysis after *Freud and Philosophy*, many of which have been published recently in the collection *On Psychoanalysis*. These later writings are characterized by a decreased influence of the energetic model and an increased emphasis on the work of interpretation. For a historical account of the full trajectory of Ricoeur's engagement with psychoanalysis, see Vinicio Busacchi, "Postface: Desire, Identity, the Other," in *On Psychoanalysis*.

4. Ricoeur, *Conflict of Interpretations*, 99.

5. Ricoeur, *Freud and Philosophy*, 46. For more details concerning this dynamic, see the "Introduction" to Hermeneutics and Phenomenology in *Paul Ricoeur: Between Text and Phenomenon*.

6. Henry, "Ricoeur and Freud: Between Psychoanalysis and Phenomenology," in *The Michel Henry Reader*. Henry originally presented this essay at a colloquium on Ricoeur in September 1988 at Cerisy-la-Salle.

7. The primary reference to Ricoeur in *The Genealogy of Psychoanalysis* is an extended footnote on page 349 of the text. So, it is easy to see why a reader, unaware of the broader context of the Henry-Ricoeur debate over psychoanalysis, would underestimate the extent of Ricoeur's influence on Henry.

8. Arguably, Henry's reading runs into difficulty due to a faulty conception of translation. Henry uses the notion of translation to mean that there is a transparent and complete transfer from one discourse to the other. But, as Ricoeur emphasizes in his later writings, although translation is possible, it is never perfect or complete. See Ricoeur's book *On Translation*.

9. To clarify a potential source of confusion, a quick note on the translation of the Freudian term *Trieb*. This term was originally translated as *instinct* in English and appears as such in the Standard Works. However, because Freud uses the German term *Instinkt* in a different sense, French interpreters opt for the term *pulsion*, which is an English equivalent to the term *drive*.

10. This is, of course, a simplification of a much more complex and interesting dynamic concerning the deployment and resistance of desire. For a rich and detailed account of the intellectual history leading to the Freudian view, see Rudolf Bernet's recent book *Force, Drive, Desire: A Philosophy of Psychoanalysis*.

11. Henry's frequent term for this is "hyper-organique," which is borrowed from Biran but doesn't find any easy equivalent in English. To convey the sense of something above or beyond nature, I opt here for the Latin term *supra* in place of the Greek *hyper* and *natural* in place of the term *organique*, though I think the term *non-natural* would also suffice.

12. For a recent assessment that is mostly positive and provides a helpful overview of Ricoeur's argument in *Freud and Philosophy*, see Richard J. Bernstein, "Ricoeur's Freud," *Etudes Ricoeuriennes/Ricoeur Studies* 4, no. 1 (2013): 130–39.

13. Henry, "Ricoeur and Freud," 129; cf. Ricoeur, *Freud and Philosophy*, 386.

14. It is worth noting that, long before Henry, Ricoeur himself identifies the limits of the Husserlian conception of consciousness, observing that it "can make room for the unconscious only by way of the theme of 'passive genesis'" and that it "remains 'capable of becoming conscious'" (*Conflict of Interpretations*, 102).

15. Henry, "Ricoeur and Freud," 133; cf. Ricoeur, *Freud and Philosophy*, 392.

16. Henry, "Ricoeur and Freud," 132.

17. Ricoeur, *Freud and Philosophy*, 69.

18. Ricoeur, *Freud and Philosophy*, 429.

19. Henry, "Ricoeur and Freud," 134–35.

20. Henry, "Ricoeur and Freud," 135; Henry's italics.

21. Henry, "Ricoeur and Freud," 136.

22. Henry, "Préface à la traduction italienne de la Généalogie de la psychanalyse," in *Phénoménologie de la vie*, vol. 5, 99.

23. Henry, "Phénoménologie et psychanalyse," in *Phénoménologie de la vie*, vol. 5, 61.

24. Henry, *The Genealogy of Psychoanalysis*, 285f.

25. This distinction is developed most fully by Henry in his article "Phénoménologie et psychanalyse." It should be noted that the same task is taken up by Ricoeur's article "Consciousness and the Unconscious," which observes that "the question of consciousness is just as obscure as that of the unconscious" (*The Conflict of Interpretations*, 99).

26. Henry, *The Genealogy of Psychoanalysis*, 286.

27. Henry, *The Genealogy of Psychoanalysis*, 286. But Henry's accusation can be answered by a similar realization in Ricoeur that "representation obeys not only a law of intentionality, which makes it the expression of some object, but also another law, which makes it the manifestation of life, of an effort or desire" (*Freud and Philosophy*, 457).

28. Henry, *The Genealogy of Psychoanalysis*, 318.

29. Just registering an interesting point of contention here over the status of Freud's energetics. Ricoeur, on the one hand, follows Freud in conceiving the energetics in naturalistic terms. Drives, forces, and energies are rooted in our biological life, and as such, their reality does not admit a phenomenological description or meaning. For Henry, on the other hand, to relegate psychic energies and forces to the natural sciences would be to miss their phenomenological reality. Henry's material phenomenology thus provides a non-naturalistic reinterpretation of Freud's energetics in which the drives, instincts, and energies of the unconscious are anchored in the auto-affective dimension of life. It thus foreshadows a debate later in this chapter over the organic and hyperorganic interpretations of desire.

30. Henry, "Ricoeur and Freud," 139.

31. Perhaps it is worth noting that Freud, in contrast, states the opposite: that "psychoanalytic work shows us every day that translation of this kind is possible" (*Standard Edition*, vol. 14, 166).

32. Henry, *The Genealogy of Psychoanalysis*, 286.

33. Henry, *The Genealogy of Psychoanalysis*, 316.

34. Ricoeur, *Freedom and Nature*, 405.

35. In this sense, Ricoeur's early discussion of the unconscious closely resembles Henry's own reading of Freud in *The Genealogy of Psychoanalysis*.

36. Ricoeur, *Freedom and Nature*, 399.

37. Ricoeur, *Freud and Philosophy*, 66.

38. Ricoeur, *Freud and Philosophy*, 438.

39. It should be noted that Ricoeur already perceived this aspect of the unconscious in *Freedom and Nature*: "In its unconscious aspect, subjectivity is like a physical nature. It imitates the object. It lends itself to the schemata of conflicts, compromises, products of forces, or as they psychoanalysts put it, of 'drives.' But 'force' in the language of subjectivity is, as we know, the thrust of a need or sovereignty of effort" (398).

40. Ricoeur, *Freud and Philosophy*, 454. On this topic, also see Ricoeur's insightful observation that "the unconscious indicates within me that not only my 'body' but also my psychic functioning lend themselves to objective treatment: there is an object-psyche as there is an object-body" (*Freedom and Nature*, 398).

41. Ricoeur, *Freud and Philosophy*, 439.

42. This point is expressed especially clearly in Ricoeur's essay "Psychoanalysis and Hermeneutics," which was first published in Japanese as "Seishinbunseki to Kaishakugaku" in *Shiso* (1978) and is included in the book *On Psychoanalysis*. The theory

has to "represent the psyche as at once a text to be interpreted and a system of forces to be manipulated" ("Psychoanalysis and Hermeneutics," 68). On this point, he notes that Freud himself uses textual metaphors (translation, substitution, overdetermination, etc.) along with energy metaphors (condensation, displacement, repression) (Ibid.). This indicates not only that Freud has a mixed epistemology of desire but that he uses a mixed discourse consisting of motives and causes.

43. The conflict between Lacan and Ricoeur over the interpretation of this statement is carried out in considerable detail by Karl Simms, *Ricoeur and Lacan* (London: Continuum, 2007).

44. Ricoeur, *Freud and Philosophy*, 400.

45. Ricoeur, *Freud and Philosophy*, 402.

46. Ricoeur, *Freud and Philosophy*, 403.

47. The theory of drives is central insofar as the drives stand at the threshold or intersection between the organic realm of forces and the conscious realm of meaning.

48. These two laws of desire are not developed in a detailed and systematic manner in Henry's work, but they find their clearest expression in Barbarism on pages 97–98. Additional clarification of these points might also be discerned in his essays on Schopenhauer.

49. Spinoza, *Ethics*, Book III, Prop. 6. Analogous to the principle of inertia in physics, the conatus is a principle of perseverance in living bodies. For Spinoza, to be a living being is to strive to persevere in being. Henry, of course, wrote his master's thesis on Spinoza, and Ricoeur often invokes the conatus in connection with his discussion of the self as a source of the power to act. See, for example, *Fallible Man* 137–41; *Freud and Philosophy*, 46–47, 454–56; *Oneself as Another*, 315–17; *Memory, History, Forgetting*, 357.

50. Henry, *Barbarism*, 97.

51. Henry, *Barbarism*, 100.

52. Henry, *Barbarism*, 101.

53. This desire for growth and the intensification of life creates a surplus of psychic energy within the self that can be discharged in acts of creation as well as destruction. Cultural products, as Henry understands them, are the expressions of this self-growth of life. But these energies can also be destructive when they turn against oneself and against life itself. This is evident in the death drive and its various manifestations in a culture of death, which are described in detail by Henry's book *Barbarism*. To overcome these destructive and self-destructive tendencies, Henry prescribes a change of life that redirects psychic energies toward creative pursuits that embrace life instead of fleeing it and seek to intensify it instead of diminishing it.

54. For some remarks on a vital teleology, see Henry, *Barbarism*, 52–53; *From Communism to Capitalism*, 79, 85, and 90.

55. "Henry, "Souffrance et vie," 149. To elaborate, life is the passion of undergoing life—it expresses the powerlessness of each individual in relation to life, the inability to give oneself life or to be someone other than oneself. Henry clarifies that "suffering is not initially a particular content of the life of the individual. It is the very fact of living, inasmuch as living is to going through, undergoing, and suffering what one is. Suffering is only the actualization of this 'suffering' that constitutes the essence of life" (*From Communism to Capitalism*, 49).

56. Henry writes, "Selon la téléologie immanente de la vie, le besoin s'assouvit dans l'activité en laquelle il se change spontanément. Tel est le movement de la vie, son auto-mouvement, selon la séquence subjective élémentaire: Souffrance-Effort-Jouissance. Depuis l'origine immemoriale de l'humanité, cette séquence élémentaire—dite objectivement: besoin-travail- consummation—s'invéstit dans la production matérielle, c'est à dire subjective, des biens indispensables, dans le 'procès réel de production'" ("Sur la crise du marxisme," 144).

57. Henry, *From Communism to Capitalism*, 25.

58. Much more could be said about this point, but in the following passage Henry makes clear that the affective weight of life is what gives rise to the force of action: "The internal connection of Force and Affectivity is not only due to the fact that, as the auto-affection of force, Affectivity forms the proper essence of every force. Because, in its auto-affection, the affect is radically passive with regard to itself and thus is laden with its own being even up to the unbearability of this weight, it seeks to discharge itself. It is thus the movement itself of the drive, which Freud rightly designates as the endogenous excitation that never ceases. In other words, it is auto-affection as constitutive of the essence of absolute subjectivity and of life" ("Ricoeur and Freud," 139).

59. Henry, *Genealogy of Psychoanalysis*, 316.

60. For the sake of focus, I have bracketed Henry's extended discussion of transference, though it is clear that Henry rightly locates the psychoanalytic cure in that process. Apart from the *Genealogy of Psychoanalysis*, Henry offers very lucid remarks on transference in *Material Phenomenology*, 129.

61. Ricoeur, *Freud and Philosophy*, 459.

62. Ricoeur, *Freud and Philosophy*, 460.

63. Ricoeur, *Freud and Philosophy*, 440.

64. Ricoeur, *Freud and Philosophy*, 452.

65. Ricoeur, *Freud and Philosophy*, 469.

66. Ricoeur, *Freud and Philosophy*, 472.

67. It is perhaps worth noting, as an aside, that Ricoeur does not emphasize only the influence of culture over desire. Elsewhere, in *Fallible Man*, Ricoeur describes the "mixed texture" of affectivity, in which affective life sometimes fights on the side of reason and sometimes takes the side of desire. Affective life thus requires a mixed

discourse that can describe both the vital affections and the rational affections. For more detail, see the chapter "Affective Fragility" in *Fallible Man*.

68. Emmanuel Falque, "Is There a Flesh without Body?," 139–66.
69. Ricoeur, *Freedom and Nature*, 85.
70. Ricoeur, *Freud and Philosophy*, 90, 93.
71. Henry poses this question in an extended footnote about the role of "representatives" in Ricoeur's reading of Freud. See *Genealogy of Psychoanalysis*, 349, note 62.
72. In *Freud and Philosophy*, Ricoeur also touches on this link in his own terminology. He observes that "effort and desire are the two sides of this positing of the first truth: I am" (*Freud and Philosophy*, 46). Effort and desire are then linked more clearly in Ricoeur's subsequent proposition that "reflection is the appropriation of our effort to exist and of our desire to be through the works which bear witness to that effort and desire" (Ibid.).

## 5. Praxis

1. While Ricoeur famously identifies Marx as one of the masters of suspicion, along with Freud and Nietzsche, who issues a challenge to the self-transparency and self-mastery of the ego, this label already points to a discrepancy between the two thinkers. Interestingly enough, Henry finds it an apt description for only part of Freud's work and not at all for Marx or Nietzsche. For him, the latter two are not guided by suspicion; they are thinkers who affirm the certitude of life.
2. Discussions of Henry's book *Marx: A Philosophy of Human Reality* must be treated with caution because there is a large discrepancy between the content of the French original and that of the English translation. Much gets lost in translation because the work was largely rewritten and condensed by Henry from two volumes to one for the English translation, as Tom Rockmore explains in his foreword. In addition to Henry's two-volume book *Marx*, a few other articles by Henry have been collected recently in a thin volume, *Marx: An Introduction*.
3. Originally published as "Le Marx de Michel Henry," *Esprit* (1978): 124–39; reprinted in *Lectures 2: La contrée des philosophes*, 265–93.
4. But it is important to insert the caveat that Ricoeur's engagement with Marx is not restricted to that period. As Johann Michel has documented, the young Ricoeur contributed essays regularly to French socialist journals. See Michel, *Ricoeur and the Post-structuralists*.
5. While this timeline might not make perfect sense on paper, Ricoeur directly states that he had "recently read" Henry's book in these 1975 lectures. See Ricoeur, *Lectures on Ideology and Utopia*, 101–02.
6. It is worth noting that, as an acknowledgement of its significance, Ricoeur also devoted part of an issue of *La Revue de la métaphysique et de la morale* to a set of critical responses to Henry's book as well.

7. This article, including responses by Mikel Dufrenne, R. P. Dubarle, and Paul Ricoeur, is published in Henry, *Phénoménologie de la vie*, vol. III, 77–104.

8. But shouldn't he have referred to Henry's book on Biran instead? That much is conceded, as we noted in chapter 3, in Henry's introduction to the second edition of *The Philosophy and Phenomenology of the Body*.

9. For Ricoeur's remark, see Henry, "La Rationalité selon Marx," 101.

10. It is surprising, though, that Henry acquiesces to Ricoeur's criticisms in their discussion. For it seems that a response is already prepared in his book, which acknowledged precisely that the origin of ideology is most often designated by the pair "the individual and conditions" in *The German Ideology*. Henry notes, however, that these conditions are nothing else than the determinations of individual life. Because individuals define these conditions and determine them, it follows that there is "a single origin, a single creative principle [*naturans*] that produces the conditions of production, classes, and ideas" (*Marx*, 171). This creative principle is what makes ideology possible. It is life that constitutes the ground of the representations of consciousness, the origin of their content, while as representations they are only modalities of consciousness itself.

11. In a letter dated June 14, 1984, Henry responds to a previous letter that Ricoeur had sent concerning his study of Marx. There, Henry refers to a "pertinent but difficult" question that Ricoeur had posed about something that Henry admits to not covering. He concedes that the aim of socialism, for Marx, is indeed the "development in living subjectivity of its own teleology." Perhaps this is related to this particular question and answer exchange. But it is difficult to determine the precise significance of this claim due to the fact that the initial question is unknown. Henry, "Lettre de Michel Henry (June 14, 1984)," 20.

12. Grégori Jean and Jean Leclercq have sided with Henry on this debate and have argued that Ricoeur's criticism completely misses the point. See their argument in Grégori Jean and Jean Leclercq, "Sur la situation phénoménologique du Marx de Michel Henry," 1–18.

13. This debate, accordingly, reiterates the divergence that surfaced earlier with regard to the interpretation of Maine de Biran. In fact, in an unpublished note Henry writes "that this book on Marx is one application of the program sketched out in *Philosophy and Phenomenology of the Body*" (Ms A 17708). Cited by Roberto Formisano, "Vie et représentation," 195.

14. In *Sens et Existence: En Hommage à Paul Ricoeur*, 138–51.

15. These reprinted parts of the text appear in volume 1 of Henry's *Marx*, "Une Philosophie de la réalité," 384 ff.

16. In *The Ego and Its Own*, Stirner argues for an unbridled egoism and is one of the prime targets of Marx in *The German Ideology*, which lampoons Stirner as a "petty bourgeois individualist intellectual."

17. Henry, *Marx*, 164.
18. Henry, *Marx*, 160.
19. Henry, *Marx*, 163.
20. Henry, *Marx*, 167.
21. Interestingly, this aspect of the debate between Henry and Ricoeur anticipates the more recent debate between Honneth and Fraser in Redist*ribution or Recognition? A Political-Philosophical Exchange*.
22. Marx, *German Ideology*.
23. Henry, *Marx*, 167.
24. Henry, *Marx*, 306.
25. Henry, *Marx*, 15. One example of Henry's equation between his understanding of life and Marx's understanding of praxis is the following passage: "Life is a dimension of radical immanence in virtue of which it experiences itself without ever separating from itself and it as such, by experiencing itself and not ceasing to do so, that it is life. This original dimension of being as exclusive of all distantiation and all difference, as life, is what Marx calls 'praxis'" (*Socialisme selon Marx*, 51).
26. See Ricoeur, "L'originaire et la question-en-retour dans la *Krisis* de Husserl," 167–77.
27. For this connection, I am indebted to Roberto Formisano's excellent article "Vie et representation: Henry et Ricoeur sur le problem de la praxis," in Hardy, Leclercq, and Sautereau, *Paul Ricoeur et Michel Henry*, 195–206.
28. Explaining the motivations for this essay, Ricoeur first credits Levinas for launching Husserlian studies in France and then curiously shifts to a second influence. He mentions obliquely that he was "invited elsewhere to interpret the style of reduction of ideologies to praxis in Marx's German Ideology" and that he then recalled Derrida's *Origin of Geometry*, which highlighted the method of "questioning back" [*Rückfrage*]. This led him to think about whether Marx and Husserl shared this method of reduction in common (see Ricoeur, "L'originaire et la question-en-retour dans la Krisis de Husserl, 361–62). I take it that the "other invitation" is a reference to his invitation to respond to Henry's book on Marx.
29. Henry, *Marx*, 16.
30. Henry, *Phénoménologie de la vie*, vol. 3, 104.
31. Ricoeur, "Le Marx de Michel Henry," 268.
32. Henry, *Marx*, 1.
33. Henry, *Marx*, 14.
34. Henry, *Marx*, 145.
35. Henry, *Marx*, 168.
36. Henry, "On the Crisis of Marxism: Two Faces of Death," 125.
37. Henry, *Marx*, 91.
38. Adler, "Neither Consciousness, nor Matter, but Living Bodily Activity," 158.

39. Henry, *Marx*, 160.

40. It's worth noting another possible account of alienation that Henry could have developed through the concept of labor power. What does *labor power* mean? It means the potential to produce. Potential as aptitude, capacity, dunamis, does not refer to any actual or specific kind of labor; instead, it refers to the aggregate of the capabilities of the living individual. This potential is what the capitalist buys. To the extent that the potential of labor power exists in the living body, it follows that capitalism seizes the subjective labor power of the individual. But it attempts to seize hold of that which it does not possess: the life of the living individual. For the development of this reading of alienation, see Virno, "An Equivocal Concept," 269–73.

41. In response to Henry's claim that all wage labor is alienating by definition, one might wonder whether it might be possible to conceive of and engage in non-alienating forms of wage labor. In a recent essay, I explore this question in the context of affective labor: "Affective Labor and the Henry-Ricoeur Debate over Marx," 27–44.

42. Henry, *Marx*, 142.

43. Ricoeur, "Le Marx de Michel Henry," 274.

44. Henry, *Marx*, 171.

45. Ricoeur, "Le Marx de Michel Henry," 274.

46. Henry, *Phénoménologie de la vie*, vol. 3, 101.

47. Henry's response to this objection, in the dialogue that ensues, is that he does not deny the role of life circumstances. Instead, he asserts that Marx shows that both the living individual and the circumstances of life are the product of life. Life produces both the subjective determination of praxis and the social circumstances in which the individual acts.

48. Henry, *Marx*, 160.

49. This view is echoed by many of Henry's critics. Bohman, for example, puts forward the following objection: "it is truly difficult to imagine any adequate description of ordinary and concrete acts of living (such as speaking, making something, even eating) that is not in some way 'objective,' mediated in a thousand ways with objectivity and sociality so as to make it 'impure'" (Bohman, "A New Phenomenological Marxism," 166–67).

50. Ricoeur, "Le Marx de Michel Henry," 291.

51. Ricoeur, "Le Marx de Michel Henry," 281.

52. Henry, *Marx*, 92.

53. Henry, *Marx*, 97.

54. Ricoeur, "Le Marx de Michel Henry," 281.

55. Ricoeur, "Le Marx de Michel Henry," 283.

56. Ricoeur, "Le Marx de Michel Henry," 282–83.

57. Ricoeur, "Le Marx de Michel Henry," 285.

58. Ricoeur, "Le Marx de Michel Henry," 291.
59. Ricoeur, "Le Marx de Michel Henry," 268.
60. Ricoeur, *Lectures on Ideology and Utopia*, 101.
61. See Ricoeur, *Lectures on Ideology and Utopia*, 68–102.
62. Note also Ricoeur's comment that "the opposition between the reading of Michel Henry and that of Althusser is thus radical" ("Le Marx de Michel Henry," 277).
63. In particular, see Althusser, *For Marx*.
64. Ricoeur, *Lectures on Ideology and Utopia*, 101.
65. Ricoeur, *Lectures on Ideology and Utopia*, 76–82.
66. Ricoeur, *Lectures on Ideology and Utopia*, 5.
67. In later developments of Marxism and especially the structuralist interpretation, this realism of life comes to be replaced by a purported body of scientific knowledge of reality (whence ideology comes to comprise what is nonscientific).
68. Ricoeur, *Lectures on Ideology and Utopia*, 77.
69. Marx, *German Ideology*, 42.
70. Ricoeur, *Lectures on Ideology and Utopia*, 77.
71. See Mannheim, *Ideology and Utopia*.
72. Ricoeur, "Le Marx de Michel Henry," 293.
73. Geertz's book *The Interpretation of Cultures* was also on the reading list for these 1975 lectures.
74. Ricoeur, *Lectures on Ideology and Utopia*, 10.
75. Ricoeur, *Lectures on Ideology and Utopia*, 10.
76. Henry, *Marx*, 168–89.
77. Henry, *Marx*, 170.
78. Henry, *Marx*, 172.

## 6. Language

1. To recall, the specific observation is as follows: "When Marx declares that 'ideology is the language of real life,' in no way does he want to reduce this life—hunger, cold, striving, suffering—to the discourse of ideology. Instead, he asserts that, while this discourse is of another order and is irreal like the meanings with which it is composed, it is unintelligible in its own order, and therefore is explained only in its reference to the multiple modalities of the life of 'living individuals'" (Henry, *The Michel Henry Reader*, 206–07).
2. By contrast, I have not found a single reference by Henry to an Anglo-American philosopher!
3. This view, which originates with Nietzsche, was developed further in Derrida's essay "White Mythology." Ricoeur enters into debate with Derrida in the final study of *The Rule of Metaphor*. For an excellent analysis of this debate, see Amalric, *Ricoeur, Derrida: L'enjeu de la métaphore*.

4. Henry, *Phénoménologie de la Vie*, vol. 5, 189f.
5. Henry, "Material Phenomenology and Language," 207.
6. Henry, "Material Phenomenology and Language," 203.
7. Henry, *I Am The Truth*, 226; *Incarnation*, 371.
8. For one development of this notion and an alternative solution to it, see Seyler, "La certitude comme enjeu éthique et épistémologique pour la Phénoménologie de la vie."
9. See Henry, *Phénoménologie de la Vie*, vol. 5, 143.
10. Henry, *Phénoménologie de la Vie*, vol. 5, 147.
11. Greisch was a friend of Ricoeur and an insightful commentator on his work, so there can be little doubt that his question is influenced by Ricoeur's treatment of metaphor. Along with his continual dialogue with Ricoeur, Greisch is the author of *Paul Ricoeur: L'itinérance du sens*.
12. Ricoeur, "Creativity in Language," in *The Philosophy of Paul Ricoeur*, 120.
13. Ricoeur, "Creativity in Language" in *The Philosophy of Paul Ricoeur*, 123; cf. 143.
14. The closing lines of Richards's book are especially suggestive in the context of the present discussion: "Words are not the medium in which to copy life. Their true work is to restore life to order" (*The Philosophy of Rhetoric*, 134).
15. Arguably, this could be the alternative into which Henry's account of the language of life lands: life as the pure as if that has abandoned all connection to the language and facts of the world. By contrast, Henry himself seems to suggest that Merleau-Ponty falls into the other trap: in ascribing flesh to the world, his view falls into the naivety of ascribing reality to the metaphor of flesh.
16. This has an important implication for the phenomenology of feeling: Henry's account of feeling emphasizes the auto-affective dimension of feeling as a pure feeling. But according to the tension theory of metaphor, the feeling associated with metaphor is not purely internal and subjective, just as much as reference does not simply denote the external world. It comes much closer to Heidegger's notion of a mood, according to which a feeling is not simply subjective but also an attunement to the world.
17. Ricoeur, *The Rule of Metaphor*, 254.
18. Berggren, "The Use and Abuse of Metaphor," 248.
19. Ricoeur, "Creativity in Language," 133.
20. Ricoeur, *The Rule of Metaphor*, 247.
21. A good example of this comes from the title of *Oneself as Another*—the self and other are not the same, nor are they wholly different, but they are alike in spite of their difference.
22. Ricoeur, *The Rule of Metaphor*, 33ff.
23. Aristotle, "Poetics," 1412a8.
24. Aristotle, "Poetics," 1448a28.

25. Aristotle, "Poetics," 1412a3.
26. I utilize the phrase *living cosmos* here because it is a phrase that Henry himself endorses in his book on Kandinsky. If Henry is willing to embrace that notion, then it doesn't seem too far-fetched to imagine that this account of metaphor could be embraced as well. Such a reconciliation would seem to require only the acceptance of a wider range of tools to get there, including metaphor but perhaps also narrative and other artistic modes of expression. I return to this important point in the book's conclusion.
27. Henry, "Four Principles of Phenomenology," 9.
28. Henry, "Four Principles of Phenomenology," 18–19.
29. Henry, "Four Principles of Phenomenology," 18.
30. Henry, "Four Principles of Phenomenology," 19.
31. Henry, "Four Principles of Phenomenology," 19.
32. Henry, "Four Principles of Phenomenology," 20.
33. In a later response to Henry's essay, Marion slightly alters the nature of Henry's critique and asserts that "none of these four formulations receive Henry's endorsement, and for one single reason: because they all remain 'purely formal concepts,' they all lack 'the pure phenomenological material' not limited by the world but which ultimately refers back to the phenomenality of life" (Marion, "The Reduction and 'The Fourth Principle,'" 43). This leads Marion to consider the question at stake to be: does the call structure necessarily admit an ek-stasis, or is it possible to conceive a call structure without any ek-stasis? But in lumping all the principles together, Marion does not capture Henry's point precisely enough. Instead, I take it that Henry is claiming that the fourth principle, when applied to a phenomenology of life, yields a different phenomenological structure, a different phenomenology of the call, from the one Marion proposes.
34. Henry, "Material Phenomenology and Language," 206.
35. Though it has not been a point of emphasis in the preceding analysis, the langue-parole distinction was common currency in twentieth-century French theory and may have guided Henry's own choice of terminology. Note that when Henry speaks about the language of life, he opts for the terminology of *parole* and *verbe*, both of which emphasize the active use and event of spoken language as opposed to language as a system or code.
36. Ricoeur, *Interpretation Theory*, 3.
37. Ricoeur, *Interpretation Theory*, 21.
38. After all, languages don't speak or refer on their own; people do (Ricoeur, *Interpretation Theory*, 13). To convey discourse in its full scope, both a semantics of meaning and a pragmatics of speech acts are needed.
39. Ricoeur, *Oneself as Another*, 40.
40. Ricoeur, *Oneself as Another*, 55.

41. Henry, *Phénoménologie de la Vie*, vol. 3, 322.

42. A brief word about how this might pertain to the Henry-Marion debate in the previous section. If this account is correct, then each is right in a sense. In one sense, Henry is right to note that the appearing of life has a distinct structure in contrast with other modes of appearing. But in another sense, Marion would be right that there is a difference opened up by the call of life just as much as with any other type of call. But perhaps both accounts fall short in the sense that they convey only the passive reception of revelation while ignoring the active role of the self in producing revelation through the living word. For a recent study of the phenomenology of revelation, see Graves, *The Phenomenology of Revelation*.

43. This prospect is not entirely antithetical to Henry's thought. It can be glimpsed in his reading of Kandinsky, which ascribes inner and outer modes to every appearance. Each color, for example, has both an outer aspect (its shade) and an inner aspect (its affective tone). For an artist like Kandinsky, the choice of color is not simply guided by an attempt to represent the world; it seeks to communicate an affect. But to the extent that a given affective tone is produced by a given color, it follows that affective life and the world are materially linked in a single expression. The subsequent work to be done would be to show how this works against the grain of the binaries in Henry's phenomenology and trace out its full implications.

## 7. Death

1. In this way philosophy, to borrow Derrida's words, can prepare us "to learn to live finally."

2. In another interesting passage, Henry seems to present death as a negation that is dependent on life:

> When we seem to see a countryside or a face that we will not see again, this new meaning, which gives the world of human intersubjectivity and the world in general its tragic nature (since we are never more than passing tourists in it) and the provisional and fugitive nature of all experience—this is possible only because of our permanent ability to access the world, an ability constitutive of our being. Even the idea of death, which represents the complete disappearance of all my body's powers, is merely a negative determination of the general significance of my experience of the world as an experience of this body, as an experience of power (*Genealogy of Psychoanalysis*, 324–24; trans. modified).

3. Ricoeur, *Critique and Conviction*, 156.

4. For an excellent clarification of this contrast in the context of Ricoeur's thought, see Worms, "Vivant jusqu'à la mort et non pas pour la mort," 304–15.

5. It is a question, then, of whether life after death—immortality—counts as what has been called a limit phenomenon for phenomenology. For an extensive

account of the role of the limit phenomenon in French phenomenology, see Sebbah, *Testing the Limit*.

6. Their projects resonate, in many ways, with that of Hannah Arendt, who, in *The Human Condition*, also privileges the reflection on life over death. She pursues the significance of immortality directly in the final section of the first chapter, where she distinguishes between eternity and immortality and toward the end of the book remarks that "what counts today is not immortality, instead it is life that is the sovereign good."

7. Again, it should be noted that this was not at all regarded as a paradox or contradiction for Husserl himself. In an appendix to *Analyses Concerning Passive and Active Synthesis* from the early 1920s, for instance, Husserl affirms the immortality of the transcendental ego: "Even if the presently 'enduring' unitary object or event can cease, the process of the 'enduring' itself cannot come to a halt. The 'enduring' is immortal.... This implies that the process of living on, and the [pure] ego that lives on, are immortal.... Immortality is now given as the incapability of crossing out the present that is being ever newly fulfilled" (467).

8. This tale is recounted in Alfred Schutz's memoir, *Husserl and His Influence on Me*. It recounts his last meeting with Husserl in December 1937, shortly before his mentor's death in April 1938.

9. See Husserl, *Analyses Concerning Passive and Active Synthesis*, 466–67. For a broader discussion of this aspect of Husserl's thought, see Paul McDonald's essay "Husserl, the Monad and Immortality."

10. It is worth noting the overlap of this concept with a remark from Derrida's last interview: "I have always been interested in this theme of survival, the meaning of which is not to be added on to living and dying. It is originary: life is living on, life is survival [*la vie est survie*]" (*Learning to Live Finally*, 25).

11. It bears noting that the early Heidegger dabbled with the philosophy of life prior to the writing of *Being and Time*. Several excellent studies of the transitions in this early period are available: Kisiel, *The Genesis of Heidegger's Being and Time*; Greisch, *L'arbre de Vie et L'arbre du Savoir*; and Arrien, *Le Jeune Heidegger*. To examine Heidegger's existential analytic from the perspective of a phenomenology of life is thus, in some sense, to work backward in time and to excavate a different potential development of his thought.

12. This notion of verticality is introduced and explored extensively by Anthony Steinbock's book *Phenomenology and Mysticism: The Verticality of Religious Experience*.

13. Note that Henry's detachment of the living flesh from the natural body has a clear parallel with the separation of the soul from the body in Plato's *Phaedo*. Just as Plato's proofs of the immortal soul separate the life of the soul from its association with the physical world, Henry's phenomenology of life separates the living flesh

from its association with the organic functions of the body as well as from its entanglement with the natural world.

14. Here too, Henry's description of Life as a cause has a clear parallel with Plato's *Phaedo*. The soul is alive for Plato not due to its presence in the world but through its linkage with the Form of Life. Just as the Forms are generative of the Life of the Soul, so too Life is generative of the living flesh for Henry. It is Life itself that brings one into the flesh and puts one in possession of one's own flesh.

15. On a related note, see Joseph Rivera, *The Contemplative Self after Michel Henry*, chapter 3.

16. See Henry, *I Am the Truth*, 106 ff.

17. Henry, *I Am the Truth*, 107. In the course of this analysis, Henry states quite directly that auto-affection in the weak sense characterizes the human life while auto-affection in the strong sense is suitable to God.

18. Another way to put this question is as follows: is the self who comes into life my self, or is it life itself? Henry responds by saying, "Well, I have to answer: both at the same time. It is my self joined to itself in the self of life or rather the self of life is found precisely there where I am joined to myself, that is, that the self of life is the permanent internal possibility of my self. . . . I say that there is no self numerically distinguishable, but that there is what I call a reciprocal phenomenological interiority, a concept that can only arise in life" (*Phénoménologie de la Vie*, vol. 4, 234). He ties this "reciprocal phenomenological interiority" to Spinoza's concept of immanent causality, which describes the situation of every living self in life. It suggests that the living self is not self-enclosed but instead radically open and that the process of generating each living self is interior and continues to be interior (*Phénoménologie de la Vie*, vol. 4, 235).

19. For references to Life's "continual creation" of the living present, see Henry, *Auto-Donation*, 56, 82.

20. To be clear, it is unclear to me whether in referencing "continuous creation" Henry is embracing the Cartesian doctrine. That is a point that would require further scholarly discussion that I'm unable to provide. Note, however, the strong parallel between Henry's description of Life with Descartes's use of the doctrine of continuous creation:

> The nature of time is such that its parts are not mutually dependent, and never coexist. Thus, from the fact that we now exist, it does not follow that we shall exist a moment from now, unless there is some cause—the same cause which originally produced us—which continually reproduces us, as it were, that is to say, which keeps us in existence. For we easily understand that there is no power in us enabling us to keep ourselves in existence. We also understand that he who has so great a power that he can keep us in existence, although we are distinct from him, must be all the more able to keep himself in existence; or rather, he requires no other

being to keep him in existence, and hence, in short, is God (Descartes, *Principles of Philosophy*, 200).

21. Henry, "The Phenomenology of Birth," 36.

22. This essay can be accessed in Grégori Jean and Jean Leclercq's book *Lectures de Michel Henry*. Note that this passage is omitted from the second version of the article, which is the one published in *The Michel Henry Reader* and in the French version of his collected works, *Phénoménologie de la vie*.

23. Henry, "Phénoménologie de la naissance (première version)," 31.

24. See Plato, *Timaeus*, 37d6-7. A more technical account of Henry's view would need to dig into the traditional contrast between eternity and sempiternity. Here, I'm using the term *eternity* in a casual manner, but my hunch is that the technical notion of sempiternity may be more suited to his account of life. This is reflected in Henry's own description of the eternal as a constant movement and pressure exerted by life. The endless flowing and movement of life seem to justify the use of the term *sempiternity* rather than *eternity* to describe the endlessness of life, but Henry himself does not seem to recognize this difference, and so I don't pursue it any further here.

25. Note that this seems to rejoin Husserl's account of the enduring now that cannot be destroyed. Going back to the anecdote relayed by Schutz about the immortality of the transcendental ego, Henry's account of the omnipresence of Life might elucidate how the transcendental ego outlasts the empirical ego. But what needs to be asked, I think, is in what sense one can continue to speak of an ego in this regard.

26. In each of these respects, Henry's conception of the life of Life parallels the features ascribed to the Platonic Forms, thereby suggesting that there may be a line of influence passing from Platonism to Henry's phenomenology of life.

27. Lacoste puts this contrast more sharply in stating that Henry's interpretation of life "brackets any interpretation of death and, above all, of a being-towards death: life is always living now" (Lacoste, "Foreword," x).

28. This is supported by Henry's statement in an interview that the human condition is such that "our life is a finite life and, precisely to this extent, is an infinite life" (Henry, "Interview with Virginie Caruana," in *Entretiens*, 122). If this reading is correct, it follows that Henry shares the same position that Ricoeur develops in *Fallible Man*. Ricoeur's main thesis is that Heidegger the human being is not defined by finitude but instead by the duality of the finite and the infinite. The same point emerges through the application of the Cartesian circle to Henry's account of the relation between the living individual and life.

29. One might even wonder whether it is problematic within his own phenomenological perspective. Does it not contradict Henry's claim in *I Am the Truth* that there is "no life without the living. No living without life" (60)? Is not the eternity of Life an indication of the separability and independence of Life from the living?

30. For more context on these writings, see Olivier Abel's "Preface" to *Living Up to Death* as well as his very interesting "Élégie à la resurrection."

31. Ricoeur, *Critique and Conviction*, 145.

32. Ricoeur, *Critique and Conviction*, 156.

33. Ricoeur, *Living Up to Death*, 18.

34. Ricoeur, *Living Up to Death*, 14.

35. Abel, "Preface," in *Living Up to Death*, x. While an eidetics of the will, as we have indicated, is well suited for analyzing the various divisions and tensions that divide and wound the self, it is not compatible with the conciliatory task of mending those fractures and restoring their unity. Such a task calls for a different method—namely, a poetics whose role will be to restore the lost unity of the self and to bring about a genuine affirmation that *I am my life*. A brief allusion to this method of a "poetics of the will" appears in a curious footnote about life:

> We must eliminate from the experience of being alive all the harmonies which already point to the "poetics" of the will. In our language, life has an ambiguous meaning: it designates at the same time the order of limits and the order of sources or creation. In this new sense life brings up a new method, namely, a "poetics" of the will which we are here abstracting. One of the crucial, difficult problems posed by such "poetics of the will" will be to know why the spontaneity of life below serves in turn as a metaphor for higher life, and what secret affinity unites those two meanings of the word "life" (*Freedom and Nature*, 415).

36. Ricoeur, *Critique and Conviction*, 161.

37. Psalms 8:5.

38. Ricoeur, *Critique and Conviction*, 159.

39. Ricoeur, *Critique and Conviction*, 159.

40. Ricoeur, *Critique and Conviction*, 160.

41. It is perhaps telling that Ricoeur recognizes this and accepts that it is simply a matter of faith while Henry does not see this as a matter of speculation at all.

42. We often specify being toward the future through kinship (blood relations) and the transmission of property/capital, but these ways of engaging the future have rightly been criticized for valorizing heteronormative reproductive activity. Proposals for queering the future rightly point to the possibility of a nonreproductive model of the future outside of kinship (see Edelman, *No Future*). In place of care for one's blood line or kin, it is also possible to express care for the future in a broader sense, such as support for institutions that advance a value or cause or other types of chosen relationship. All are various ways in which we make a specific investment in a future that is not our own. These different expressions are situated against the background orientation of living after or life as survival or as being toward life.

43. Ricoeur, *Critique and Conviction*, 161.

44. Ricoeur, *Critique and Conviction*, 159.

45. Ricoeur, *Critique and Conviction*, 161.

46. Scheffler, *Death and the Afterlife*, 32.

47. The belief in immortality as survival—as a life after our own—is itself a "noble risk"; it is a belief—or, better, an orientation—that makes us better, helping us to lead more rich and meaningful lives, leading us to aspire to accomplish more than we would without it. It shows that we are not beings who are primarily preoccupied with our own existence. Instead, we are in some fundamental way preoccupied with our own existence in relation to lives and a life in general that will continue to persist after ourselves. In this respect, it broadens the sphere of care to include a care for life.

48. Let me highlight a passage by Derrida that overlaps with the analysis developed here:

> Survival is an originary concept that constitutes the very structure of what we call existence, Dasein, if you will. We are structurally survivors, marked by this structure of the trace and of the testament. But having said that, I would not want to encourage an interpretation that situates surviving on the side of death and the past rather than life and the future. No, deconstruction is always on the side of the yes, on the side of the affirmation of life. Everything I say—at least from "Pas" on—about survival as a complication of the opposition life/death proceeds in me from an unconditional affirmation of life. This surviving is life beyond life, life more than life, and my discourse is not a discourse of death, but on the contrary, the affirmation of a living being who prefers living and thus surviving to death, because survival is not simply that which remains but the most intense life possible (Derrida, *Learning to Live Finally*, 51–52).

## 8. For an Integrated Phenomenology of Life

1. T. S. Eliot, "Choruses from the Rock."

2. Jacob, *The Logic of Life*, 294.

3. This feeling can be illustrated by one of the key moments in Rousseau's The Reveries of the Solitary Walker. As Anne Devarieux points out, Rousseau describes the "feeling of one's own existence" as follows: "What do we enjoy in such a situation? Nothing external to ourselves, nothing if not ourselves and our own existence. As long as this state lasts, we are sufficient unto ourselves, like God. The sentiment of existence, stripped of any other emotion, is in itself a precious sentiment of contentment and of peace which alone would suffice to make this existence dear and sweet to anyone able to spurn all the sensual and earthly impressions which incessantly come to distract us from it and to trouble its sweetness here below" (Reveries, 69).

4. This duality is already implicit in Henry's distinction between two types of auto-affection in the weak (life) and strong (Life) senses. The lowercase sense of life refers to the lived experience of the self, who experiences the fact of its own living and who enters into possession of its power to express itself in and through life. Here, the self is positioned as a nominative—the individuation of the self is the necessary

starting point for the expression of life. The uppercase sense of Life, by contrast, refers to the way in which Life originally generates the self and brings the self into itself; this perspective exposes the radical passivity of the self in its exposure to life. The double genitive thus explains how the auto-affection of life can be redescribed in such a way that it retains these two different senses as well as their unity.

5. This is the underlying confusion that motivates Renaud Barbaras's critique of Henry. Barbaras assumes (as much of Henry's writing would admittedly lead one to believe) that his phenomenology of life is only about the pathos of life and that it lacks an active dimension. What such an interpretation cannot explain are the many passages, from his thesis on Maine de Biran onward, in which Henry speaks about the force of life.

6. If this claim concerning the pathos and praxis of life is granted, one might wonder whether this self-differentiation undermines the conceptual architecture of Henry's phenomenology. The simple answer is no; quite the contrary, it improves it. Without some form of self-differentiation, how could Henry speak meaningfully about the growth or decline of life, the increase or decrease of its powers, and the satisfaction or frustration of its strivings? By admitting an internal self-differentiation, it becomes possible to speak intelligibly about life in developmental terms as becoming, growth, and decline. These gradations are internal to the self-development of life.

7. To illustrate the significance of this point, consider the difference between a contract and a gift. A contract is entered into by consent; it is an expression of the will of two or more parties to exchange goods and services. The individual parties exist independently prior to their agreement, and the contract is an expression of their mutual volition. The contract establishes the conditions under which it can be fulfilled as well as dissolved. A gift or inheritance, by contrast, is the expression of the will of one individual alone: the giver. The gift is given without the recipient's prior consent, and its contents are determined without the recipient's knowledge.

8. This discussion of meritocracy is heavily indebted to the critique of meritocracy developed in Michael Sandel's recent book, *The Tyranny of Merit: What's Become of the Common Good?*

9. Note that Eliot adds further that there is "no community not lived in praise of God" ("Choruses from the Rock").

# BIBLIOGRAPHY

Abel, Olivier. "Élégie à la resurrection." *Études* (spring 2000): 192–94.
Adler, Pierre. "Neither Consciousness, nor Matter, but Living Bodily Activity." *Graduate Faculty Philosophy Journal*, 10, no. 2 (1985): 147–61.
Althusser, Louis. *For Marx*. Translated by Ben Brewster. London: Verso, 1979.
Amalric, Jean-Luc. *Ricoeur, Derrida: L'enjeu de la métaphore*. Paris: Presses Universitaires de France, 2006.
Arendt, Hannah. *The Human Condition*. 2nd ed. Chicago: University of Chicago Press, 1998.
Arrien, Sophie-Jan. *Le Jeune Heidegger: 1909–1926*. Paris: Vrin, 2011.
Barbaras, Renaud. *Introduction to a Phenomenology of Life*. Translated by Leonard Lawlor. Bloomington: Indiana University Press, 2022.
———. The Essence of Life: Drive or Desire? In *The Affects of Thought*, edited by Jeffrey Hanson and Michael R. Kelly, 40–61. London: Bloomsbury, 2012.
Bernet, Rudolf. *Force, Pulsion, Desir: Une autre philosophie de la psychanalyse*. Paris: Vrin, 2013.
———. *La vie du sujet: Recherches sur l'interprétation de Husserl dans la phénoménologie*. Paris: Presses Universitaires de France, 1994.
Berggren, Douglas. "The Use and Abuse of Metaphor, I." *Review of Metaphysics* 16, no. 2 (1962): 237–58.
Bernstein, Richard J. "Ricoeur's Freud." *Etudes Ricoeuriennes/Ricoeur Studies* 4, no. 1 (2013): 130–39.
Bohman, James. "A New Phenomenological Marxism." *Human Studies* 13, no. 2 (1990): 163–72.
Brennan, Eileen. "Paul Ricoeur's Hermeneutics of the Self." *Tropos VIII* 2 (2015).

Carter, James. *Ricoeur on Moral Religion: A Hermeneutics of Life*. Oxford: Oxford University Press, 2014.

Davidson, Scott. *A Companion to Ricoeur's* Fallible Man. Lanham, MD: Lexington, 2020.

———. "Affective Labor and the Henry-Ricoeur Debate over Marx." In *The Practical Philosophy of Michel Henry*, edited by Jeffrey Hanson, Brian Harding, and Michael R. Kelly, 27–44. London: Bloomsbury, 2022.

———. "Book Review: The Test of the Limit." *Bulletin de la Société de la Philosophie Française* XIV, no. 1 (spring 2004): 105–09.

———. "Is a Hermeneutic Phenomenology Wide Open Enough?" *Journal of Speculative Philosophy* 28, no. 3 (2014): 315–326.

———. "La phénoménologie de la vie: Entre Ricoeur et Henry." In *Paul Ricoeur et Michel Henry: Entre héritages et destinées phénoménologiques*, edited by Jean-Sébastien Hardy, Jean Leclercq, and Cyndie Sautereau, 33–48. Louvain, Belgium: Presses Universitaires Louvain, 2016.

———. "The Phenomenon of Life and its Pathos." In *A Companion to Ricoeur's* Freedom and Nature, edited by Scott Davidson. Lanham, MD: Lexington, 2019: 157–72.

———. "Michel Henry (1922–2002)." In *Encyclopedia of Phenomenology*, edited by Nicolas de Warren and Ted Toadvine. Cham: Springer, 2023: 1–7.

———. "The Husserl Heretics: Ricoeur, Levinas and the French Reception of Husserlian Phenomenology." *Studia Phaenomenologica* 13 (2013): 209–29.

———. "The Life of Consciousness: Between Henry and Ricoeur." *Pli* 28: 32–52.

Davidson, Scott, and Frédéric Seyler, eds. *The Michel Henry Reader*. Evanston, IL: Northwestern University Press, 2019.

Davidson, Scott, and Marc-Antoine Vallée, eds. *Hermeneutics and Phenomenology in Paul Ricoeur: Between Text and Phenomenon*. Cham: Springer, 2016.

De Biran, Pierre Maine. Oeuvres: Tome 7. *Essai sur les fondements de la psychologie*. Edited by F. T. C. Moore. Paris: J. Vrin, 2001.

———. Oeuvres: Tome 11. *Commentaires et marginalia XVIIIe siècle*. Paris: J. Vrin, 1993.

———. *The Influence of Habit on the Faculty of Thinking*. Translated by Margaret Donaldson Boehm. Baltimore, MD: Williams & Watkins, 1929.

De Jaegher, Hanne. "How We Affect Each Other. Michel Henry's 'Pathos-With' and the Enactive Approach to Intersubjectivity." *Journal of Consciousness Studies* 22, 1–2 (2015): 112–32.

De Leeuw, Marc. *Paul Ricoeur's Renewal of Philosophical Anthropology*. Lanham, MD: Rowman & Littlefield, 2022.

Deroo, Neal. *The Political Logic of Experience*. New York: Fordham University Press, 2022.

Derrida, Jacques. *Edmund Husserl's Origin of Geometry: An Introduction*. Translated by John P. Leavey. Lincoln: University of Nebraska Press, 1989.

———. *Learning to Live Finally*. Translated by Pascal-Anne Brault and Michael Naas. Hoboken, NJ: Melville House, 2007.

———. *On Touching—Jean-Luc Nancy*. Translated by Christine Irizarry. Stanford, CA: Stanford University Press, 2005.

———. "White Mythology: Metaphor in the Text of Philosophy." In *Margins of Philosophy*, translated by Alan Bass. Chicago: University of Chicago Press, 1984: 207–72.

Descartes, René. *Principles of Philosophy* [1644]. Translated by Valentine Rodger Miller and Reese P. Miller. Dordrecht: Kluwer, 1982.

Devarieux, Anne. "L'exil des affections pures. A propos d'une formule d'Ovide et de sa reprise biranienne." *Revue Philosophique de Louvain* 103, no. 1–2 (2005): 139–58.

———. *L'intériorité réciproque: L'hérésie biranienne de Michel Henry*. Paris: Millon, 2018.

Dierckxsens, Geoffrey. "Imagination, Narrativity and Embodied Cognition: Exploring the Possibilities of Paul Ricoeur's Hermeneutical Phenomenology for Enactivism." *Filosofia Unisinos* 19, no. 1 (2018): 41–49.

Dosse, François. *Paul Ricoeur: Les sens d'une vie*. Paris: La Découverte, 1997.

Edelman, Lee. *No Future: Queer Theory and the Death Drive*. Durham, NC: Duke University Press, 2004.

Falque, Emmanuel. *Ça n'a rien à voir: Lire Freud en philosophe*. Paris: Cerf, 2018.

———. *Hors phénomène: Essai aux confins de la phénomenalité*. Paris: Hermann, 2021.

———. "Is There a Flesh without Body?" *Journal of French and Francophone Philosophy* 24, no. 1 (2016): 139–66.

Fink, Eugen. "The Problem of the Phenomenology of Edmund Husserl." In *Apriori and World: European Contributions to Husserlian Phenomenology*, edited by William McKenna, Robert M. Harlan, and Laurence E. Winters, 21–55. The Hague: Martinus Nijhoff, 1981.

Franck, Didier. *Flesh and Body: On the Phenomenology of Husserl*. Translated by Joseph Rivera and Scott Davidson. London: Bloomsbury, 2014.

Fraser, Nancy, and Axel Honneth. *Redistribution or Recognition? A Political-Philosophical Exchange*. London: Verso, 2003.

Freud, Sigmund. *Standard Edition of the Complete Psychological Works of Sigmund Freud*. 24 volumes. Edited by James Strachey. New York: Vintage, 1999.

Geertz, Clifford. *The Interpretation of Cultures*. New York: Basic, 1973.

Graves, Adam J. *The Phenomenology of Revelation in Heidegger, Marion, and Ricœur*. Lanham, MD: Lexington, 2021.

Greisch, Jean. *L'arbre de Vie et L'arbre du Savoir*. Paris: Cerf, 2000.

———. *Paul Ricoeur: L'itinérance du sens*. Paris: Jérôme Millon, 2001.

Gschwandtner, Christina M. *Degrees of Givenness: On Saturation in Jean-Luc Marion*. Bloomington: Indiana University Press, 2014.

———. "Revealing the Invisible: Henry and Marion on Aesthetic Experience." *Journal of Speculative Philosophy* 28, no. 3 (2014): 305–14.

———. "What about Non-Human Life? An 'Ecological' Reading of Michel Henry's Critique of Technology." *Journal of French and Francophone Philosophy* 20, no. 2 (2012): 116–38.

Haldane, John B. S. *What Is Life?* New York: Boni & Gaer, 1947.

Hanson, Jeffrey, and Michael R. Kelly, eds. *Michel Henry: The Affects of Thought*. London: Continuum, 2012.

Hanson, Jeffrey, Brian Harding, and Michael R. Kelly, eds. *Michel Henry's Practical Philosophy*. London: Bloomsbury, 2021.

Hardy, Jean-Sébastien, Jean Leclercq, and Cyndie Sautereau, eds. *Paul Ricœur et Michel Henry: Entre héritages et destinées phénoménologiques*. Louvain, Belgium: UCL Press, 2016.

Hefty, Karl. "Is There a Body without Flesh?" *Crossing: The INPR Journal* 1 (2020): 54–72.

Heidegger, Martin. *Being and Time*. Translated by Joan Stambaugh. Albany: State University of New York, 1996.

Henry, Michel. *Barbarism*. Translated by Scott Davidson. London: Continuum, 2012.

———. "Does the Concept 'Soul' Mean Anything?" *Philosophy Today* 13, no. 2–4 (Summer 1969): 94–114.

———. *Entretiens*. Arles, France: Sulliver, 2008.

———. *I Am the Truth: Toward a Philosophy of Christianity*. Translated by Susan Emmanuel. Stanford, CA: Stanford University Press, 2003.

———. *Incarnation: A Philosophy of the Flesh*. Translated by Karl Hefty. Evanston, IL: Northwestern University Press, 2015.

———. "Lettres de Michel Henry à Paul Ricoeur." *Revue Internationale Michel Henry* no. 1 (2010): 15–20.

———. "Life, Death: Marx and Marxism." In *Marx: An Introduction*. Foreword by Frédéric Seyler. Translated by Kristien Justaert. London: Bloomsbury, 2018.

———. *Marx: A Philosophy of Human Reality*. Translated by Kathleen McLaughlin. Bloomington: Indiana University Press, 1983.

———. *Marx*, 2 vols. Paris: Gallimard, 1976.

---. *Material Phenomenology.* Translated by Scott Davidson. New York: Fordham University Press, 2008.

---. Phénoménologie de la naissance (premie version) in *Lectures de Michel Henry.* Edited by Grégori Jean and Jean Leclercq. Louvain: Presses universitaires de Louvain, 2014, https://books.openedition.org/pucl/2400.

---. *Phénoménologie de la vie.* 5 volumes. Edited by Jean Leclercq et al. Paris: Presses Universitaires de France, 2004–115.

---. *Philosophie et Phénoménologie du Corps: Essai sur l'ontologie biranienne.* 2nd edition. Paris: PUF, 2014.

---. *Philosophy and Phenomenology of the Body.* Translated by Girard Etzkorn. The Hague: Martinus Nijhoff, 1975.

---. *Seeing the Invisible: On Kandinsky.* Translated by Scott Davidson. London: Continuum, 2009.

---. *The Essence of Manifestation.* Translated by Girard Etzkorn. The Hague: Martinus Nijhoff, 1973.

---. "The Four Principles of Phenomenology." *Continental Philosophy Review* 48, no. 1 (2015): 1–21.

---. *The Genealogy of Psychoanalysis.* Translated by Douglas Brick. Stanford, CA: Stanford University Press, 1993.

---. *The Michel Henry Reader.* Edited by Scott Davidson and Frédéric Seyler. Evanston, IL: Northwestern University Press, 2019b.

---. "Un parcours philosophique." In *Auto-Donation: Entretiens et conferences* 159–70. Paris: Beauchesne, 2004.

Husserl, Edmund. *Analyses Concerning Passive and Active Synthesis: Lectures on Transcendental Logic.* Translated by Anthony J. Steinbock. Dordrecht: Kluwer: 2001.

---. *Cartesian Meditations: An Introduction to Phenomenology.* Translated by Dorion Cairns. The Hague: Nijhoff, 1960.

---. *Grenzprobleme der Phänomenologie: Analysen des Unbewusstseins und der Instinkte. Metaphysik. Späte Ethik (Texte aus dem Nachlass 1908–1937).* Edited by Rochus Sowa and Thomas Vongehr. Springer, 2014.

---. *Idées Directrices pour une Phénoménologie.* Translated by Paul Ricoeur. Paris: Gallimard, 1950.

---. *The Idea of Phenomenology.* Translated by Lee Hardy. Dordrecht: Kluwer, 1999.

Jacob, François. The Logic of Life: A History of Heredity. Princeton, NJ: Princeton University Press, 2022.

Janicaud, Dominique. *Phenomenology "Wide Open": After the French Debate.* Translated by Charles N. Cabral. New York: Fordham University Press, 2010.

———. "The Surprises of Immanence." In *Phenomenology and the "Theological Turn": The French Debate*. Translated by Bernard G. Prusak. 70–86. New York: Fordham University Press, 2000.

———. "Toward a Minimalist Phenomenology." *Research in Phenomenology* 30 (2000): 89–106.

Jean, Grégori, and Jean Leclercq. "Sur la situation phénoménologique du *Marx* de Michel Henry." *Journal of French and Francophone Philosophy* XX, no. 2 (2012): 1–18.

Jean, Grégori. *Force et temps: Essai sur le vitalisme phénoménologique de Michel Henry*. Paris: Hermann, 2015.

———. "Habitude, effort et résistance: Une lecture du henryan concept de passivité." *Bulletin d'analyse phénoménologique* VIII, no. 1 (2012): 455–77.

Jonas, Hans. *The Phenomenon of Life: Toward a Philosophical Biology*. Evanston, IL: Northwestern University Press, 2001.

Kant, Immanuel. *Anthropology from a Pragmatic Point of View*. Edited by Robert Louden. Cambridge, UK: Cambridge University Press, 2006.

Kearney, Richard, and Brian Treanor, eds. *Carnal Hermeneutics*. New York: Fordham University Press, 2015.

Kern, Iso. "The Three Ways to the Transcendental Phenomenological Reduction in the Philosophy of Edmund Husserl." In *Husserl: Expositions and Appraisals*, edited by Frederick Elliston and Peter McCormick, 126–49. South Bend, IN: University of Notre Dame Press, 1977.

Kisiel, Theodore. *The Genesis of Heidegger's Being and Time*. Berkeley: University of California Press, 1995.

Lacoste, Jean-Yves. "Foreword." In Michel Henry, *Words of Christ*, translated by Christina M. Gschwandtner. Ix–x. Grand Rapids, MI: William B. Erdmans, 2012.

Leclercq, Jean. "Biographie de Michel Henry." In *Michel Henry. Pour une phénoménologie de la vie. Entretien avec Olivier Salazar-Ferrer*. Edited by Olivier Salazar-Ferrer, 9–29. Clichy, France: Éditions de Corlevour, 2010.

Levinas, Emmanuel. *Of God Who Comes to Mind*. Translated by Bettina Bergo. Stanford, CA: Stanford University Press, 1998.

Lind, Andreas Gonçalves. "Michel Henry's Notion of *Bodily-Ownness* in the Context of the Ecological Crisis." *Religions* 13, no. 9 (2022): 8–34.

Madison, Gary B. *Sens et Existence: En Hommage à Paul Ricoeur*. Paris: Seuil, 1975: 138–51.

Mannheim, Karl. *Ideology and Utopia*. Translated by Louis Wirth and Edward Shils. New York: Harcourt, Brace, and World, 1936.

Marion, Jean-Luc. "Descartes et la question de la technique." In *Le discours et sa méthode*, edited by Nicolas Grimaldi and Jean-Luc Marion, 285–301. Paris: Presses Universitaires de France, 1987.

———. *Reduction and Givenness*. Translated by Thomas A. Carlson. Evanston, IL: Northwestern University Press, 1998.

———. "The Invisible and the Phenomenon." In *The Affects of Thought*, edited by Jeffrey Hanson and Michael R. Kelly, 19–39. London, Continuum, 2012.

———. "The Reduction and 'The Fourth Principle.'" *Analecta Hermeneutica*, vol. 8 (2016): 41–63.

McDonald, Paul. "Husserl, the Monad and Immortality." *Indo-Pacific Journal of Phenomenology* 9 (2007): 1–18.

Michel, Johann. *Homo Interpretans: Towards a Transformation of Hermeneutics*. Translated by David Pellauer. Lanham, MD: Rowman & Littlefield, 2019.

———. *Ricoeur and the Post-structuralists*. Translated by Scott Davidson. Lanham, MD: Rowman & Littlefield, 2016.

Moran, Dermot. "Husserl's Transcendental Philosophy and the Critique of Naturalism." *Continental Philosophy Review* 41, no. 4 (2008): 401–25.

Nabert, Jean. *L'expérience intérieure de la liberté et autres essais de philosophie morale*. Paris: Presses Universitaires de France, 1994.

Nurse, Paul. *What Is Life? Five Great Ideas in Biology*. New York: Norton, 2021.

O'Byrne, Anne. *Natality and Finitude*. Bloomington: Indiana University Press, 2010.

Pellauer, David. *Ricoeur: A Guide for the Perplexed*. London: Continuum, 2007.

Ravaisson, Félix. *Of Habit*. Translated by Clare Carlisle and Mark Sinclair. London: Continuum, 2009.

Reagan, Charles E., and David Stewart, eds. *The Philosophy of Paul Ricoeur: An Anthology of His Work*. Boston: Beacon, 1978.

Reagan, Charles E. *Paul Ricoeur: His Life and Work*. Chicago: University of Chicago Press, 1996.

Richards, I. A. *The Philosophy of Rhetoric*. Oxford, UK: Oxford University Press, 1936.

Ricoeur, Paul. *A Key to Edmund Husserl's Ideas I*. Milwaukee, WI: Marquette University Press, 1986.

———. *A l'ecole de la phenomenologie*. Paris: Vrin, 1986.

———. *Critique and Conviction*. New York: Columbia University Press, 1998.

———. *Fallible Man*. Translated by Charles A. Kelbley. New York: Fordham University Press, 1986.

———. *Freedom and Nature: The Voluntary and the Involuntary*. Translated by Erazim Kohák. Evanston, IL: Northwestern University Press, 1966.

———. *Freud and Philosophy: An Essay on Interpretation*. Translated by Denis Savage. New Haven, CT: Yale University Press, 1970.

———. *From Text to Action: Essays in Hermeneutics, II*. Translated by Kathleen Blamey and John B. Thompson. Evanston, IL: Northwestern University Press, 1991.

———. *Husserl: An Analysis of His Phenomenology*. Evanston, IL: Northwestern University Press, 1967.

———. "Intellectual Autobiography." In *The Philosophy of Paul Ricoeur*, edited by Lewis E. Hahn, 3–53. Chicago and LaSalle: Open Court, 1995.

———. *Interpretation Theory: Discourse and the Surplus of Meaning*. Fort Worth: Texas Christian, 1976.

———. "L'attestation: entre phénoménologie et ontologie." In *Ricoeur: Les métamorphoses de la raison herméneutique*, edited by Jean Greisch and Richard Kearney, 381–403. Paris: Cerf, 1991.

———. *Lectures 2: La contrée des philosophes*. Paris: Seuil, 1999.

———. *Lectures on Ideology and Utopia*. Edited by George H. Taylor. New York: Columbia University Press, 1986.

———. "Le Marx de Michel Henry." In *Lectures 2: La contrée des philosophes*, 265–93. Paris: Seuil, 1992.

———. *Living Up to Death*. Translated by David Pellauer. Chicago: University of Chicago Press, 2009.

———. "L'originaire et la question-en-retour dans la *Krisis* de Husserl." In *Textes pour Emmanuel Levinas*, edited by François Laruelle, 167–177. Paris: Jean-Michel Place, 1980.

———. *Memory, History, Forgetting*. Translated by Kathleen Blamey and David Pellauer. Chicago: University of Chicago Press, 2004.

———. *Méthode réflexive appliqué au problème de Dieu chez Lachelier et Lagneau*. Paris: Cerf, 2017.

———. *Oneself as Another*. Translated by Kathleen Blamey. Chicago: University of Chicago Press, 1992.

———. *On Psychoanalysis*. Translated by David Pellauer. Cambridge, UK: Polity, 2012.

———. *On Translation*. Translated by Eileen Brennan. London: Routledge, 2006.

———. *The Conflict of Interpretations: Essays in Hermeneutics*. Edted by Don Ihde. Evanston, IL: Northwestern University Press, 1974.

———. *The Rule of Metaphor*. Translated by Robert Czerny. Toronto, Canada: University of Toronto Press, 1975.

———. *Time and Narrative*, volume 3. Translated by Kathleen Blamey and David Pellauer. Chicago: University of Chicago Press, 1988.

Ricoeur, Paul, and Jean-Pierre Changeux. *What Makes Us Think? A Neuroscientist and a Philosopher Argue about Ethics, Human Nature, and the Brain*. Translated by M. B. DeBevoise. Princeton, NJ: Princeton University Press, 2000.

Peter Vandecasteele and Frans Vansina, eds. *Paul Ricoeur: Bibliographie primaire et secondaire. Primary and Secondary Bibliography 1935–2008*. Leuven, Belgium: Peeters, 2008.

Rivera, Joseph. *The Contemplative Life after Michel Henry: A Phenomenological Theology*. South Bend, IN: University of Notre Dame Press, 2015.

Romano, Claude. "Must Phenomenology Remain Cartesian?" *Continental Philosophy Review* 45, no. 3 (2012): 425–45.

Rousseau, Jean-Jacques. *The Reveries of the Solitary Walker*. Translated by Charles E. Butterworth, New York: New York University Press, 1979.

Sandel, Michael J. *The Tyranny of Merit: What's Become of the Common Good?* New York: Farrar, Straus & Giroux, 2020.

Sartre, Jean-Paul. *Being and Nothingness*. Translated by Hazel E. Barnes. New York: Philosophical Library, 1956.

Savage, Roger W. H., ed. *Paul Ricoeur and the Lived Body*. Lanham, MD: Rowman & Littlefield, 2020.

Scheffler, Samuel. *Death and the Afterlife*. Oxford, UK: Oxford University Press, 2013.

Schott, Robin May, ed. *Birth, Death, and Femininity*. Bloomington: Indiana University Press, 2010.

Schrift, Alan D. *Twentieth-Century French Philosophy: Key Themes and Thinkers*. Oxford, UK: Blackwell, 2006.

Sebbah, François-David. *Testing the Limit*. Translated by Stephen Barker. Stanford, CA: Stanford University Press, 2012.

Serban, Claudia. "De l'hylétique à l'herméneutique." In *Paul Ricœur et Michel Henry: Entre héritages et destinées phénoménologiques*, edited by Jean-Sébastien Hardy, Jean Leclercq, and Cyndie Sautereau. Louvain, Belgium: UCL Press, 2016.

Seyler, Frédéric. "La certitude comme enjeu éthique et épistémologique pour la Phénoménologie de la vie." In *La Vie et les vivants*. https://books.openedition.org/pucl/2715.

Simms, Karl. *Ricoeur and Lacan*. London: Continuum, 2007.

Steinbock, Anthony. *Home and Beyond: Generative Phenomenology after Husserl*. Evanston, IL: Northwestern University Press, 1995.

———. *Phenomenology and Mysticism: The Verticality of Religious Experience*. Bloomington: Indiana University Press, 2012.

Stirner, Max. *The Ego and Its Own*. Edited by David Leopold. Cambridge, UK: Cambridge University Press, 2009.

Taylor, George H. "Delineating Ricoeur's Concept of Utopia." 3, no. 1 (spring 2017): 41–60.

Vansina, Frans D. *Paul Ricoeur Bibliography (1935–2008)*. Leuven, Belgium: Peeters, 2008.

Varela, Francisco J., Evan Thompson, and Eleanor Rosch. *The Embodied Mind and Human Cognition*. Revised Edition. Cambridge, MA: MIT Press, 2017.

Virno, Paolo. "An Equivocal Concept: Biopolitics." In *Biopolitics: A Reader*, edited by Timothy Campbell and Adam Sitze, 269–73. Durham, NC: Duke University Press, 2013.

Wahl, Jean. "Preface to *Toward the Concrete*." In *Transcendence and the Concrete: Selected Writings*, edited by Alan D. Schrift and Ian Alexander Moore, 32–53. New York: Fordham University Press, 2016.

Worms, Frédéric. "Vivant jusqu'a la mort et non pas pour la mort." *Esprit* (Avril 2006): 304–15.

Zimmer, Carl. Life's Edge: The Search for What It Means to Be Alive. New York: Penguin, 2021.

# INDEX

alienation (Marxism), 27, 57, 112, 206n40
Althusser, Louis, 117
*apophansis*, 125
appearance, 9, 88–89, 210n43
Arendt, Hannah, 189n27, 211n6
Aristotle, 62, 132–133, 143
*askesis*, 154–156
Austin, J. L., 140–141
authenticity, 148, 152
auto-affection, 215n4; eternal, 150–151, 202n58; Henry's distinction, 149; versus hetero-affection, 90

Barbaras, Renaud, 3–5, 181n15, 182n37, 193n36, 216n5
*Being and Nothingness*, 107
being-in-the-world, 148
being-towards-death (Heidegger), 148
being-towards-life, 16, 144, 146–148, 151–152, 162
Berggren, Douglas, 130–131; poetic schema and textures, 131–132
*Bildung*, 100

biology, 1, 13, 45, 55, 57–58, 179nn1–2; inheritance, 7, 11, 13, 55–57, 99, 157, 171, 216n7; genetics, 13, 27, 56–57, 60
bodily movement, 1, 4, 13, 28, 62–63, 65–71, 78–82, 111, 193n31. *See also* locomotion
body, Ricoeur's notion, 24–27; bodily movement, 62–75; 78, desire, 101; docile body, 14, 66, 74–75, 78, 81, 195n58, 196n71; living body, 3, 4, 12–13, 23, 26, 52, 62–63, 81, 110, 127, 139, 149, 206n40, 211n13; transcendental, 13, 52, 59, 65, 67

Cartesian circle, 44–48, 52–53, 60–62; *ordo cognoscendi*, 13, 46, 48, 52–53, 58, 60, 79, 80, 94, 121, 142, 148, 168–169; *ordo essendi*, 13, 142, 149, 168–169
Changeux, Jean-Pierre, 180n12
*Children of Men, The*, 160
Christianity, 188n10
class (social), 109, 113, 115–117, 204n10

cogito (original), 29, 31–32, 40–49; Biranian vs. Cartesian, 68, 70; bodily cogito, 13, 20, 24, 28, 39, 66, 68, 79–81, 149; cogitatum, 29, 31–32, 46–48; *res cogitans*, 68
consciousness (intentional), 30–31, critique of intentionality, 20–38, 84–110
*corps propre*, 13, 64, 67, 70, 72, 79

Dalbiez, Roland, 198n3
Dasein, 49–50, 144, 146–148, 154, 162, 215n48
death, 144–164, 210nn1–48
*Death and the Afterlife*. See Samuel Scheffler
de Biran, Maine, 13, 63–74
Derrida, Jacques, 72–73, 189n28, 194n46–47, 205n28, 207n3, 210n1, 211n10, 215n48
Descartes, Rene, 29–33, 44–48, 76, 80, 212n20; *Meditations*, 22–23, 29, 44–46, 66, 188n3
desire, 83–103, 197nn1–72
developmental psychology, 26
difference (separation), 43–44; external, 44, 53, 59–61; internal, 44–45, 53, 60–61, 78, 168–170
drive. *See* force

ego (psychoanalysis), 22, 36–38; *ego cogito*, 29; transcendental, 37, 51, 145, 211n7
eidetic reduction, 20, 29–30. *See also* phenomenological reduction
*Ego and Its Own, The*, 106, 204n16
ek-stasis, 49, 89, 134, 150, 209n33
Eliot, T. S., 165–166, 176–177, 216n9
embodied cognition, 39, 187n75, 192n19
enactivism, 187n75

energetics, 86–87, 89, 92, 200n29
Epicurus, 145, 160
*epoche*, 20–21, 28, 38, 108–109, 145
*Erleben*, 12, 25, 158

Falque, Emmanuel, 4, 101
false consciousness, 84–85
fault, 20, 180n13, 192n14
filial, 55–57, 189n32, 190n35
finitude, 144, 148, 151–153, 159, 162–164, 168, 180n14, 213n28
force, 61, 69–70, 79, 83, 87, 92, 171, 190n42, 200n29, 200n39, 201n47, 202n58; of labor 110; illocutionary, 141
Foucault, Michel, 195n58
Franck, Didier, 33
*Freud and Philosophy*, 7, 83–85, 91, 98
Freud, Sigmund, 14; Henry-Ricoeur debate over, 83–103; unconscious, 14, 24–25, 84–95, 98–99, 102, 116, 198n2–3, 199n14, 199n25, 200n29, 200nn39–40

Geertz, Clifford, 119
*Genealogy of Psychoanalysis, The*, 84, 88, 91, 198n3
genetics, 13, 27, 56–57, 60
*German Ideology, The*, 104–105, 113, 116–118, 204n10, 205n28
givenness, 12, 31, 33–37, 134–136
God, 155–157
Greisch, Jean, 128–129, 132, 208n11

Hegel, Wilhelm Friedrich, 99, 107
Heidegger, Martin, 49, 144–148, 151–152, 154, 162, 180n14
Henry, Michel, and Maine de Biran, 63; on language, 10, 14–15, 43–44, 92–93, 117–119, 122–143, 207nn1–43; immanent

teleology of life, 95–97; *Material Phenomenology*, 19, 33
hermeneutics, in relation to phenomenology, 9–10; hermeneutic circle, 55, 121; critical and constructive, 98
hetero-affection, 90
history, 8, 10, 114–115
homo umbilicus, 59
horizontal resurrection, 155, 157–159, 162–163
*How to Do Things with Words. See* J. L. Austin, 140–141
Husserl, Edmund, Ricoeur's critique of, 18–25; "Husserlian heretics," 19; *Ideas I*, 18, 21, 33, 134; lifeworld, 11, 18, 29, 61, 108, 187n70; phenomenological reduction, 20–21, 29–30, 32, 134 183n3. *See also* eidetic reduction

id (psychoanalysis), 92
Idealism (critique of), 20–41, 44–45, 188n3; transcendental idealism, 21–22, 28
ideology, 15, 104–108, 112–122, 204n10
immanence (radical), 10-11, 33, 35, 82, 114; in relation to transcendence, 121–127
infinite, 46–49, 80, 188n3
intentionality, 32–35, 136, 184n23

James, P. D., 160–161
Janicaud, Dominique, 9–10, 47

Kant, Immanuel, 3–5, 65, 82, 180n7, 180n12; anthropology, 3–5, 11, 180n12, 180n14
*kath'-auto*, 127
kinship, 57, 59, 214n42

labor, 110–112, 206nn40–41; Marx's critique of wage labor, 111–112
labor power, 121, 206n40
Lacan, Jacques, 92
language, debate on, 123–144, 207nn1–43
law of growth, 93–97
law of preservation, 93–97
*Leben*, 11–12, 180n9
*Lectures on the Internal Consciousness of Time*, 33–34
Levinas, Emmanuel, 16, 40, 48, 184, 188n3, 196n69, 205n28
Life, discussion of birth, 42–61; gendered assumptions, 189n13; living individual, 3, 11–16, 37–61, 93–177, 206n40, 206n47, 207n1, 213n28–29
linguistic turn, 124
living after (concept), 153–164. *See also* Scheffler, Samuel
*Living Up to Death*, 8, 146, 153–159
locomotion, 62, 79. *See also* bodily movement

Mannheim's paradox, 118–119,
Marburg School, 29
Marion, Jean-Luc, 9, 9, 16, 124, 133–136
 *Reduction and Givenness* 133–136, 185n53
*Marx* (book by Michel Henry), 14, 104, 109, 112, 203n2
Marxism, Ricoeur contra Marx, 109
Marx, Karl, 1,7, 14–15, 63, 104–123, 167, 196n74, 203n1–78; *Capital*, 109
Masters of Suspicion, 1, 7, 84, 104, 187n77, 203n1
meritocratic thinking, 174–176
Merleau-Ponty, Maurice, 4, 191n5, 208n15

metaphor, 124–133, 143, 182n37, 201n42, 208n11, 208nn15–16, 209n26; metaphorical tension, 130–132
metaphysics, 9, 88
Michel, Johann, 180n11
MRS GREN, 2, 179n2

naturalism, 3, 21, 25, 180n12
necessity, 25–28, 122
Nietzsche, Friedrich, 1, 7, 203n1, 207n3

Other, the (concept), 16, 22, 72, 82, 100, 102, 107, 134, 146–147, 155, 157–158; discussion of mother and child, 55–60
Ovid, 3

Parmenidean One, 43
Parmenides, 188n2
Phenomenology, classical, 1, 102, 165; Hermeneutical relation, 11, 87; Husserlian, 7, 12, 18–38, 186n62, 187n74; hyletic data, 25, 34–35; maximalist, 9–11, 14, 19, 28, 40–42, 103, 120, 121, 125, 133, 142, 149, 167–168; minimalist, 9, 11, 13, 15–16, 19, 23, 40–42, 136–142, 153, 167–168
phenomenological reduction, 20–21, 29–37, 134
*phi*-system, 90
*phusis* (nature), 133
Plato, 151, 211n13, 212n14, 213n24, 213n26
positivism, 130
*pragma*, 110, 120
pragmatics, 125, 137–139
proprioception, 68
*psi*-system, 90

Psychoanalysis, 7, 14, 84–93, 98, 102, 198n3, 200n42
*pulsion*, 83, 199n9. *See also* force

*ratio cognoscendi*, 46, 48, 52–53, 58, 60, 79, 80, 94, 121, 148
*ratio essendi*, 46, 48, 52, 58, 60, 80, 94–95, 121
reflexive philosophy, French, 7, 64–65, 78–79, 81–82, 192n12, 192n14, 192n18
Richards, I. A., 130, 208n14; tension theory 130–131, 208n16
Ricoeur, Paul, *Freedom and Nature*, 7, 9, 19–20, 23–25, 28, 40, 54, 64–65, 72–75, 81, 91, 98; *Husserl: An Analysis of His Phenomenology*, 18, 20; *Lectures on Ideology and Utopia*, 15, 104, 116; *Living Up to Death*, 8, 146, 153–159, 163; *Memory, History, Forgetting*, 8

Sartre, Jean-Paul, 107–108
Saussure, Ferdinand de, 137
Scheffler, Samuel, 16, 146, 158–162
science, 2, 62, 117, 166, 200n29
self-division, 187n77
Self, 13, 32, 36; active, 22–23, 39, 45–46, 52, 70–71, 76–77, 90, 142, 196nn68–69; passive, 22, 51–52, 71. *See also* ego
semantics, 137–138, 209n38
speech act(s), 15, 137–142, 209n38
Spinoza, Baruch, 93, 201n49, 212n18
Stirner, Max, 106, 204n16
suffering, 12–13, 39–40, 46, 51, 95–97, 102–103, 115, 127–129, 196n71, 202n55
superego (psychoanalysis), 100
symbolic(s), 86–87, 92, 114–116, 118–120

temporality, 148, 156, 186n62
thrownness, 49, 146–148

transcendence, 11, 20, 29, 32–33, 35, 44, 53, 82, 103, 111, 114, 121–122, 124, 182n37, 187n77, 196n68

*Umstände*, 15, 105, 113, 115
*Ur*-birth, 50
utterance, 15, 125, 127, 138–139, 141. *See also* speech act

values, 100–102, 161–162
vertical resurrection, 155–159, 163
*Vor-stellung*, 30

Will, voluntary and involuntary, 19, 21, 23–28, 37–39, 52, 60, 64, 66, 70–73, 80, 195n65
Worms, Frédéric, 9

**SCOTT DAVIDSON** is Professor of Philosophy and Director of Multidisciplinary Studies at West Virginia University. His recent publications include *The Michel Henry Reader* (coedited with Frédéric Seyler) and three volumes on Ricoeur's philosophy of the will: *A Companion to Ricoeur's Freedom and Nature* (2018), *A Companion to Ricoeur's Fallible Man* (2019), and *A Companion to Ricoeur's The Symbolism of Evil* (2020).

*For Indiana University Press*
Tony Brewer, Artist and Book Designer
Dan Crissman, Editorial Director and Acquisitions Editor
Anna Francis, Assistant Acquisitions Editor
Anna Garnai, Editorial Assistant
Katie Huggins, Production Manager
David Miller, Lead Project Manager/Editor
Dan Pyle, Online Publishing Manager
Pamela Rude, Senior Artist and Book Designer
Stephen Williams, Assistant Director of Marketing